PRAISE FOR *BALANCE*

"*Balance* is one of the best personal finance books you'll ever read—because it's so much more than that. Andrew Hallam has written an insightful guide to spending and investing money, not to impress others but to build a life of satisfaction and significance."
DANIEL H. PINK, #1 *New York Times*–bestselling author of *When, Drive,* and *To Sell Is Human*

"Decades ago, Andrew Tobias gave us *The Only Investment Guide You'll Ever Need*. It's still a good read. But *Balance*, by Andrew Hallam, ups the game and takes us many steps further. *Balance* gives us a complete, modern context for the role of money and investing in our lives. Beneath a rich collection of anecdotes and stories, this short book provides a depth of research into the realities of investing and the errant relationship between money and happiness."
SCOTT BURNS, personal finance columnist and creator of the Couch Potato Portfolio

"Entertaining and well-written yet solidly rooted in science, *Balance* offers a fresh look at what it means to be truly successful in life."
MARTA ZARASKA, bestselling author of *Growing Young: How Friendship, Optimism, and Kindness Can Help You Live to 100*

"In *Balance*, Andrew Hallam describes what it means to be 'successful.' And it's not what you might expect. If you want a healthy mindset with respect to money, health, relationships, and purpose, you'll learn a lot from this humorous, impressively researched book."
LEON LOGOTHETIS, bestselling author of *The Kindness Diaries*

"A must-read! *Balance* is a remarkable road map for overcoming the greatest challenge in life: finding happiness. You will learn, laugh, and be inspired by the personal stories and the science revealing the intersection of wealth, health, and happiness. Andrew Hallam is the best friend who tells you the truth about money, and you'll be wealthier for it. Equal parts investing smarts and wellness savvy, this rare book tells you how to have it all. A flat-out great read."
KERRY K. TAYLOR, founder, Squawkfox.com

"*Balance* is a must-read, filled with humorous stories and scientific, evidence-based tips. Andrew Hallam explains how to spend and invest your money to maximize life satisfaction—for you, your children, and your grandchildren. I highly recommend it."
LARRY SWEDROE, co-author of *Your Complete Guide to a Successful and Secure Retirement*; chief research officer, Buckingham Strategic Wealth

"If you're feeling baffled by how to approach money in a post-pandemic world, spend a few hours with Andrew Hallam. His new book, *Balance*, offers a master class in how to invest wisely, but it goes well beyond the normal stocks and bonds stuff. It offers a wise meditation on how to think of money as part of your larger life plan. Whether you're a multimillionaire entrepreneur or a fitness buff living in his car by choice, you'll find insights here that can reshape both your portfolio and your priorities."
IAN MCGUGAN, investment editor, *Globe and Mail*

"Imagine there was a multiverse where the most content, satisfied, happiest future version of yourself traveled back in time to give you the blueprint to lead a fulfilling life. That's this book."

PREET BANERJEE, financial educator, YourMoneyDegree.com

"Andrew Hallam isn't just a fabulous personal finance writer. His book *Balance* invites us to go deeper to consider one of the oldest, most important questions of all time: 'How should I live my life?' The right questions matter, and Andrew knows which ones are worth asking."

ADRIAN JURIC, filmmaker and psychotherapist, Vancouver Walk & Talk Therapy

"In *Balance*, Andrew Hallam offers a simple and sensible approach for a secure and satisfying life. He provides a guide to achieving financial success, while promoting physical, emotional, and spiritual well-being. It is a thoughtful and thought-provoking book that I will strongly encourage my young adult children to read."

JOHN S. WOERTH, former chief spokesperson, Vanguard

"Low-cost index funds may be the smartest investment for most people, but they won't tell you how to live a good life. Andrew Hallam's excellent book, *Balance*, will."

BENJAMIN FELIX, portfolio manager, head of research and client education, PWL Capital

BALANCE

BAL

ANCE

How to Invest
and Spend
for Happiness,
Health, and
Wealth

ANDREW HALLAM

● ● PAGE TWO

Some names and identifying details have been changed to protect the privacy of individuals.

This book is for educational purposes and is not intended as a substitute for professional financial advice. Additionally, the author does not claim to be endorsed by, nor does he endorse any product, business, firm, organization, or trademark contained in this document.

Cataloguing in publication information is available from Library and Archives Canada.
ISBN 978-1-77458-075-2 (paperback)
ISBN 978-1-77458-076-9 (ebook)
ISBN 978-1-77458-077-6 (audiobook)

Page Two
pagetwo.com

Edited by Amanda Lewis
Copyedited by Lesley Cameron
Proofread by Alison Strobel
Cover design by Peter Cocking
Interior design by Jennifer Lum
Printed and bound in Canada by Friesens
Distributed in Canada by Raincoast Books
Distributed in the US and internationally by Macmillan

22 23 24 25 26   5 4 3 2 1

andrewhallam.com

*This book is dedicated to everyone who's brave enough
to dance to the beat of their own drum.*

CONTENTS

"Happiness will never come to those who fail
to appreciate what they already have."

BUDDHA

INTRODUCTION

IF I HAD asked, "Why do you not want to pee your pants?" they would have given me the same stare.

I was speaking to a group of high school students at an elite private school. Most of their parents had Ivy League ambitions for their kids, as if Harvard, Yale, and Stanford were parachutes in a crashing plane. So my opening question rattled them: "Why do you want to do well in school?"

After a long pause, one of the students said, "We want to get into a good college."

I then asked, "*Why* do you want to get into a good college?"

Several students replied, "So we can get a good job."

The rest of the conversation went something like this:

"*Why* do you want a good job?"

"So we can be successful."

"*Why* do you need a high-paying job to consider yourself successful?"

As their teacher, I supported their Ivy League ambitions. But I learn a lot by asking *why*, and I hoped my students would too. Whether I'm talking to students, corporate CEOs, or a ripped person at the local gym, I ask a lot of questions. Aren't you glad you're reading this book and not stuck on a train with me?

My friends sometimes take advantage of this quirk. They might ask, "Andrew, why does that guy with the giant fish hook in his cheek have a purple butterfly tattooed on his back? Can you go and ask?"

Here's what I've learned from asking why. When I ask people why they want to do something, buy something, achieve something, or help someone, the responses vary—at first. But when I continue to ask "Why. . . ?" the answers begin to sound the same.

People hope their actions or decisions will make them happy, safe, or secure. In other words, they're motivated by their life satisfaction. Consider the most selfless acts you could imagine—acts of pure kindness—and ask people why they do them. From my experience, when I keep asking, "Why. . . ?" they might start by saying, "It's just the right thing to do." But when I ask, "*Why* is it the right thing to do? *Why* do you do it?" eventually they say it makes them feel whole, purposeful, or happy.

Plenty of people seek success, but they don't define it holistically. To many, like my students, success means money in the bank, a great career, or a big house on the hill. How often have you heard (or even said) something like, "That woman is so successful. She owns a massive house, a BMW, and her own law firm"?

Unfortunately, this picture defines only one element of success: monetary. As I see it, there are four quadrants to a successful life:

- Having enough money
- Maintaining strong relationships
- Maximizing your physical and mental health
- Living with a sense of purpose

Think of success as a four-legged table, with each leg representing a quadrant. Each quadrant depends on the other. If they don't all play their part equally, the table collapses. If one leg is spindly or cracked, it's tough to maximize your life satisfaction, no matter how solid you might be in the other three quadrants.

Unfortunately, when defining success, we often focus too much on the money leg. For example, I enjoy watching television shows like *America's Got Talent*. Winners are reported to receive a million dollars. But I often cringe when contestants gush, "This money will change my life forever," as if this waterfall of cash could cure everything from chronic hemorrhoids to toxic relationships.

I didn't think about these things when I first began investing as a nineteen-year-old. By my late thirties, I had built a million-dollar investment portfolio on a schoolteacher's salary. For the past twenty years, I've been writing personal finance articles for magazines, newspapers, and online publications. I wrote an international bestselling book, *Millionaire Teacher: The Nine Rules of Wealth You Should Have Learned in School*. I also taught a high school personal finance class, and I give dozens of talks around the world every year, showing how people can invest their money, while helping them figure out how much they need for retirement.

When my wife, Pele, and I quit our Singapore-based teaching jobs in 2014, we planned to take a year off to travel. But one year led to two, which soon led to six. We stayed in short-term rentals in Mexico, Thailand, Bali, and Malaysia. We spent several months cycling on our tandem around Europe. We even spent seventeen months in a camper van in a failed quest to drive from Canada to Argentina. We joke that we almost killed each other only once.

The only real threat to us was a civil conflict that broke out when we got to the Honduras/Nicaragua border. Unlike several braver adventurers who filled their RVs' fuel tanks and raced breathlessly across the country, we chose to venture south again only when the bullets stopped flying.

During these travels we often stored our van (sometimes in sketchy places) while we flew across the world to give financial talks. I spoke at international schools and corporations, like Facebook in Dubai and the Radisson Blu resort in Malta. I spoke at technology companies, investment firms, and insurance companies.

But over those six years, something piqued my curiosity. I met plenty of conventionally successful people (measured by money and career) who appeared less satisfied than, say, a family of Argentinians traveling through Mexico in a motorhome. I'm not saying Type-A career personalities live less successful lives. But if holistic success were a four-legged table, a surprisingly high number of conventionally successful people appeared to have one or two fractured legs. For some, the damaged leg was their health and fitness. For others, it was their relationships, as they prioritized work over family and friends.

This doesn't mean the rich are miserable and the poor are happy. It does mean that we often strive for things that don't boost our happiness. We fall into conventional ways of thinking that hamper our life satisfaction and harm our natural environment.

I've written this book to help you on your personal quest for wellness. I draw on stories and research to describe the relationships between money, health, happiness, and purpose while offering suggestions that will help you live the best life possible. If you're willing to keep an open mind, respect the research, and sometimes dance to a beat that might differ from your neighbor's, this book is for you.

In chapter 1, we explore how to best spend your money for the biggest life-satisfaction buck. (Pro tip: Be nice to Mr. and Mrs. Jones but don't copy their consumption habits.) Chapter 2 describes the surprisingly quirky relationship between income, happiness, and the place you choose to live. (Note: I use US dollars throughout the book unless otherwise specified.)

In chapter 3, we'll discuss our relationships with other people. Chapter 4 weaves in studies about and tips for maximizing physical and mental health, while chapter 5 shows why we should spend money on what we value most. What we think we value on the surface and what we actually value deep down are often quite different.

Chapters 6 to 9 focus on investing in the stock and bond markets. I'll explain how to do this right, so you won't have to spend much time thinking about investing. Those who follow my strategies of consumption and investing won't have to work at jobs they despise if they want financial independence. They could follow their professional passions (even if they pay less money) and live more fulfilling lives. I start from ground zero, so you won't require any prior investment knowledge. I'll show how to pick a good financial advisor or (if you want to go solo) beat the performance of most financial advisors and professional traders without following the stock market at all. I'll show you exactly what to do, what to buy, and what pitfalls to avoid so you can spend time on more important things. After all, spending more than an hour a year thinking about investing is a massive waste of time. And time is the only nonrenewable resource that you have.

Chapter 10 explains how, using a similar investment philosophy, you can invest in environmentally sustainable (SRI, or socially responsible investing) funds and still trounce most investment pros without any effort. It also describes some of the risks our planet faces because of some of the seemingly harmless things we do and offers solutions to give Mother Earth a break.

Following the future theme, chapter 11 shows how to help your children succeed. Several little things, like assigning household chores, strongly impact their development. I also explain exactly how they can invest at an early age, filling their sails with the magic of compound interest.

Finally, chapter 12 focuses on the relationship between human longevity and retirement. If you're worried you won't have enough money to retire, this chapter is for you. It explains the health benefits of working part-time in your golden years and illustrates out-of-the-box solutions for stretching a retiree's hard-earned money while expanding your life experience.

The book's overriding premise is this: When you choose to buy something, live somewhere, do something, or accept a specific job, start by asking, "Why. . . ?" Then focus on your core values and learn how behavioral science might help boost your life satisfaction.

Thank you for joining me in this journey toward holistic success.

1

THE GRIM REAPER ASKS
What Do You Value More, Your Stuff or Your Life?

M Y FRIEND Andrew Chacko and I were walking through a
hotel lobby in Varadero, Cuba. It was an all-inclusive resort
where booze flowed as freely into the guests as it did from taps
at the bar.

We overheard a middle-aged Russian tourist chatting about ice
hockey with a young Canadian. As we walked by the pair, we heard
a heavy slap. The Russian had the Canadian in a headlock on the
ground. Two hotel clerks pulled the older man off the younger guy,
likely saving him from some expensive dental work. Despite his age
and obvious drunkenness, the Russian pummeled the younger man
like a UFC pro.

That evening, we ate dinner at one of the resort's restaurants.
Nearby, a man ate with his wife and two young children. As the father
was digging into his pickled vegetables (a staple at most Cuban
resorts), another guy walked behind him and slapped his head. It
didn't just happen once. The slapper stood above the family man,
slurring something in Russian, and whacked him every ten or twenty
seconds. The seated man winced but otherwise was stoic.

This was weird stuff, and we half-expected another fight. But
Andrew and I didn't fly to Cuba to watch vodka-fueled battles, so the

following day we caught a taxi to Havana. After spending a couple of days exploring this iconic city, we left for the country's southern coast. It wasn't long before we ran out of Cuban cash. We couldn't find an ATM, but I had several crisp $50 bills. I tried to exchange the money in a small town where a woman at the post office scrutinized each bill, as if she feared we were in the business of counterfeiting.

Each bill, though perfect to my eye, had a tiny tear in the exact same spot. Her eyes widened and her finger wagged back and forth. "No," she said. "These bills aren't good." Unfortunately for us, no vendor within miles would accept our credit cards either.

Our flight was scheduled to leave the next day—and here we were, stuck without money, over 60 miles (at least 100 kilometers) from Varadero. Fortunately, we managed to beg our way onto a bus that took us back to the resort... where we vowed to avoid any Russians on the sauce.

Here's the point of this story: If Andrew and I were sharing stories around a campfire with friends today, we might talk about the crazy fight in the hotel lobby. We might laugh about begging our way onto a local Cuban bus while the driver stopped to pick up milk and chickens. But we wouldn't likely talk about anything we bought that year. We value our experiences over the things we buy. Yes, we might be a couple of dorky dudes, but most people prefer life experiences over stuff.

When I give talks about happiness and money, I ask attendees to recall their most memorable material purchase. Sometimes, I ask them to write down what they felt when they first acquired that purchase. I recall one gentleman saying, "I love tech gadgets. When the first iPhone came out, I was one of the first to buy one. I loved it. I thought it was amazing."

Then I ask attendees to think about their favorite experiential purchase: something they enjoyed with a friend or with their family. This same guy said he and his son once flew to New Zealand and spent a week mountain biking.

Next, I present the following scenario: You have one more month to live. The Grim Reaper says, "I'm going to erase one of your memories. It's going to be the memory of your favorite material purchase or the memory of your favorite experiential purchase."

Not surprisingly, the man said he would sacrifice the memory of any "thing" he bought before relinquishing a memory of an enjoyable time with his family.

Most people would say the same, according to Professor Thomas Gilovich and Professor Leaf Van Boven. Their research found that we prefer experiences instead of things because our experiences become part of our identities. As a result, we often think about them later.[1] That's why, when I see my friend Andrew, we often laugh about that trip to Cuba. We talk about the fun we had together when we were kids. But we don't reminisce about things we bought.

I know what you might be thinking: Some of the things we buy do offer an experience. That's true, and I'll come to that later. But most of the unneeded stuff we buy offers nothing but a sugar rush.

Being human is such a pain. Here's why. We often buy things to feel good. But hedonic adaptation sets in. In other words, the excitement of buying something new soon wears off when that new iPhone or purse becomes, well, just another phone or purse. We adapt to what we own, sometimes without realizing we're doing so. That puts us on a treadmill of consumption. To make us feel better, we then buy something else, not realizing that it won't boost our life satisfaction either. And then we start the cycle all over again.

Here's something you could try: Find one of your old credit card statements. For each item you purchased, write down a number between 1 and 10, based on how much happiness you felt when you took it home (or took it out of its packaging). Then beside that number, write down a number that reflects how happy the item makes you now. You might even ask yourself, "Years from now, would these purchases make their way into a campfire story?" Most of the time they wouldn't. But if you spent money on an experience, you would more often tell stories about that experience. And if you're anything like my friends (I'll just say that they're "creative") such tales get better every year.

When Borrowing Money to Buy Stuff Can Really Drag Us Down

In most cases, buying stuff doesn't improve our life satisfaction. In fact, it can even bum us out when we borrow money to do it. We might tell ourselves, "Credit card consumer debt is normal. Everyone has it." But debts are like garden weeds. Unless we attack them at the roots, they just keep growing.

If we want to live the best lives we can, we shouldn't normalize credit card debts or auto loans. In 2005, the University of Nottingham's Sarah Bridges and Richard Disney published a report titled *Debt and Depression*.[2] During their research, they asked more than seven thousand British mothers to rate their overall well-being. They also asked if a doctor had ever diagnosed them as suffering from anxiety or depression. The researchers found that those with lower debts were more satisfied with their lives compared to those with higher debts.

One of the biggest sources of debt is auto loans. According to an April 2021 report by Experian, Americans owe about $1.2 trillion on their cars.[3] In fact, about 85 percent of new cars are financed. Plenty of people believe newer, faster, smoother, or higher-status cars will boost their life satisfaction, so they borrow money to buy something that's flashier than they need.

Yet research suggests most people who own high-status cars don't enjoy their driving experience any more than people who drive lower-end cars. That pesky hedonic adaptation chips away at their fun.

For example, Professor Norbert Schwarz, from the University of Michigan, and Professor Jing Xu, from Peking University, asked research participants to rate their most recent driving experience in terms of how it made them feel. After rating their levels of happiness, the participants were then asked what kind of cars they drove. Some drove high-end cars. Others didn't. But there was no correlation between the happiness participants felt while driving and the cars they drove. In other words, high-end cars didn't make people happier on the road.[4]

Quoted in the *Michigan News*, Professor Schwarz says, "During the test drive of a new car, our attention is focused on the car, and the more luxurious it is, the better we feel while driving it. This experience is real, visceral and compelling. What we miss, however, is one simple thing. Once we have owned the car for a few weeks, it no longer captures all of our attention and other things will be on our minds while driving. As soon as that happens, we would feel just as well driving a cheaper alternative."[5]

And if an expensive car includes an auto loan as a built-in accessory, the net happiness achieved is usually less than zero.

What Message Are You Sending with the Car You Drive?

Plenty of people pine for nice cars. But cars are the greatest personal wealth destroyer. We often borrow to buy them, and they lose value every month.[6]

In some cases, we might think having the right car makes us part of a certain social group. But we might be fooling ourselves. Think about the people you love or respect. Now consider whether you would love or respect them less if they didn't have a car (and weren't constantly bumming rides). And what if they owned a high-status car? Would you love or respect them more because of what they drove? I hope these questions answer themselves.

Plenty of people splash out on fancy cars to impress other people. But that can backfire.

One of my neighbors owns a new Corvette; his license plate reads "UR2ND." I haven't met him yet. He might be a really nice guy whose dying Aunt Matilda bought him that license plate and insisted that he use it. Unfortunately, she wouldn't have known that his car and license plate combo flips the middle finger to his neighbors.

When I speak to people about the habits of the wealthy, I often ask, "What are the favorite cars driven by the rich?" Most people yell out names like Ferrari, Maserati, Tesla, Mercedes-Benz, Audi, BMW, or Porsche. But research says that's wrong.

The marketing professor Dr. Thomas J. Stanley began compiling information on the habits, professions, and purchases of US-based millionaires in 1973. In 1996, he co-authored the groundbreaking book *The Millionaire Next Door* with William D. Danko. Stanley continued collecting data on millionaires until his death in 2015. The year he died, he and his daughter, Sarah Stanley Fallaw, were collecting research for another book. She continued their work and published *The Next Millionaire Next Door* in 2018 (with her father listed as co-author).

The twenty-first-century research by Stanley and his daughter confirmed Stanley's previous findings: Most millionaires don't drive flashy cars. The three most popular vehicle brands among American millionaires are Toyota, Honda, and Ford. Only two high-end brands made the top ten: BMW ranked fourth and Lexus sixth. Among millionaires, Hyundais and Kias are more popular than Porsches, Mercedes-Benzes, and Teslas. Plenty of people think most rich people buy expensive cars. Meanwhile, most millionaires might be saying, "I don't think an expensive car will make me smile more often." Instead of spending six figures on a set of wheels, the average millionaire paid about $35,000 for their latest car.

OK, so we're talking about millionaires: mere mortals who, perhaps, might just be trying to stretch a buck. But what about the world's richest billionaires? Surprisingly, nine of the seventeen world's richest people drive cars worth less than $50,000.[7]

According to CNBC, Mark Zuckerberg's favorite car is his Acura TSX. He also owns a Volkswagen GTI and has been seen driving a Honda Fit. None of these cars are worth more than $30,000.[8]

Not everyone who works at Facebook earns an Everest-like income. Perhaps Zuckerberg would feel silly driving a Bentley or a Rolls-Royce into his workplace parking lot. Whether that's true or not, plenty of the world's richest people drive equally modest cars.

In Table 1.1, I list the seventeen richest people in the world, based on a 2020 *Forbes* list.[9] I include the cars they drive, and the approximate prices for each of these cars if purchased new in 2021.

TABLE 1.1

What Cars Do the Rich Drive?

2020 Global Wealth Rank	Name	Net Worth in Billions	Car	Approximate Price New
1	Jeff Bezos	$113	Honda Accord	$26,000
2	Bill Gates	$98	Porsche Taycan	$185,000
3	Bernard Arnault	$76	BMW 7 Series	$86,450
4	Warren Buffett	$67.5	Cadillac XTS	$46,000
5	Larry Ellison	$59	McLaren F1*	$2,200,000*
6	Amancio Ortega	$55.1	Audi A8	$83,525
7	Mark Zuckerberg	$54.7	Acura TSX	$30,000
8	Jim Walton	$54.6	Dodge Dakota	$25,000
9	Alice Walton	$54.4	Ford F-150 King Ranch	$49,000
10	Rob Walton	$54.1	N/A**	
11	Steve Ballmer	$52.7	Ford Fusion Hybrid	$24,365
12	Carlos Slim	$52.1	Bentley Flying Spur	$214,600
13	Larry Page	$50.9	Toyota Prius	$39,000
14	Sergey Brin	$49.1	Toyota Prius	$39,000
15	Françoise Bettencourt Meyers	$48.9	N/A**	
16	Michael Bloomberg	$48	Audi R8	$83,525
17	Jack Ma	$38.8	Roewe RX5 SUV	$15,000

*The McLaren Speedtail is the successor to the McLaren F1
**I could not find vehicle brands for Rob Walton or Françoise Bettencourt Meyers

How Much Should You Spend on a Car?

Sam Dogen, the man behind the popular blog *Financial Samurai*, says most people pay far too much for vehicles. This self-made millionaire's financial tips have been published in *Forbes*, the *Wall Street Journal*, *Business Insider*, the *Chicago Tribune*, and the *Los Angeles Times*.

He has a rule for buying cars that's seriously countercultural.[10] He says nobody should buy a car that costs more than 10 percent of their gross annual income. In other words, if someone earns $40,000 a year, they shouldn't spend more than $4,000 on a car. If someone earns $100,000 a year, they shouldn't spend more than $10,000 on a car. Anyone earning $600,000 a year shouldn't pay more than $60,000 for a car.

These are low limbo bars. And I'm not saying everyone should follow Dogen's rule. But that doesn't mean you can't. In 1986, I paid $2,400 for a 1980 Honda Civic. I earned $6,000 that year, so 40 percent of my income went toward that car. Fortunately, as a sixteen-year-old, I was still living at home and I wasn't paying rent.

But since then, I've limbo-danced under Dogen's bar. I bought my current car five years ago for $4,500. It's a 2004 Volkswagen Golf that still looks and drives as if it had just rolled out of a showroom. My wife and I also own a 2007 Toyota Yaris that cost us $6,000. They're both reliable, low-mileage vehicles. We can afford to buy higher-priced cars, but I know that wouldn't make us happier. Besides, if we spent $50,000 on a car, it might annoy me if an errant shopping cart rolled into its door. My lower-priced cars also make it easier to relax when I'm driving in tight traffic. And I don't have to worry about wrecking expensive wheels if I get too close to the curb while parallel parking. I'm not saying everyone should follow my lead, or Sam Dogen's. But by worrying less, I live well.

Beware the Slippery Upgrade Slope

As we saw earlier, research suggests that spending money on experiences boosts life satisfaction more than spending money on stuff (like cars). But that might leave you asking, "Can't a thing provide an experience?" That's a subtlety worth considering.

In 2020, my wife and I were stuck in British Columbia, Canada, due to the COVID-19 pandemic. Granted, it's not a bad place to be stuck. At one point, we were helping my parents find an RV for their own adventures. A salesperson at one dealership noticed we had arrived in our camper van: our wheels of adventure in Mexico and Central America.

"I'm guessing you might be interested in upgrading that," he said.

Our van hadn't come cheap, and it was only a few years old and still in great condition. To his eye—and his commission-hungry pocketbook—it made sense for us to upgrade to a $170,000 Mercedes Era. It's similar to our Winnebago Travato, but its price tag is steeper. It had a better solar power system, high-tech heating, and, of course, an expensive Mercedes engine.

You might have found yourself in a similar position. You own something that provides an experience (maybe it's a kayak, a camper van, or a bicycle) and wonder if upgrading it will enhance your experience.

In our case, I knew that a Mercedes Era van wouldn't allow us to experience anything we couldn't experience in our Winnebago Travato. It wouldn't allow us to see more places, meet more friends, or embrace a wider array of cultures. It would, however, cost more money to maintain. Most people trade time for money. They work at jobs to pay for what they need or want. Material upgrades that don't provide new experiences (beyond the initial sugar fix) often cost more not only to buy but also to maintain. As a result, people have to work harder to pay for these things—sucking time from their lives. And as I've mentioned, time is the only nonrenewable resource we have.

Unfortunately, we live in a culture of upgrades. Plenty of people upgrade their bikes, their RVs, their homes, and their cars. But we should always ask ourselves whether the upgrade would allow us to do something we couldn't have done before.

In some cases, the answer will be yes. But often it won't.

When I was young, I dreamed of racing in the Tour de France. I wasn't good enough to turn professional but I still won plenty of bike races. Recently, I became reacquainted with the sport. I paid $1,000 for a used racing bike (if you're a bike fan, it's a carbon fiber Norco with a Shimano Dura-Ace groupset).

About seven years ago, this bike was top of the line. It weighs 16 pounds (around 7 kilograms). That's just a single pound (less than 0.5 kilograms) heavier than the safe, minimum weight requirement for bikes in the Tour de France. If I were young enough and good enough to be knocking on the door of the Olympic team, that single pound *might* make a difference. But as a fifty-year-old guy without a time machine, a new and lighter bike won't provide me with a new experience. If I can't keep up with my friends on a 16-pound bike, I won't keep up on a 15-pound bike either.

Sometimes, though, spending more money on something can enhance the experience, especially if it's a big part of your life.

For example, one of my friends enjoys mountain biking with his buddies about four times a week. His bike cost about $2,000. But it didn't have rear shocks. As a result, on long technical descents with drops and roots, he couldn't keep up with his friends. After struggling in their dust for several months, he splashed out on a quality, full-suspension bike with front and rear shocks. That made a difference right away. Thanks to the suspension system, the bike doesn't beat up his body, and he can now keep up.

The popularity of e-bikes is another case in point. When I was in my twenties, I enjoyed cycling with a friend who was ten years older. He still loves to ride his bike. But he struggles with his health, so we rarely ride together. When he was healthy enough to ride, he was too self-conscious to ride with me. He worried that he would slow me down and I wouldn't enjoy the ride.

Recently, however, he bought an e-bike. It wasn't cheap. But as a result of that purchase, he can now ride with his friends again, enjoy their company, and... when he chooses to, leave us in his wake.

So here's how to test whether a purchase might provide an experience that boosts your happiness or well-being. Ask yourself if it creates experiences you wouldn't otherwise have. A new phone, purse, brand-name clothes, or car likely wouldn't do it, simply because of hedonic adaptation. Plenty of upgraded purchases (like a new racing bike for me) wouldn't provide more than a short-term boost. If a thing could improve your experience and you would use it a lot (like my friend's e-bike), purchasing the item makes sense. But be ruthless when assessing how much you'll use your "thing."

Most people with boats, for example, don't use them much. But they cost a lot to buy and maintain. So, if you'll only use a boat for two weeks a year, rent one instead. You'll enjoy the same experience at a fraction of the cost. That applies to many of the things you might want to buy but could rent instead, such as a tuxedo, wedding dress, or prom dress (unless you can alter and repurpose them).

For other things, I recommend the desert island litmus test.

The Desert Island Litmus Test

When Rob Fooks was a boy, he dreamed of owning a Porsche 911. When he became a lawyer, he was one step closer to achieving that dream. But unlike many young, high-salaried professionals, he refused to add additional debts to his student loans. Instead, he decided to wait.

He built his career, paid off his student loans, and saved enough money to buy his Porsche. He ordered the car and waited. But here's where the story takes a twist. When the sales rep finally called Rob to announce that his car had arrived, Rob didn't jump to pick it up. A few days later, the dealer called again. Still Rob stayed home. When the dealer called a third time, Rob did nothing. More than one week after the dealer's first call, Rob's wife, Tana, said, "Rob, the dealership called again. You need to get that car."

The Porsche was exactly what he wanted, a charcoal gray C4S Cabriolet. But when Rob finally arrived to pick it up, the salesperson noticed his lack of excitement. The dealer asked if there was a problem. "Don't worry," Tana said. "He loves the car. It's just him."

Rob parked the car in his garage and only drove it once or twice during the first two months. Recalling his favorite drive, he says, "The first time I really enjoyed the Porsche was on a long highway drive to British Columbia. I was alone with the car and I knew nobody was watching me. I know this sounds strange, but I felt a bit embarrassed to drive it."

Rob kept the car for several years but drove it less and less. "I saw the car more as an obligation and liability than a source of accomplishment or enjoyment, so I decided to get rid of it," he says.

This sounds like a midlife crisis in reverse. But many of us have complicated relationships with things we buy and own. If Rob lived on a desert island filled with winding mountain roads, he might have driven that Porsche every day. After all, he didn't buy it as a status symbol. Instead, he didn't want anyone to see him behind the wheel. When we're considering a high-status item, we should ask ourselves if we would still buy it if nobody else could ever see it. In Rob's case, the answer would have been yes. He would have bought—and kept— the Porsche. But I suspect that in most other cases, the answer would be no. Plenty of people buy high-status items to be seen having them, at least in part.

My wife and I recently met a woman named Deanne while we were mountain biking. As I pedaled behind her up a series of switchbacks, the athletic mother of two chatted about COVID-19. "It has one silver lining," she said. "It forced me to slow down and reflect on what's important." Before the pandemic, she spent plenty of time shopping for things she didn't need. I mentioned my desert island litmus test for high-status purchases. "That's interesting," she said. "I bought a Tesla Model S a couple of months ago. And if I'm really honest with myself, I don't think I would have bought it if nobody else could see it. I would have still bought an electric car if I lived on a desert island. But it would have been smaller and more modest."

This is worth thinking about when you're buying or upgrading a home, too. If nobody could ever see your home, would you still buy it or spend money on the upgrade? Our friends and family aren't going to love us any more or any less if we choose to buy a mansion on a hill, rent a swanky apartment, or update our living room. That's why the desert island question is a soul-searching litmus test. If you would still buy a bigger home or renovate your home if nobody outside your live-in family could ever see it, then go for it. But be honest with yourself. Ask yourself if these changes will enhance your overall life satisfaction. In most cases, they won't.

The *New York Times* referenced a German study where researchers tracked thousands of people in Germany who upgraded to different homes between 1991 and 2007. Five years after each person had bought their new home, the researchers asked them if the new homes had increased their overall levels of happiness. Overwhelmingly, respondents answered that it hadn't.[11]

The stuff we buy rarely makes us happier. More often, it actually has the opposite effect, whetting our appetites for even more because, for some reason, we think bigger, fancier, or newer things will make us happier. And if we borrow money to buy stuff, that can compound our misery. This is why, instead of buying more, or "better," stuff, consider spending your money on experiences. You might choose to take dancing, guitar, or cooking lessons. Perhaps you'll travel somewhere and learn a foreign language. Or maybe you'll save enough money to take some time away from work. It could be a sabbatical you spend with your family, exploring the country or enjoying a series of activities together. After all, the most important key to living well is having good relationships. We'll focus on that next.

Singles, What Are You Really Looking For?

Having read up to this point, some single people might say, "If I'm careful with my money, others might think I'm cheap. That might not help me when I'm dating and trying to find a life partner." But research says the opposite is true.

When I spoke with thirty-three-year-old Stephanie Weber, she was single and living in San José, California. Stephanie dated several high-income earners who work in the tech industry. She says the biggest spenders believe they impress their dates when they spend big, signaling their consumer power—but Stephanie finds it "a giant turnoff."

"One guy, who worked for Apple, invited me to an expensive steakhouse," she says. "And that was really nice. But he went out of his way to send clear signals about how much money he made and spent. He said he flew to LA every weekend in a private jet and asked if I wanted to come along." Stephanie comes from a family of business owners. But she says her family isn't foolish with their money.

"I've met so many high-income guys who spend everything they earn," she says. "Some of them rent gorgeous homes, yet they spend about 75 percent of their salary on their rent. That's irresponsible. I don't want to spend a lot of time with a person like that."

I also spoke with Gavin Taylor, a thirty-three-year-old single who lives and works in China. "I live down the street from a huge store that sells name-brand knockoffs," he says, "so I wouldn't really know if one of my dates spent more than they could afford. But if I were dating someone who spent $5,000 on a purse and $2,000 on their shoes, it might ring some alarm bells for me."

When I interviewed Jenna Nelson, a forty-seven-year-old single woman living in Kansas City, she said, "I always notice when someone is spending unwisely. If I see a profile photo of someone leaning against an expensive car or posting a photo of a bottle of ridiculously expensive wine, I won't even consider going out on a date with them. That might sound judgmental, but I've dated people who spent too much and struggled financially. So big-spending types are a deal-breaker for me." The research suggests most people agree with Stephanie, Gavin, and Jenna.

Jenny G. Olson, an assistant professor of marketing at Indiana University's Kelley School of Business, and Scott I. Rick, an associate professor of marketing at the University of Michigan's Ross School of Business, dug in to the dating scene. They wanted to see if singles preferred big spenders or people who were responsible with their money.[12]

Some of their experiments took place in online dating venues and others in traditional face-to-face environments. Of course, the study participants knew that the whole point of the exercise was to see how they evaluated romantic partners, rather than have them enjoy an actual date. In one experiment, single heterosexual students from a large Midwestern university pulled four questions at random from a container. They asked those questions to a participant of the opposite sex. One of the questions was "When it comes to money, would you say you're more of a saver or more of a spender?"

The research team then asked singles to alternate their responses each time: claiming to be a *spender* during one session and a *saver* during the next. This reduced bias toward physical attractiveness, which might have skewed the results.

After each question session, the researchers got the participants asking the questions to fill out a confidential online survey. One of the questions was "Which of these participants would you prefer to date?"

Overwhelmingly, the participants favored savers.

Olson and Rick also ran several online dating experiments where subjects chose a gender of their preference rather than restricting the research to heterosexual students. The profiles showed whether each person was more of a saver or a spender. Sometimes, spending habits were implied, rather than explicitly stated. The profiles revealed, for example, what each subject would do if they won a financial windfall.

In addition, the researchers altered the profile pictures, changing the subjects' levels of physical attractiveness. They didn't want the subjects' appearances to interfere with the variable they were studying. Once again, the subjects indicated they preferred to date people who appeared to be more responsible with money.

If this experiment had been conducted forty years ago, the results might have differed. Back then, most people who spent a lot of money actually had a lot of money. But credit card use (abuse), looser mortgage regulations, and auto loans have created a smoke-and-mirrors show.

"Spending is not necessarily an 'honest' signal of financial resources," say Olson and Rick. "Credit allows people to spend beyond their means, and observers may question whether big spenders are actually able to afford the items they buy. Moreover, savers are likely perceived as more capable of amassing and retaining wealth over the long run."

The researchers surmised another factor too. Subconsciously, the tendency to save might tell a prospective mate, "Hey, this person has self-control. It [self-control] might help them stay fit and healthy. It might help them commit to their promises and keep their temper under control when they have disagreements."

A Few Tips for Living Well

- The stuff you buy won't make you laugh more or love more, or help you attract a life partner.

- Material things rarely boost life satisfaction. But if an item provides an experience you couldn't ordinarily enjoy, especially if it enhances time with your friends, it might be worth the money. However, if you won't use it regularly, consider renting instead of buying.

- Spend less money on stuff and more on memorable experiences. When you're sitting around with a group of old friends, you'll almost never reminisce about the stuff you bought ten years ago. Instead, you'll talk about the things you did.

- Beware the slippery slope of upgrading what you own. This is often a waste of money because we get used to things quickly. Upgrades only make sense when your current item no longer works or the new one will make possible regular experiences with friends that you otherwise couldn't enjoy.

- Before purchasing something, consider the desert island litmus test. Ask yourself, "Would I still buy this if nobody else could see it?"

- Understand hedonic adaptation. Most of the things we buy—and that we don't really need—offer a short-term sugar high from which we quickly slump. That slump often drives us to then buy something else, and the process repeats itself ad infinitum.

2

WOULD YOU SAY NO TO A HIGH-PAYING JOB?

Binding Happiness, Health, Income, and Location

ANITA SUTTON WAS enjoying a bottle of wine with a friend when the words first tumbled out of her mouth: "I don't enjoy my job." Three years before, she'd been working as a primary school teacher, but now she had an educational leadership position. It was a job she had wanted, and it didn't hurt that it doubled her income.

At first she enjoyed the challenges of her new job. She learned new skills, took on new responsibilities, and thrived with a new set of co-workers. The extra income allowed her to buy finer things, take fancier holidays, and save more money for her retirement. But after only a couple of years, the role began to change. "More expectations kept being placed on me," she says, "And I didn't know how to say no without thinking it made me look like a failure." Anita's job took up an increasing amount of time—time away from friends and some of her passions, like salsa dancing, painting, cycling, and hiking.

Three years after accepting her promotion, she's back teaching. She preferred working with kids and didn't mind accepting a 50 percent drop in pay to do what she loved. Depending on who you are, where you live, and how much money you're making now, you'll either relate to Anita or think she wasn't thinking straight.

If someone doesn't have enough money to put food on their table or pay for decent shelter and medical care, more money will almost certainly make their life better. But there's a point at which more income doesn't increase life satisfaction.

You might have heard this income threshold is about $90,000 a year in the United States. Costs of living rise, so that number does too. However, we shouldn't all aim for that income level. To understand why, consider a pair of jeans. The average American man's waist size is 40.2 inches (or just over 1 meter) (a different kind of inflation that also rises every year). But only a tiny percentage of the male population has a waist that size. The vast majority is either slimmer or wider. Most men wouldn't tell an employee at a clothing store, "I'm interested in jeans with a 40.2-inch waist" just because that's the national average. That's as logical as saying, "I want to earn $90,000 a year because research suggests that will make me happiest." Your specific circumstances, much like your specific waist size, are the key factor.

Mindset, Money, and Happiness Extremes

Casey Coleman doesn't fit the stereotype of a homeless man. He's well read. His white hair is neatly cropped. He dresses in clean, casual clothes, and his eyes twinkle when he speaks. He looks more like a college professor or retired business executive. But the fit seventy-seven-year-old has lived in his car for the past twenty-seven years.

He doesn't drink, smoke, or do drugs. Nor is he a babbling conspiracy theorist (I've met several of these folks living off the grid). Casey is one of the clearest-thinking people I've ever met. Yet, every night, he sleeps in the passenger seat of his 2014 Subaru Outback.

When my wife and I met Casey, we were beginning a seventeen-month-long trip, exploring the United States, Mexico, and Central America in our camper van. As far as vans go, our 21-foot-long

Winnebago Travato is a roving Shangri-La. It has a shower, toilet, bed, two-burner propane stove, large refrigerator, TV, generator, microwave, air conditioner, and fancy electric awning. It also has a solar panel on the roof.

Casey's car doesn't have any of those things. He says he doesn't need them. He spends most of his time parked in the Kaibab National Forest, a quarter of a mile from the north entrance of Grand Canyon National Park, where it's free to camp. He also likes the mountains of the Anza-Borrego Desert State Park in southern California.

We met Casey at a mutual friend's home in Redlands, California. "Casey is the most consistently happy person I know," says his longtime friend Ingrid Dahlgren. The retired teacher loves it when Casey rolls up her driveway. She used to offer him the guest room. But he prefers to sleep in his car.

Casey meditates every morning. He also stretches and does push-ups. He then takes a long walk, often for two to three hours at a time. If he finds an abandoned item that he thinks might help someone, he brings it back to his car. At one point, while Pele and I were talking with Casey, she said I should buy a pair of shoes that I could slip on and off. "What's your shoe size?" Casey asked. When I told him, he walked over to his car and brought back a pair of slip-on Salomon running shoes. They fit perfectly.

"Where did you find these?" I asked.

"I found these one morning when I was walking along the beach. It's amazing what party-going kids will leave behind at night."

During his long walks, he often finds abandoned jackets or "trash" that people put at the end of their driveways for pickup in the morning. He then wanders into homeless communities and gives the stuff away. Often, he'll find a homeless person, hand them a jacket, and say, "It looks like you need a plan. Let's figure something out together." That's Casey Coleman's purpose.

After we'd spent a few days together with him at Ingrid's home, Casey asked, "Do you want to go on an adventure?" Few people have intrigued us more than Casey, so we jumped at the chance. We left Ingrid's home and followed Casey along the freeway before turning onto a much quieter road. Two hours later, we merged onto a dusty, narrow mountain track. Cacti and thorny plants scraped the sides of our van as we climbed high into the hills. We stopped when Casey found a free camping spot he liked.

For several days, we walked together every morning, exploring desert canyons and climbing high hills.

At the time, Casey had been "retired" for about twenty-six years. "I enjoyed plenty of jobs," he said. "I worked as a bartender, a lifeguard, a condominium maintenance worker. I raised funds for Greenpeace International and made candy in a factory." He's also a business graduate from the University of Southern California. He qualified for the Olympic trials as a swimmer, and thanks to his daily fitness routine and healthy eating, his physique doesn't look much different to how it must have looked in his prime.

Casey spends about $500 a month on living costs, including food, fuel for his car, insurance, and entertainment. He earns retirement income of $600 a month from the US government's Social Security plan and an additional $1,000 a month from money he invested in a lifetime annuity. Ironically, this homeless man saves about $1,100 a month.

I'm not saying you should ditch the "normal life" (whatever that is) and move into a car. However, we can learn a lot from a guy like Casey Coleman. I never expected, for example, that he would fit my definition of success. His four-legged table is strong and sturdy: he has enough money (based on his standards), he enjoys amazing health and great relationships, and he has a strong sense of purpose.

When Billionaires Meet Misery

To a large extent, once we have enough money for our basic needs, increases in income do little to boost our life satisfaction. In fact, sometimes extra money has the opposite effect, especially when it comes as a result of added workload or responsibility.

Other times, money can fuel flames of materialism that lead to misery. For example, a friend of mine owns an interior design company. To protect her privacy (and her career) I'm going to call her Janice. For the past twenty years, Janice has worked with the world's richest people. She says, "We don't typically work with clients who have less than $150 million." Hugh Grant would barely make the cut.

I still remember the first time I entered Janice's villa. On the wall, near the entrance, she had photographs of some of the work she had done. They included gorgeous interiors of palatial homes, yachts, and one interior I couldn't place.

"Janice," I asked, "what is this?" She grinned and said, "That's a private plane." It didn't look like any Learjet I had seen on TV. Instead, it was a 737 with an interior that looked like a five-star spa.

Janice loves to design, especially when the client pays with a fire hose of money. Her clients scream success—based on an incomplete definition of the concept. They have money and flashy things. But Janice says they're failures on emotional life support: "Over the past twenty years, I think I've only worked with one client who seemed happy." Many of her friends also design the interiors of billionaires' homes and super-yachts. When she gets together with those friends, they often share stories of misery and dysfunction among the uber-rich.

"When they have $500 million, they're only slightly psychotic," says Janice. "But once they hit $1 billion, most of them are completely crazy." She adds, "Many of them lose control of their lives. Their relationships are built on impressing other people with their fancy homes, yachts, airplanes, cars, and collectables. It's isolating because they have trouble establishing or maintaining real relationships with people who will love and respect them for who they are as people."

I don't believe most multimillionaires or billionaires are unhappy or psychotic. Plenty of them live healthy, balanced lives. But people who spend millions of dollars on self-wiping toilets (hey, you never know!) diamond-studded dog houses, and golden chandeliers might be different. They might place an unhealthy emphasis on material things.

And reams of research prove that highly materialistic people are far less happy than nonmaterialistic people. Janice's clients might sulk at one extreme while the ascetic Casey Coleman dances at the other.[1]

Could Too Much Income Make You Less Successful?

At the beginning of this chapter, I introduced the educational-leader-turned-schoolteacher Anita Sutton. Arguably, after she went back into the classroom (and had her salary cut in half) she was more successful. She had enough money, renewed health, strong relationships, and a sense of purpose. That doesn't mean educators in leadership positions are less successful than teachers. But it was true for Anita because the demands of her high-income job took time from the things she enjoyed.

Research from Purdue University suggests that Anita Sutton isn't unusual at all. A group of researchers assessed Gallup World Poll data from 1.7 million people. Like several previous studies, this study showed that happiness increases with income, but only to a point. For example, according to the Purdue study, North Americans who earned $105,000 a year reported higher levels of life satisfaction on average than those who earned $60,000 a year. But those who earned more than $160,000 a year reported lower levels of happiness on average than those who earned $105,000 a year.[2]

The Purdue University researchers say people with higher incomes often spend more money on material things. Like Janice's clients, a strong focus on "things" could detract from their life satisfaction. As previously mentioned, research reveals that materialistic people tend be far less happy than nonmaterialistic people. The Purdue researchers also surmised that the added responsibility and time commitments of higher-income jobs can take time away from what people enjoy most: connections with friends and family, healthy amounts of sleep, hobbies, and physical activity, for example.

Table 2.1 shows the highest relative income points at which happiness plateaus (at least, according to the Purdue study). However, it isn't until people earn significantly above these levels that reported happiness starts to drop. For example, the typical North American who earned above $160,000 a year reported being less happy than the typical North American who earned $105,000 a year.

TABLE 2.1

Happiness Satiation Points

Region	Satiation Point, Annually
Western Europe/Scandinavia	$100,000
Eastern Europe/The Balkans	$45,000
Australia/New Zealand	$125,000
Southeast Asia	$70,000
East Asia	$110,000
Latin America/The Caribbean	$35,000
North America	$105,000
Middle East/North Africa	$115,000
Sub-Saharan Africa	$40,000

Source: Andrew T. Jebb et al., "Happiness, Income Satiation, and Turning Points around the World."

You'll notice that people in different parts of the world require different levels of income before hitting their life-satisfaction highs. I should clarify that when the researchers conducted these surveys, they weren't asking, "How much money would you require to reach your highest level of happiness?" If they did, almost everybody (no matter how much money they make) would likely say they wanted more. That's human nature.

And there's another significant element that's worth reflecting on.

Income, Happiness, and the Power of Your Neighbors

Your income might be enough to cover your basic needs. But your life satisfaction might be determined by how much your neighbors make. Whether we admit it or not, most of us consciously or subconsciously compare ourselves to others. And we tend to be happier when we earn more than our neighbors. You might be above such behavior, like my buddy Casey Coleman. But even if it's your subconscious making these comparisons, your health could be affected.

I'll offer some helpful tips in this vein. But let me first share a story about a guy named Don Tetley. I arranged to interview Don for a story that I was writing for a financial magazine. He had retired in Cha Am, Thailand, where he lived on his US Social Security payments. Don pulled up at our prearranged meeting point in his Toyota truck, parking between a rusty scooter and an ancient Honda Civic. He had the classiest vehicle on the block by far. The lean sixty-five-year-old walked toward me, smiling as I shook his outstretched hand.

"I love living here," Don said, "because I don't have to keep up with the Joneses. In Thailand, I get to be Jones." As previously mentioned, research suggests Americans hit their income/happiness satiation point at about $105,000 a year. But Don is living proof that one size doesn't fit everyone. When we met, he earned far less than $105,000 a year. But he earned more than most of his Thai neighbors.

I'm not saying you should move to a low-income part of your country, or even to a different country, where crime might be high and people struggle day to day. But in Cha Am, Thailand, crime is low, and most of the residents earn enough money to live in relative comfort. What's more, Don can afford a lifestyle on his Social Security checks that he could never afford in the United States. Eating out at a restaurant could cost him as little as $4, including a beer. Massages cost about $12 an hour. Pedicures and manicures often cost half that.

You don't have to move to a foreign country to experience happiness. But I've learned a lot about happiness from some of the people I've met abroad. When my wife and I spent seventeen months in a camper van, traveling around Mexico and Central America, we met plenty of North American and European retirees like Don Tetley, living large in countries with a lower cost of living. We also met adventurous families raising their children in RVs as they toured countries like El Salvador, Guatemala, and Belize. The adventurers were some of the happiest people we've ever met.

One such family of adventurers is Stacey Joy, Matheu DeSilva, and their three young sons. They live in a 1979 Airstream motorhome. Stacey is originally from California. Her husband, Matheu, grew up in the UK. We met them in Ajijic, Mexico, where the couple performed a Joni Mitchell tribute concert. They invited us to their camping area for dinner and shared their story over a delicious chicken curry. The couple homeschool their children while traveling throughout Mexico and Central America, playing various gigs. Stacey also sells her music through several online retailers. They don't carry clutter or personal debts. They have everything they need, and they're able to save money. When they were stuck in Oaxaca, Mexico, during the COVID-19 lockdown, they didn't have to stress about feeding their children. Their simple living (not to mention money in the bank) probably resulted in their experiencing far less stress than most people felt when unemployment soared during the pandemic.

Unlike Janice's billionaire clients, Stacey and Matheu don't run on treadmills of consumption. Their success is much like that four-legged table. They don't earn a lot of money. But they earn enough to live and save. They're healthy. They nurture strong relationships and have a sense of purpose. Besides creating music, they're passionate about helping others. Matheu volunteers with several environmental projects, often traveling to South America to help local villagers protect their communities from illegal mining, deforestation, and poaching.

When High Incomes Aren't High Enough

After driving through Central America, we turned north, eventually reaching the United States. We met a couple (I'll call them John and Kathy) who live in Portola Valley, California. It's close to San Francisco. Hoping to strike up an easy conversation with John, I pointed to his Porsche 911 and said, "That looks like a really nice car."

John and Kathy both worked for a big tech company. They were lovely. But they had little in common with the nomadic families we met in Mexico and Central America. I was wearing what you might wear camping (if you weren't a glamper). My New Balance running shoes had holes in the side, from which my socks waved hello. There was a hole in my faded t-shirt from an old campfire that tried to set me ablaze. And my faded running cap looked like a dumpster-dive special. John didn't know anything about me. But he innocently asked if I also owned a Porsche. Clearly, he lived in a world where Porsches, Teslas, and Maseratis were regular runabouts.

As we saw earlier, happiness, related to income, is supposed to peak at about $105,000 a year in the United States. But I wondered how people who earned $105,000 would feel if they lived next to John and Kathy. In all likelihood they would struggle to pay the rent. If they wanted to buy a home in Portola Valley, they probably wouldn't qualify for a mortgage without outside help. As I'm writing this, the median listed home price in Portola Valley is $4.2 million.

Imagine this conversation between a student and his fifth grade teacher:

"Where do you live, Mrs. Smith?"

"Well, Tommy, I used to live 50 miles away. But I got tired of driving so far, so I found a nearby bridge and pitched a tent beneath it."

That sounds far-fetched. But I once knew a schoolteacher in Whistler, British Columbia, who lived in a treehouse because she couldn't afford the sky-high local rent.

Without an especially unique mindset, residents of Portola Valley might require far more than $105,000 a year to maximize their happiness. After all, several studies confirm that happiness and income are relative: that people with middle-class or upper-middle-class incomes can feel miserable if their neighbors swim in much bigger pools of cash—or even just much bigger pools.[3]

That's why people who earn $30,000 a year in Cha Am have higher odds of enjoying happiness when compared to people who earn $105,000 a year in Portola Valley. When we live in regions where the average person earns much more than we do, the higher earners (usually without intending to) often rub it in our faces. Parents in high-income regions can probably relate. They'll hear comments like: "Hey, Mom and Dad, all my friends got a new [insert a stupidly expensive gift here] on their sixteenth birthday. Why didn't I get one?"

Not everybody is in a position to choose to live where they want. That's why mindset is key. We need to focus on what we have and not on what we don't. Otherwise, living among higher-salaried people could also affect our health.

When Health and Money Clash

Imagine this scene. Camila and Kiara meet at a pub for a drink. Camila is a CFO in a small company. She earns about $120,000 a year. She bought a fine home in a neighborhood filled with much higher wage earners. Kiara is a nurse. She earns about $60,000 a year and lives among factory workers, teachers, and healthcare workers. Most of her neighbors earn slightly less than she does.

Suddenly, Camila leans back on her bar stool, burps, farts, then collapses in a heap. Heart attack. She's dead. Her income was high.

But her neighbors earned more, and that jeopardized her health. Camila's odds of dying in the pub (or anywhere else, for that matter) were higher than Kiara's. That's according to Michael Daly, an associate professor in behavioral science at the University of Stirling in the UK.

Daly's research team asserted that people's income rankings, among specific groups, predicted levels of health.[4]

Trying to keep up with higher-income neighbors (whether we do it consciously or subconsciously) hurts our health and our wealth. In fact, researchers have found that people who live next to lottery winners often end up bankrupt.[5]

Like frogs not leaping from soon-to-be boiling pots of water, they begin to follow the consumption habits of their newly wealthy neighbors. No, it doesn't make sense. But people still do it. And that leads to added debts and stress. And unfortunately, unnecessary stress can make us kick the bucket sooner than we otherwise might have done.

Even billionaires fall prey to peer-pressure spending. My friend Janice counts on that. "Obviously, we maximize our business income when our clients pay more. If someone is worth $1 billion, and they suggest a [relatively!] low budget for work they want us to do, we suck in our breath, mention someone they know who went for the higher-priced option, and that usually does the trick. They loosen their purse strings further." Janice says this strategy works because her uber-wealthy clients are hyper-competitive. They determine their personal value based on what others might say about the "stuff" they own.

Many wealthy people also socialize in circles where they aren't among the highest earners. As previously mentioned, happiness, as it pertains to wealth, is relative. For example, according to the *Forbes* list of richest Americans, Donald Trump's wealth ranked 265th in 2019. Some years, the 45th US president doesn't crack the top 400, so this is a pretty good ranking for The Donald. *Forbes* pegged his wealth at $3.1 billion.

Trump isn't known for having a big, happy smile. But if he lived in a neighborhood alongside Jeff Bezos, Bill Gates, and Mark Zuckerberg, he might scowl even more. After all, in 2019, the poorest of these guys, Zuckerberg, had twenty times as much money as Trump.

It might be especially tough on Trump if Warren Buffett lived next door. Imagine this scene: Buffett grabs a Cherry Coke from his fridge before wandering over to Trump's back porch. "Hey, Donald," he says. "I'm feeling pretty good today. I just donated $3.6 billion to charity." That's how much Buffett gave away in 2019. Between 2006 and 2020, he donated a staggering $37 billion, most of it to the Bill & Melinda Gates Foundation.[6]

Would Trump feel like a loser if he lived next to a man whose annual charitable donations exceeded his own net worth? If Trump were Gandhi or the Dalai Lama, maybe not. But he doesn't look or sound like either to me.

Matrimony and the Long Commute

So, research suggests we can be happier if our incomes match or exceed our neighbors' income levels, as long as we don't have to work too hard. There might, however, be at least one exception: if you commute long distances to work. Perhaps you decide to move to where houses are more affordable and your neighbors earn less. Based on happiness studies, this sounds like a decent move. But if you spend too much time commuting, your soulmate might leave you for a postal worker. The Swedish researcher Erika Sandow conducted a longitudinal study on commuters and relationships from 1995 until 2005. She found that divorce rates were highest among couples when at least one partner commuted a minimum of forty-five minutes to work.[7]

The journalist Annette Schaefer referenced several commuting-related studies in her article in *Scientific American*. She says people with longer commutes are less happy. They spend far less time with their families and on their hobbies. Commuting also affects their health. This could lead to fewer future birthdays as they kick the bucket young.[8]

Remember, time is the only nonrenewable resource we have. That's why we should treasure it. If we choose to work at a job we hate because it pays a lot of money, we're trading something precious for something that won't necessarily improve our lives. If we want to maximize our health and happiness, that's worth remembering.

A Few Tips for Living Well

- Don't chase a new position purely for the extra income if you already earn enough to cover your basic needs with a bit left over for savings. A higher-paying job might reduce your life satisfaction if it takes too much time away from your family, friends, hobbies, and health pursuits.

- If possible, consider jobs and careers that align with your passions so they don't feel a lot like work.

- Consider living in neighborhoods where your financial resources are aligned with, or slightly higher than, those of your neighbors. Just make sure it doesn't result in a long commute to work.

- If you can't choose where you live, remember that mindset is key. Focus on what you have and not on what you don't.

3

YOUR REAL SUPERPOWER

Building Social Relationships
to Live Better and Longer

NOT LONG AGO, when Corona was just a beer, Pele and I cycled around Costa Rica on our tandem. We enjoy splashing out on the occasional resort, especially after pedaling up the shoulder of a volcano or battling a rocky dirt road for 30 miles (one that our travel app claimed was paved).

But backpacker haunts are our favorite places to stay. That's usually where we meet the most interesting people. During our final week in Costa Rica, we walked along a near-deserted Caribbean beach a few miles from our hostel. It was run by some Argentinians who had come to the area as tourists and then decided to stick around.

It was easy to see why they stayed. The local food was great. The cost of living wasn't expensive and, unlike a resort-packed town, the place didn't have many tourists. As the sun started to set, we saw an American family practicing yoga on the beach. They laughed as three of the four family members toppled from a pose onto the still-warm sand.

Amy Halloran-Steiner was the last one standing. She and her husband, Silas, live on a small farm near McMinnville, Oregon. They brought their two children, fourteen-year-old Ukiah and twelve-year-old Metolius, to Costa Rica for more than just a vacation in the sun. "We decided to plan for a life pivot," says Amy. "I took an extended leave from my job as a clinical social worker/mindfulness teacher, and Silas left his job as director of Yamhill County Health and Human Services."

Amy and Silas planned to stay in Costa Rica for several months. They don't have high incomes, but smart life choices helped them save enough money to take a long break from work. "I've never spent more than $8,000 on a car," says Silas. Instead of spending money on material things, they prefer to spend it on having experiences together. "Time goes so fast," says Amy. "By saving that money, we are able to eke out precious moments with our family."

An extended family trip to a foreign country might not appeal to everyone. But the research on life satisfaction says Amy and Silas have the right idea. Prioritizing time to nurture our relationships is the single greatest key to a happy life.

In Brené Brown's bestselling book *Daring Greatly*, she writes, "Connection is why we are here. We are hardwired to connect with others. It's what gives us purpose and meaning to our lives, and without it there is suffering."[1] Brown's research aligns with findings from the Harvard Study of Adult Development.[2]

The ongoing eight-decade-long Harvard study started with 268 male Harvard sophomore students in 1938 (the college didn't allow women at the time). Researchers tracked them to see what circumstances and behaviors led to healthy and happy lives. Eventually, they expanded the study to include the subjects' children. In the 1970s, the research expanded again to include 456 Boston inner-city residents. The researchers compiled their early findings through questionnaires and interviews with both the subjects and their families. The ongoing research now includes a battery of medical tests, like CT scans and MRIs, methods that would have seemed like science fiction when the study began. As you might expect, some of the original subjects ended up wealthy, while others went broke.

Some led stable lives at first, only to come off the rails later. Others started off rough but got their lives on track.

However, one theme rings true for every demographic group in this near-century-long study: Close relationships—far more than money—are the single greatest influence on a happy life. In fact, personal relationships are better predictors of happiness, health, and longevity than social class, IQ, or even genetics.

This is why spending time with friends and family makes so much sense. It's why Amy and Silas set a goal and then followed through with their plan to spend several months with their children in Costa Rica. But the benefits extended beyond the effects on their immediate family. Amy and Silas also volunteered at an orphanage, which let them connect with the local community. At home in Oregon, they also organize their friends and general community to plant trees together each year.

In developing countries, communities rely on each other more. As regions become more affluent, the inhabitants begin to pull away from each other—much to our personal and collective detriment.

The Roseto Effect

In 1964, research published in the *Journal of the American Medical Association* claimed that the town of Roseto, Pennsylvania, was a medical marvel.[3]

The researchers found that residents in this small town lived far longer than people elsewhere in the United States. Mortality rates were 30 to 35 percent lower than they were in nearby towns. It was rare for anyone under the age of sixty-five to suffer from heart disease. Scientists studied the town's water and found it was no different to the water in neighboring communities. They initially assumed Roseto residents' diet might be better but learned that wasn't the case. The residents loved sugary foods. Many smoked cigarettes and were overweight. Nothing they ate or drank explained why they lived so long.

Several years later, scientists found the answer: Roseto was phenomenally social. The residents took care of each other and stuck to the old Italian traditions of their ancestors. They lived in multigenerational homes. They were always socializing in each other's homes, reportedly wandering in and out as if the community were one giant family. They also often cooked and celebrated together in large groups.

Roseto had a population of about two thousand people—and twenty-two civic organizations, including fishing and hunting clubs, library groups, sports clubs, and Christian youth organizations. The people in Roseto who had a lot of money didn't show it off. That was considered poor taste, so they lived in modest homes and drove modest automobiles.

There are several documented locations in the world where people live impressively long, happy lives. Known as Blue Zones, they include Okinawa, Japan; Sardinia, Italy; Nicoya, Costa Rica; Ikaria, Greece; and Loma Linda, California.[4] Their community social fabrics are much like Roseto's—at least, they're much like Roseto's used to be.

In the 1970s, Roseto began to change. More of the town's young residents began to pursue the American Dream. They built bigger houses, farther from their neighbors. They began to drive more instead of walking. The town's highly social culture began to crumble. By 1980, heart disease and mortality rates had jumped. Today, Roseto still has about two thousand residents. But their highly social lifestyle, widespread robust health, and impressive longevity are now just footnotes from their past.[5]

We can learn a lot from Roseto. In Dan Buettner's book *Blue Zones*, the journalist and community developer doesn't just explain where the Blue Zones are and why they exist; he also encourages community-driven projects to boost health and longevity in US towns and cities. He does that with his Blue Zones Project work, which encourages communities to mirror the strong social fabrics that are common in every Blue Zone region. In one sense, he's trying to re-shape communities to mirror the old Roseto. And so far, the results have been impressive. For example, in Beach Cities, California, local officials employed the Blue Zones Project in 2010 because obesity was high among children and adults. Surveys also showed community stress levels were high. The Blue Zones Project focused on bringing people together and encouraging physical activity. Seven years after the project started, adult obesity levels had dropped by 25 percent and childhood obesity had dropped by 68 percent. The number of Beach Cities residents who exercised for at least thirty minutes a day, three days a week, had increased by 9 percent. Perhaps the most impressive improvement was shown in a 2015 well-being survey conducted on 190 metropolitan areas in the United States. Beach Cities took the #1 spot.[6]

In a post-pandemic world we should open our doors (or at least our backyards) to neighbors in ways that we haven't done before. We can increase our number of community barbecues, block parties, clean-up projects, tree-planting projects... anything that brings people together. After all, we crave real connections. Not having them can shorten our lives, make us less happy, and lead to regrets in our final years.

Embracing Other People and Yourself

The best relationships are honest and forgiving. They include the relationships you have with other people and the relationship you have with yourself. Bronnie Ware is an Australian nurse who worked in palliative care for several years. She spent a lot of time with patients in their last twelve weeks of life. Ware interviewed her patients about their lives and subsequently wrote her book *The Top Five Regrets of the Dying*.

When asked about their regrets in life, the dying patients didn't say they wished they had lived in a bigger house, driven better cars, worn better clothes, or owned more stuff. They didn't wish they had had better-paying jobs. Their top five regrets were more relationship-based.

- They wished they had lived true to their values, instead of living lives that others expected of them.

- They wished they hadn't worked so hard.

- They wished they had the courage to express their feelings.

- They wished they had stayed in touch with old friends.

- They wished they had let themselves be happier, instead of falling into boring routines.[7]

One of the five points Bronnie Ware listed might bring back memories of your childhood. At one point, a friend of yours likely urged you to do something stupid. In response, your parents might have sounded much like mine: "If your friend stuck his head in a fire, would you do that too?" We all faced early peer-pressure tests. And in plenty of cases, as Bronnie Ware learned, people go through life still influenced by others. Are we true to ourselves? Or are we living a life and doing things that others expect of us?

Parents try to prepare their children for the realities of life. Sometimes, their strategies are really messed up, though. For example, my friend Joe grew up next door to a boy named Chris, who was bigger than he was. One day, when they were about ten years old, the pair got into a fight. Chris pummeled Joe, who came home with a bloody nose. But instead of consoling his son, Joe's father yelled, "Stop your crying. Get back over there and give *him* a bloody nose!" While Joe and I laugh about it now, going back for more didn't help his relationship with Chris.

Unlike Joe's dad, my father didn't focus on raising a physically tough son. Instead, he tried to toughen me up socially. He didn't want his kids losing themselves to what others expected of them. But his teaching methods (if we could call them that) would have humiliated even the most freakishly stoic kid.

When I was fifteen years old, I sometimes hung out with friends at the local mall's food court. Streams of other kids—some from our school, some from other schools—often did the same. I had the deluded idea that we could pick up girls there. We had great hopes. But we were like tennis players swinging fly swatters. One weekend, my dad and I went to that same shopping mall. Like many teenagers, I usually tried to avoid my dad when my peers were around. Sensing my weakness, he chose to exploit it for his own entertainment and to socially toughen me up.

We walked past the food court, which was filled with teenaged kids. Then my dad took my hand. My father was a mechanic with a viselike grip. Without trying to attract attention, I said from between my teeth, "Dad, let go of my hand." He just smiled and squeezed harder. "Dad," I seethed, with quiet desperation. "Let go of my hand." I thought every kid was looking. If they weren't, they soon would be. Releasing his grip, he stepped back, put his hands on his hips, and announced, "Just because I'm so much older than you doesn't mean you should be ashamed of our relationship!"

If that happened today, some kid would film it and the whole scene would go viral on YouTube. I might have needed lifetime psychiatric treatment. Luckily for me, it was the 1980s. And although nobody should ever do this to their kids, his antics, of which there were many, really might have worked. I grew increasingly immune to social pressure. (I got him back in my twenties. My dad was on a packed public bus that I stopped with my car. I flashed a bogus credential and paraded him off the bus while claiming to be saving everyone from a dangerous escaped patient from a mental health hospital.)

OK, so maybe my dad did mess me up. But being true to ourselves and not allowing ourselves to be swayed by other people's expectations lets us create a healthier relationship with ourselves. Peer-pressure influences can be good if you're encouraged to be honest, eat well, exercise, and be kind to other people. Unfortunately, they're often negative.

When Societal Pressures Harm Our Relationship with Ourselves

When people are in their early twenties, plenty of them feel they can do almost anything. I recall seeing this with my former high school students in Singapore. They graduated from high school and then left for elite colleges in the United States. Because their expatriate parents still lived and worked in Singapore, they would come back to see their families, often returning to the school to visit us, their former teachers. They arrived confident, like triumphant conquerors. I recall one of my former students visiting from Yale. We went out for lunch, and she said, "I'm going to change the world!" But over time these same students began to change. In the years that followed, they came back less confident.

At least one piece of research suggests this is normal. The economics professor David Blanchflower says life satisfaction among adults tends to hit one high when we're in our early twenties and another after we've passed fifty. He assessed data from 132 countries and found the data was consistent across developed countries.[8]

Not everyone rides the same life-satisfaction swing. Dispositions differ. Some people view the world as a half-full glass. Others are the opposite. But on average, the research is consistent. In our early twenties we radiate strength and confidence. We hit a point (laughably early) when we're deluded enough to think we know more than our parents. We live to party and have sex. Mortgages, bills, and retirement planning are vague forms in the distance.

But careers, student loans, marriage, children, divorce, bills, and retirement planning can make us feel like Atlas, carrying the world. By our late thirties and forties, insecurity is peaking. Our stresses are mounting. We're pining for the artificially enhanced highlights (often outright lies) that we see on Facebook and Instagram—and working hard to maintain our own artificial images. There are plenty of benefits to social media. But according to research, the more often we use it, the more miserable we become.[9]

In Jonathan Rauch's book *The Happiness Curve: Why Life Gets Better after 50,* he says people in their thirties and forties grind away on metaphorical treadmills. They try to boost their happiness with an increase in status or status-oriented stuff.[10]

We might seek a higher-status job, buy a better car, or upgrade our home, expecting it to improve our lives—and then we often post about it on Facebook. But these things don't improve our lives. Unfortunately, though, we're often slow learners. It takes longer than it should for us to learn that status and stuff don't make us happier. As a result, we might shift jobs again, buy an even better car, upgrade our kitchens again, or fill our lives with other material acquisitions. Deep down we think, "I'm really going to enjoy this."

But as Rauch says, "The same ambition that made us status hungry makes us hungry for more status. We're on the hedonic treadmill." However, by the time we're in our fifties, he says, we don't typically feel the same need to pursue status. We begin to care a lot less about what other people think. It's like a slow weight being lifted from our shoulders.[11]

Research suggests we also narrow our social circles as we age. We decide to spend less time with people who don't enhance our lives, socially, emotionally, or spiritually, and more time with people we've formed deep connections with. This could be one more reason for increased life satisfaction after middle age.[12]

Fortunately, you don't have to be in your fifties, sixties, or seventies before you figure this out. You could choose to focus on mutually nurturing relationships at a much younger age. You could be true to yourself and not chase the shadow of an image. That's easier said than done. But we can do it. We can also improve how we feel about ourselves when we're kind and generous.

Being Kind Can Help Us Live Longer and Better

When I was in my twenties, I often secretly paid for restaurant meals for other people. I wasn't trying to be a saint. At the time, it was entertainment. I might be eating lunch with a friend or one of my sisters. We would then surreptitiously scour the lunch crowd to figure out whose lunch we should pay for.

We spent half our mealtime cycling through prospects. Sometimes we chose people who looked kind, sad, or lonely. Other times we selected someone who was belligerent to a server. We smiled at the thought of messing with an angry person's head. Once we agreed on a person or couple, we asked the server to secretly bring us their bill. We enjoyed watching from afar as the server said, "Someone in this restaurant just paid for your lunch." Nobody ever suspected us.

I've done plenty of things for laughs. My friends often say, "Do you remember the time you [fill in something stupid here]?" Sometimes I remember. Sometimes I don't. But I recall almost every time I anonymously paid for someone's meal.

Studies suggest there might be a reason for that. According to research published by the American Psychological Association, we gain more pleasure when we spend money on other people, compared to when we spend it on ourselves.[13]

In one experiment, the researchers asked passersby to rate their current levels of happiness. The researchers then gave them an envelope containing either a $5 bill or a $20 bill. They asked the passersby to spend the money before 5:00 pm. Half were told to buy a treat for themselves, and the other half were told to spend the money on someone else.

When the researchers called at 5:00 pm, they asked each participant to rate their level of happiness. Those who'd spent the money on someone else reported higher levels of happiness than those who'd spent the money on themselves. It didn't matter whether they spent $5 or $20.

The optometrist Dr. Elaine Kerr had a similar experience. She was at a multiday conference at Pan Pacific Vancouver when some friends convinced her to join them on a shopping trip to the Fluevog shoe store in Gastown. Caught up in the moment, she bought a pair of expensive shoes. But she began to feel uncomfortable as she walked past street people panhandling for food and money.

At the end of the second day of the conference, she noticed plenty of bagged lunches that the attendees hadn't taken, so she decided on a plan. She grabbed as many bags as she could carry and headed back toward the shoe store. Along the way she greeted the homeless people she encountered and offered them a lunch bag. "I asked them if they were hungry," she says. "I gave out all those bags and people really appreciated it. It wasn't just the food; they seemed genuinely amazed that somebody noticed and spoke to them. I felt great."

She returned her expensive shoes for a refund and donated that money to the food bank. It wasn't that she didn't love the shoes, but making a small difference in someone's day gave her much more joy. "It felt amazing. It reinforced my thoughts about what gives me joy. I never missed those shoes or regretted returning them." She told me this is a memory she won't forget. It simply made her feel good.

Elaine's happy sentiment supports summarized findings compiled in a Harvard Business School paper. In one such example, a Gallup World Poll asked more than 200,000 people whether they had donated money to charity over the previous month. The survey also asked them to rate their levels of happiness. In 120 out of 136 countries, those who donated money reported being happier. This trend emerged in both rich and poor countries. The giver's income level didn't matter.[14]

However, the study didn't specify different types of charitable giving. Elizabeth Dunn, a psychology professor at the University of British Columbia and co-author of *Happy Money*, says that when people give money and they see the results of their generosity, it gives them far more pleasure than donating money to a faceless organization. She calls this "prosocial giving."[15]

Prosocial Spending Might Be Best

As a happiness researcher, Dunn knew that donating money is supposed to make people feel happier. But when she donated money, she found it didn't boost her mood. She describes this in her TED Talk, "Helping Others Makes Us Happier—but It Matters How We Do It."

She says we're happier when we can witness our generosity in action. In her case, she joined a group of twenty-five people who helped a family of Syrian refugees move to Canada. They raised money as a group (providing a social, team-like element) and sought additional help from a corporate sponsor. They found a home for the family, filled the refrigerator with food, and met the family when they arrived at the airport. To this day, she says these refugees are part of her extended family.

In her TED Talk she adds that prosocial giving, such as what she did for the Syrian family, affects the giver more positively compared to how the giver feels when they can't see the benefit. "Back in the lab, we had seen the benefits of giving spike when people felt a real sense of connection with those they were helping and could easily envision the difference they were making."[16]

This brings me back to those secret restaurant meals. We had fun trying to figure out who would get a free lunch. You and your friends could do something similar. But to boost the benefits of prosocial giving, you might share lunch and a conversation with an elderly couple. You might pool money for a laptop so a teen from a low-income family could do their school assignments. You might make bagged lunches and gift them to people living on the street.

You might also enjoy lending money to small business owners in a global region of your choice through Kiva.org. In some ways, this beats donating money. After all, the recipients use your money to empower themselves. For example, you could lend as little as $25 to a woman in Bangladesh who's trying to open a bakery, or a man in the Philippines who's opening his own roadside food stall. Assume they required a total of $200. In that case, your $25 would get pooled with loans from other people who chose to lend money to the same person. There are more than a dozen categories of people you can help on Kiva's website. For example, there's a category for helping single parents, buying livestock, and helping people with expenses related to education. You can also select recipients in specific regions: North America, Central America, South America, Africa, Eastern Europe, the Middle East, or Asia.

When you donate via Kiva, a separate loan company vets the applicants and charges the loan recipient interest. As the lender, you don't receive interest, but if the recipient defaults on the loan, you'll often get most of your money back. The loan company often ponies up the money to limit your losses. That way you don't feel discouraged and (they hope) you'll continue to use Kiva to loan money to other people. It becomes a form of empowerment instead of charity.

You could have coffee or lunch with a few friends and select someone on Kiva whose plight and challenge speak to you. If each of you lends money to the same person, you'll feel like a team making a difference. It's something you could do together for a different person every month. According to research, this act might even boost your health, your strength, and help you live longer.

Boosting Health and Strength

While conducting research for her book *Growing Young*, the journalist Marta Zaraska asked a couple of scientists to help her conduct an experiment. She had read plenty of research studies suggesting that acts of kindness boost people's health and wanted to conduct one on herself. The scientists mailed her plastic tubes to collect her saliva three times a day (morning, noon, and night) for seven consecutive days. Zaraska then mailed her spit back to the Stress, Psychiatry and Immunology Lab (otherwise known as the SPI-Lab) at King's College London, where the scientists measured her cortisol levels.

Cortisol is part of a chain reaction that contributes to stress. Too much of it can affect our mood, which can in turn lead to health complications. During four of the saliva collection days, the researchers asked Zaraska to live as she normally would. But on the other three days, they asked her to commit to performing specific acts of kindness.

The third day of the week-long experiment was her first conscious kindness day. She explains in *Growing Young*:

> As I sat down at my desk planning what fun things I could do for others, I felt my spirits lifting... I bought and delivered a small box of chocolates for the nice lady at our local library. At a grocery store, I rushed to open the doors for an elderly woman with a heavy shopping bag. And in the evening I left five-star Google Maps reviews for all my favorite local restaurants and services.[17]

Not only did she feel happier during her three kindness days, but she also recorded cortisol levels that were 16 percent below her baseline level. This meant she was less stressed. Consequently, if she continued such kindness, she might boost her longevity.

This experiment involved only one person, but several large, peer-reviewed scientific studies have produced the same conclusions: kindness and generosity make us stronger and happier, and they boost human longevity.

For example, researchers at the University of British Columbia conducted experiments on seniors who suffered from hypertension. Every week for three weeks, they gave each senior $40. They split the subjects into two groups: one group had to buy something for themselves, the other had to spend the money on someone else. At the end of the three weeks, the group who were asked to spend the money on someone else recorded lower blood pressure levels.[18]

Some might point to a 1999 study on mortality rates among elderly people who looked after their disabled spouses and argue that kindness and helping others won't extend your life. But one of that study's original researchers told Marta Zaraska that they only studied the very old and frail.[19]

Zaraska's book references several large studies confirming that caring for others helps us live longer. In one such briefly titled study, "Family Caregiving and All-Cause Mortality: Findings from a Population-Based Propensity-Matched Analysis," researchers found that mortality rates for caregivers were 18 percent lower than for non-caregivers in similar demographic groups.[20] And grandparents who spend time caring for their grandchildren appear to experience similar benefits. The Berlin Aging Study found "mortality hazards for grandparents who provided non-custodial childcare were 37% lower than for grandparents who did not provide childcare and for non-grandparents." And it wasn't because they were healthier when they began. The research controlled for physical health, age, socio-economic status, and various characteristics of the children and grandchildren.[21]

Caring for others could also improve your strength. Here's something you could try with your children before a sports competition. Give them an opportunity to do something kind before they compete. It might help them win.

Kurt Gray, a psychology professor at the University of Maryland, led a team of researchers who asked people in a Boston subway station if they wanted to conduct a strength experiment with a 5-pound (2.3-kilogram) weight. Subjects held the weight away from their bodies with a fully extended arm. The researchers asked them to hold it there as long as possible. After testing the subjects' muscular endurance, they let the subjects rest. Then they gave them a dollar for their help. But while doing so, they asked the subjects if they wanted to donate that dollar to UNICEF or keep it for themselves. Then they tested their strength again. Those who donated the money were able to hold the weight 15 percent longer than they did before. Those who kept the money did not show any improvement.[22]

Many people set career-oriented goals, money-related goals, or personal health goals. If you asked, "Why do you want to achieve these goals?" they would provide a variety of reasons. But if you kept asking, "*Why* do you want that?" most people would likely zero in on the same thing: "I think it will make me happy."

Yet how many times do we set goals to help other people? Some people do it naturally, just like some people find it easy to exercise and eat healthy foods. But many others (me included) often get distracted. That's why we should focus on the research. Our relationships—with ourselves and with others—impact our life satisfaction and health more than any fitness regime or diet.

A Few Tips for Living Well

- Increase the amount of time you spend with people you love and respect.

- Go narrow and deep with your relationships (a few good friends), not broad and shallow (many acquaintances).

- Be true to yourself as a person. Don't chase status or a lifestyle you think others expect from you.

- Limit the time you spend on social media. Your life satisfaction and your health will benefit.

- Be kind and generous with other people. If possible, make it a prosocial experience.

- Support and participate in activities that promote social and/or community interaction.

4

WHO ARE YOU GOING TO FOLLOW?
Learning from Gratitude

A FEW YEARS AGO, a Channel NewsAsia reporter interviewed
me for a story on my book *Millionaire Teacher*. She asked about
my upbringing and my 2009 bout with cancer. When she asked
about my illness, I looked straight at the camera and said something
that rattled the reporter. In fact, the producers cut my words from
the interview. I've said plenty of dumb things in my life (haven't we
all?), but they omitted one of the wisest things I've ever said.

In 2009, I was thirty-nine years old. I was fit and, as far as I knew,
healthy. In each of the previous five years, I had tried to win one of
the biggest running races in Singapore: the JP Morgan Chase Corporate Challenge. I was never far behind the winner, but I had never
broken the winner's tape. I was getting a little long in the tooth for
such a short, fast event. But I hoped 2009 was going to be my year.

After they fired the starting gun, I ran with the lead pack until the
halfway point. More than eleven thousand others were strung out
behind us. I surged ahead with Melvin Wong, a man who would soon
represent Singapore on the international stage. We stayed together
until the final mile (just over 1.5 kilometers). Then I began to inch

ahead. We each knew the race was supposed to be 5.6 km. But that year, the organizers had chosen to move the finish line. Unfortunately, they hadn't properly measured the new course. It was half a kilometer longer than expected. That might not sound like much. But when you're trying to empty the tank, learning there's an extra 500 meters to go brings on a lot of hurt.

I pushed myself and won, becoming the oldest winner in the event's history.

Then my life fell apart. A few months later, I was diagnosed with bone cancer.

Cancer affects everyone. You, your friends, or your parents might have had it. In my case, a routine scan found a cancerous tumor engulfing three of my ribs.

I soon had surgery to partially remove the three ribs, some vertebral bone, and some of my lung lining. The surgeon also cut a large, healthy muscle in my back (the lower left part of my latissimus dorsi) and folded it over the hole they created when they extracted the three ribs. After the operation, the surgeons asked, "Can you move your toes?" To my horror, they seemed happy, even surprised, that I could.

After months of physical therapy, I was able to run again.

This brings me back to the reporter. She said, "Now that you've had a life-threatening illness, I suppose it makes you value life more." I looked straight at the camera and said, "No. It doesn't matter how high someone's IQ is supposed to be. If they need their own life-threatening illness to recognize that one day they're going to die, then that person is an idiot."

Yeah, it was a harsh thing to say. Part of me understood why they cut that comment. Perhaps the word "idiot" wasn't fair. Perhaps, if I had tempered my judgment just a bit, I could have shared what I believed to be the most important message: We're all going to die. Our friends and loved ones are going to die. That's why we should live with gratitude, being thankful for our lives and the lives of our friends and loved ones. It's easier to do this when we remind our-selves daily that we're all here temporarily.

My oncologist, Dr. Steven Tucker, joked about this when he told me, "People always ask me, 'Am I going to die?' I feel like saying, 'Yeah, of course you will. If you were creeping around two hundred years from now you would freak people out.'"

Your life is like a dark hourglass. It gets tipped at birth, and nobody knows how much sand they have left. That's why we should live with the knowledge that every day is precious. If we're going to emu-late the lifestyles of others, who do we choose to follow, and why?

Abandoning an Unhealthy Path

When Ashley MacPherson was in her early twenties, life seemed almost perfect. She had enjoyed herself as a student and then as a young working professional. She had mounting student loan debts, but they didn't bother her at the time. "It was a blissful time of life where I just dug deeper and deeper into [student loan] debt and didn't worry about paying it back," she remembers. She figured she would pay it back eventually but she wasn't worried, because almost everyone she knew was swimming in a pool of debt too.

When she and her husband, Morgan, began their careers, their combined student loans topped $125,000. The couple spent money on things they couldn't afford: too many restaurant meals, trips, expensive clothes and purses, brand-name watches, and a luxury car. Ashley says, "These things weren't making life better, and here I was, three years after graduating. I was making a great salary and I had hardly put a dent in my student loan. Was this the life we wanted to set up for ourselves and our kids?"

In many ways she followed the same well-worn path that most of her friends were following. But her stress levels soared after the couple had their first child and their credit card bills hit an all-time high. While Ashley was on maternity leave, their household income plunged. The couple also still had large mortgage payments, car payments, and oppressive student loans. "I suddenly realized I wasn't going to have enough money to pay all the bills at the end of the month," she says.

Ashley could have buried her head in the sand or blamed others for her neck-high debt. But she took action instead. She temporarily put her student loan payments on hold and stopped going to Starbucks. She also began to purge. "We sold a lot of stuff—purses, dresses, baby stuff we weren't using, motorcycle gear, my beloved Michael Kors watch that I had to have but only wore about five times in three years. I also told my husband that we shouldn't buy lunch or even coffee when we're out of the house. It was an eye-opening month, but we scraped by and I'm proud to say that we did not go further into debt during my maternity leave."

Soon after, they sold their house and now they're renting a home in a lower-priced area. Ashley and Morgan did something else that helped them succeed. They continued to socialize with friends and family instead of keeping their noses to the grindstone at the expense of their relationships.

Shawn Achor was a teaching assistant for the most popular course in Harvard University's history: Tal Ben-Shahar's Happiness course. After spending several years at Harvard, he founded GoodThink, a research and corporate training firm. He also wrote several best-selling books, including *The Happiness Advantage: How a Positive Brain Fuels Success in Work and Life.*[1] Achor says when we face tough challenges we shouldn't hide in a cave. If we have high debts, for example, we shouldn't shut off our social networks to focus on that debt. Instead, we should keep every social channel firing. As waves of research say, we're social animals. We thrive when we're social. We're happier and healthier when we spend time with friends and family. This also helps us to achieve our goals.

Ashley and Morgan continued to see their friends. They just met where it didn't cost money, or where it didn't cost them too much.

And when they eventually resumed their trips to Starbucks, they didn't go several times a week, as they had in the past. Instead, they made it a special treat.

As a result, they're now completely debt-free. They're saving money to buy a home and they're investing money. They ditched their quest to keep up with other people. Consequently, they can now build wealth, which in turn can boost their life satisfaction if they spend their money right.

Mind over Money

I was born in 1970. I'm part of the so-called Generation X. My parents were born in the mid-1940s, representing the first of the Baby Boomers. My parents' generation bought more stuff than their parents did. And Gen-Xers typically buy more than Baby Boomers do. Each subsequent generation has earned higher levels of disposable income. This is a common trend in most developed countries. According to Economic Research, Federal Reserve Bank of St. Louis, real median household income in the United States increased 30.4 percent between 1984 and 2019. In other words, after adjusting for inflation, a person's buying power increased by almost one third.[2]

However, according to the US General Social Survey, Americans aren't as happy today as they were in 1984. Each year since 1976, the survey has asked Americans to rate whether they were "very happy," "somewhat happy," or "not too happy." The trend has been downward since 1993.[3]

Research suggests our insatiable quest for more stuff might be making us less happy. And the debts we acquire might compound the problem.

In 2020, the average American owed $6,194 in credit card debt.[4] Their northern neighbors weren't much better. The average Canadian owed about $3,636 (in USD) in credit card debt.[5] And when you factor in the *Financial Post*'s report that Canadians pay a higher percentage of their income to service all debts—including credit cards, auto loans, and mortgages—compared to residents in any G7 country, it's a dire picture, no matter how you slice it.[6]

And why do US houses keep getting bigger? American households have fewer children than they did fifty years ago. Logic therefore suggests new houses should be smaller. But the average house size increased by 1,000 square feet (almost 93 square meters) between 1973 and 2015.[7]

Unfortunately, many people struggle to make mortgage payments on these bigger homes. In 2017, *Bloomberg*'s Alexandre Tanzi reported that 9.1 percent of US homeowners had mortgage debt that was higher than their homes were actually worth.[8]

Americans also stretch themselves financially to drive cars they can't afford. According to *The Psychology of Money* author Morgan Housel, the average car loan, adjusted for inflation, doubled between 1975 and 2003. Household debt, as a percentage of income, more than doubled between 1972 and 2007. Interest rates dropped. But the percentage of income that people put toward their debt is near an all-time high. And in 2020, auto loan debt hit an all-time peak, with the average loan reaching $33,739.[9]

Rampant consumerism has spread far beyond North America. It's also tough to dodge—especially when we see plenty of our colleagues, friends, and neighbors who appear to have so much more than we do. If that's how you sometimes feel, here's a story that might help you feel better.

Our Spending Culture Reveals a Mirage

For many people, swimming at a popular beach is a self-conscious experience. Stripping down to our bathing suits, we reveal all our bumps, folds, and jiggles. Some men and women show off Greek god–like physiques. Thanks to a combination of genetics and hard work (sometimes even pharmaceuticals and implants), they reveal rock-hard abs, perfect chests, strong back and shoulders, and super legs. In Thailand, I once met an Australian guy who looked like a young Arnold Schwarzenegger. We posed together for a photo: the sand kicker beside the sand kickee.

But what if most of the perfect bodies were holographic images or muscled-up bodysuits? If we knew that most of these images were fake, we might be at least a bit more comfortable in our own skin. And how does this relate to money and the stuff we buy?

A couple of years ago, a company's director asked me to speak to his employees about saving and investing. Before the talk, he invited me out to lunch. He said, "I've asked you to speak because I don't want my employees to make the same mistakes I did." He was in his late fifties, and for more than a dozen years he had earned several million dollars a year. He had a villa in France with a monstrous mortgage. He wore a Rolex, drove a Maserati, and flew first class to ski on glaciers every summer. Most people think he's rich. That's what I expected too. But he isn't. In fact, many of my schoolteacher friends have more money than him. He spends almost everything he makes.

I asked, "What would happen if you lost your job? How long could you support your lifestyle on your savings?"

He said, "Just a few months."

Most of your friends and colleagues likely don't earn millions of dollars a year. Yet many—perhaps even most—likely spend more than they should. And that won't be apparent on the surface. There's a wide chasm between what people can afford and what they buy. That's why, if you want financial security, it's important to know the background story.

Spending Like the Rich Might Be Smarter Than You Think

In chapter 1, I mentioned that most rich people don't drive high-status cars. Instead, high-salaried people with low levels of wealth are mostly behind the wheels of Mercedes-Benz, Tesla, Porsche, Audi, and BMW cars. Some rich people, of course, do drive these cars. But the price of a person's car is a poor indicator of their personal wealth.

Instead of spending like a pretender, develop the mindset of the average wealthy person. I'm not talking about those who pay my friend Janice millions to redesign their bathrooms. As mentioned previously, her clients represent a subset of the wealthy. They define themselves by what they own, but most wealthy people aren't like that.

According to Thomas J. Stanley's four decades of research, most millionaires don't buy expensive cars or flashy homes. That's why you shouldn't buy them either—unless you really can afford them and would buy them even if nobody else could see them. I'm not talking about *affording payments*. Determining whether we can afford something, based on monthly payments, is like getting dropped in the middle of the ocean and saying, "I'm OK. I can swim." In terms of a car, ask yourself if you could afford to buy it outright. With a home, ask yourself if you could still afford the mortgage if the interest rate doubled or you were out of work for six months. If the answer to these questions is no, then you really can't afford them.

In some cities, median home prices are more than a million dollars, so if you live in one of these places, you likely can't escape from buying a high-priced home. But despite the cost of real estate, most of the people living in these regions aren't rich. They're leveraged with debt instead. Consider Vancouver, British Columbia. It's Canada's most expensive major city. According to MLS real estate data reported by Zolo, the median sale price for a stand-alone home was $2.17 million ($1.79 million USD) in May 2021. The typical townhouse sold for $1.27 million ($1.05 million USD) and the median condo sale was $716,450 ($592,246 USD).[10]

But despite how much their homes are worth, most people in Vancouver are not millionaires. According to Statistics Canada, families in Vancouver had a median net worth of $521,500 in 2019 ($408,798 USD). That figure includes their home equity (almost 64 percent of Vancouverites own a home) and the money they have in investments. It's fair to assume that plenty of the million-dollar homeowners in Vancouver have huge mortgage debts.[11]

And despite low interest rates at the time of writing, that debt would be tough to service. After all, according to Vancouver's 2020 *City Social Indicators Profile*, the median family household in Vancouver earned about $92,000 ($72,117 USD) a year—before taxes! The median household income for couples with children was $112,000 ($87,795 USD) a year, and the typical lone-parent-led family earned $53,000 ($41,546 USD) a year. Only 15 percent of households in Vancouver had pre-tax income of above $150,000 ($117,583 USD) per year.[12] Servicing a million-dollar debt, even on that income, could add a lot of stress.

If we rounded up everyone in the United States who owned homes valued above $1 million, we would learn that most of the expensive homeowners aren't millionaires either. In *Stop Acting Rich*, Thomas J. Stanley wrote, "My research has found that most people who live in million-dollar homes are not millionaires. They may be high-income producers but, by trying to emulate glittering rich millionaires, they are living a treadmill existence. In the United States, there are three times more millionaires living in homes that have a market value of under $300,000 than there are living in homes valued at $1 million or more."[13]

Stanley published that book in 2009. Home prices have risen a lot since then. But most wealthy people aren't as flashy as you might think when it comes to the homes they buy. In their 2018 book *The Next Millionaire Next Door*, published after Stanley's death, Stanley and Sarah Stanley Fallaw revealed that just 64.8 percent of American millionaires live in seven-figure homes.[14]

In *Stop Acting Rich*, Stanley also revealed that most millionaires don't buy expensive wines or expensive watches or dine out at Michelin five-star restaurants, either. Some do, of course. But most wealthy people don't.

Trying to spend responsibly is especially tough when your friends and colleagues don't. New lawyers and doctors feel pressure to live like lawyers and doctors, just like the older lawyers and doctors felt the urge to do so before them. It's one of the reasons Stanley's research shows that doctors, for example, have among the lowest levels of wealth, relative to their income. He found that most doctors are big spenders.[15]

No matter our profession or income, we should think twice before following the consumption habits of our friends and neighbors. This goes double or triple for our sports heroes, whose own copycat examples could lead them to poverty. For example, CNBC reports that most NBA players make millions of dollars a year. But 60 percent of retired NBA players go broke five years after they stop playing basketball and 78 percent of NFL players are broke or financially struggling within two years of their retirement.[16] *FourFourTwo* reporter Alec Fenn explained why such a high percentage of professional soccer players go broke too. They have little, if any, financial common sense. And like most people, they copy the lifestyles of others in their professional and social circles.[17]

This is why mindset is important. Most of the things we buy don't boost our life satisfaction. And high debts drag us down emotionally. So, when you see someone with more, don't envy them. They might be living on an edge. Instead, follow the consumption habits of minimalists or the less-flashy rich. Also, appreciate what you have instead of stumbling after others on treadmills of consumption. And do your best to find your financial team.

Find Your Financial Team

Anytime you want to achieve something, whether it's running a marathon or earning a degree, having a support network can help. That's why athletes often train together and students do course work together. And for anyone trying to overcome an addiction, support networks like Alcoholics Anonymous and Weight Watchers can help keep them on track.

Financial goals and wellness are no different. When I first moved to Singapore, I had to find my financial team. My school's community had an online service where people could ask questions about pretty much anything. When I was looking for places to stay during an upcoming vacation to Thailand, I posted, "Hey, any suggestions on clean, modestly priced hotels in Phuket?" Suggestions streamed in. But most of them were expensive. In some cases, the five-star resort recommendations came from people I knew and really liked. But I made a mental note: "Enjoy free activities with these people but don't regularly dine out or take vacations with them."

Other people offered ideas that aligned with my pocketbook. I took advice from them when I wanted to find delicious, low-cost restaurants. I took the public bus with them instead of paying for taxis. They spoke about passions, not stuff, saving money for their futures instead of spending almost everything they earned. We encouraged each other to save, invest, seek magical vacations, and exercise. We socialized at home and outdoors instead of at country clubs.

That doesn't mean I don't have friends who spend a lot of money. I do. But I don't typically travel with them, frequently dine out with them, or shop with them. After all, social groups establish their own sets of norms. That's why, if you're seeking financial wellness, it's best to find people whose goals align with yours. And if you can't find friends who are responsible with money, find a group online. For example, you can find several financial independence groups on Facebook. Just search "Financial Independence" or "FI" and the name of your town or city.

Embrace What You Have

A couple of years ago, Pele and I were looking for a place to stay in Portugal. While scrolling through the Airbnb website, we saw an advertisement for a camper van. Impressed by the owner's creativity, we decided to rent it for a week.

It was a red Renault Kangoo van. The owner had built a bed inside, and she had drawers that held a small propane stove for cooking, a pot, a skillet, two cups, two plates, two sets of silverware, and other essentials. The Kangoo was far too small for us to sit upright in bed. But it was long enough to sleep in without curling up.

We drove it around the southern Algarve region of Portugal. We sought the most idyllic locations, sleeping off the beaten track. One time, we slept beside a lake where we bathed in our birthday suits without a soul in sight. Another time, we joined a cluster of other campers parked for free above a gorgeous beach. Because the van had curtains, we even slept in several town squares and a few parking lots.

There was just one problem: the van didn't have a toilet. In rural wooded regions, we could handle that. With a smile, our host had given us a small shovel and a roll of TP.

But when nature called in the morning, if we had slept in a town square, we often had to wait for one of the local cafés to open. Portugal isn't what I would call a morning place. There are no Starbucks coffee shops opening for busy workers at 6:00 am. It's a go-slow culture. To the Portuguese, takeout coffee is as attractive a prospect as a wedding reception at McDonald's. As a result, I spent twenty tense minutes pacing Costa da Caparica's streets, holding my breath as I searched for a bathroom. When a café opened up, I forced myself not to sprint for their toilet. I strolled in, ordered a cup of tea, sat down at a table with my drink... and then bolted for the bathroom.

I realize I'm sharing some pretty basic, normally private stuff. But I'm sure you can relate. When you're practically cramping with a desperate urge to go, finding a bathroom is like winning the lottery. For at least an hour, I would ride that high, feeling glad I wasn't older. (I hear bladder and sphincter control gets tougher down the road.)

After spending a week in the van, we booked two nights at one of the best boutique hotels in Faro. It had running water. And not just cold water, but hot water too. It had a bathroom. It had a huge shower. I marveled, with gratitude, at these things we usually take for granted.

Gratitude is a key to life satisfaction. Some people are born with a glass half-full. They might even practice gratitude. While driving to work on a cold winter's day, they might take a moment to appreciate their car's heater. While getting on a bus, they might reflect on the marvel of public transportation. When opening their phone, they might mentally take themselves back a few years to a time before people could walk around with a single device that took photos, played music, and allowed them to text and find a date on Friday night. Instead of pining for the next new iPhone, they might take the time to say, "Wow, look at some of the things my current phone can do!"

When practicing gratitude we can also express how much we love or appreciate a friend or family member. Life is better when we appreciate what we have.

Who Are You Going to Follow?

With respect to gratitude, I follow my friend Bill Green. I met Bill when I was a twenty-six-year-old middle school teacher. Bill was forty, and the vice principal at my school. But despite his relative youth, he suffered ongoing battles with painful kidney stones. Often, he had to be hospitalized to have them lasered or blasted. He joked about the stones, saying, "Pain is my friend."

He also battled chronic hip pain. The former amateur football player, baseball player, and triathlete had a hip replaced when he was just forty-one. A few years later, he had his other hip replaced. Several years later, he had the first hip replaced again.

This all came on the tail of something much more devastating. His lovely wife, an elementary school teacher, suffered a debilitating stroke when she was forty years old. That changed her life, Bill's life, and their son's life forever.

Despite this, however, Bill Green is the most positive guy I know. Every Monday morning he asked me, "How was your weekend?" I typically reported a mixed bag of good and bad. Bill always listened, and when I asked him about his weekend, he only focused on the good. He isn't the kind of guy who's afraid to get real. When I asked about his challenges, he opened up. But he always did it in a way that expressed appreciation.

He also made his health woes sound like an Olympic sport. "You know, I met an amazing doctor at the hospital this weekend. I have a kidney stone that's killing me. But this guy gave me some strategies to try to pass this bastard on my own. I can do this! And this guy. . . he's now part of my team."

I recently caught up with Bill, now in his mid-sixties, and asked about his health. Summing up the past several years, he said, "They yanked out a kidney. I've had three hip replacements. But I'm good now! I'm able to work out every morning. I'm just so glad I can do this stuff."

You might know somebody like Bill. In many cases, their positivity is genetic. But Bill trains himself too. He writes what he's grateful for on sticky notes. He pastes them on the mirror so he sees them every morning. Then he reads them out loud, reminding himself of what he appreciates. "Most people think they're too busy to do that," he says. "But people can't afford not to do it! We need to keep reflecting on the things we're thankful for. If we don't, we become complacent. And when we're complacent, we don't get the most out of life."

This strategy works. In fact, it doesn't just work for people like Bill, who might be predisposed to seeing a half-full glass. It works for people who struggle with depression too.

Research shows that practicing gratitude boosts well-being.[18] Most of these studies were done on people who weren't previously struggling, but at least one of them took a different approach. Joshua Brown is a professor of psychological and brain sciences at Indiana University. In 2017, he published a summary of research in *Greater Good Magazine* with Joel Wong, an associate professor of counseling. They studied nearly three hundred adults with clinically low levels of mental health. Most suffered from anxiety and depression.

They divided the patients into three groups. Each person in each group received counseling services. In addition, the researchers asked two of the three groups to perform a writing task. They asked the first group to write a letter of gratitude to another person once a week for three weeks. They asked the second group to write about their deepest thoughts and feelings about negative experiences once a week. They didn't ask the third group to write anything.

The researchers found that the participants who wrote gratitude letters (whether they sent them to their intended recipients or not) reported far higher levels of mental health than the other two groups, four weeks and twelve weeks after their writing exercises ended.

Brown and Wong wrote: "This suggests that gratitude writing can be beneficial not just for healthy, well-adjusted individuals, but also for those who struggle with mental health concerns. In fact, it seems, practicing gratitude on top of receiving psychological counseling carries greater benefits than counseling alone, even when that gratitude practice is brief."[19]

Gratitude Tips That Work

Robert Emmons is one of the world's leading experts on the science of gratitude. The professor at the University of California, Davis, says gratitude journaling works. And the good news appears to be that less is more. Those who journal about what they're grateful for once a week report higher life satisfaction compared to those who journal daily. Here are some other tips for using a gratitude journal:

- Set a conscious goal to feel gratitude. The journaling works best for those who are mindful of their intent to improve their happiness.

- Go narrow and deep, not broad and shallow. When describing your gratitude, don't list several things. Focus on just one thing and explain why you're grateful for it.

- Focus on people over things. When we write about our gratitude for people, it has a far bigger impact on our well-being.

- Write about what your life would be like without certain things. This might be your job, your access to hot water, or (even more important) your friends and loved ones.

- Record happy events that were surprising or unexpected.

- Write in your gratitude journal just once or twice a week. Doing this activity more often doesn't result in better outcomes.[20]

Yes, We Can Have Gratitude for Stuff

Material acquisitions don't boost life satisfaction unless they provide us with a novel experience or bring our loved ones together. Otherwise, the more materialistic we are, the less happy we become. We also know that we shouldn't be envious of people with high incomes who exhibit expensive tastes. After all, they aren't necessarily happier. And according to Thomas J. Stanley and Sarah Stanley Fallaw's research, most people with a lot of expensive stuff don't have a lot of wealth. In many cases, they swim in debt. And debts bum us out.

Still, knowing all this doesn't stop us from sometimes pining for something new. We might see others buying new cars, upgrading their homes, or buying the latest iPhones, and we might want these things too. Or we might just want to have the financial means to pay for them.

Whether we buy these things or not, we should practice gratitude. For example, if you decided to buy a new car, use gratitude to fight off hedonic adaptation. At least once a week, drive your car without a destination in mind. Feel the comfort of the seat. Make a note of the acceleration, the smooth ride, and the effective braking. Stop at some point to step outside and admire your car (just don't post a humblebrag on Facebook or Instagram).

Take care of your car. Wash it yourself regularly and then admire it. Don't let that new car become just another tool. Don't let it become something that just takes you from place to place. Take time to appreciate it.

Even better, appreciate what you have without entertaining any thoughts of buying something new. I've never bought a new car. But often, when I'm driving my 2004 Volkswagen Golf, I take mental notes to appreciate what I have: the smooth acceleration, the sharp handling, the sunroof in the summer, and the heated seats in the winter. I take care of that car (it doesn't have rust, scratches, or dents) and I keep it clean.

Instead of focusing on people who own newer, more expensive cars, I recall how much better my car is compared to some of the cars I had when I was younger. I sometimes imagine a twenty-year-old me (in 1990) getting behind the wheel of my 2004 Volkswagen Golf. The electronic door locks alone would have blown my mind. But I also know that if I took this car back in time and gave it to my former self, hedonic adaptation would have quickly taken hold. Some twenty-year-olds are evolved enough to practice gratitude. I wasn't one of them.

A Few Tips for Living Well

- Life really is like a dark hourglass. Nobody knows when their sand will run out. That's why we should strive to live the best lives we can, today, tomorrow, and onward.

- Realize that most people live unhealthy financial lives. They spend too much and usually borrow money to do it. Don't be envious of people who have more things. Material things don't boost happiness and most of the people who buy expensive things don't have a lot of money.

- Take time to appreciate what you have. Start a gratitude journal.

- Talk to people about money. You'll eventually find somebody whose lifestyle aligns with your philosophy.

5

AFFORD ANYTHING, BUT NOT EVERYTHING

Spending Decisions That Are Worth a Million Dollars

I USED TO RUN home after work in Singapore, keeping an eye out for crocodiles. One of my friends said he once saw one beside the lake that I ran past. It was in a military zone, used for training soldiers. I never saw a crocodile by that lake. But my paranoid eye made me keenly aware of the less harmful, wondrous sights: monitor lizards, monkeys, wild boars, and occasionally reticulated pythons (known to eat people, but not very often).

Wednesday was my favorite day of the week. When I arrived home, I had a quick shower, tossed on a pair of shorts, and then lay on the massage table where Juliana—a freakishly strong-fingered Malay Singaporean woman—waited to torture me. She worked on my knots like a sadist. And sometimes she recorded my wimpy squeals, playing the recording for my friends whom she was scheduled to hurt next.

It might sound horrible. But it wasn't. Most of the time I was in a deep, relaxed state. And by the time she was done, you had to practically peel me from the table. One of my friends once said, "Andrew, for a guy who's supposed to be good with money, you spend a stupid amount on massages every year." My wife and I both did. Besides our weekly routine, we often treated ourselves to foot reflexology sessions. When we visited Thailand or Indonesia on weekend trips we often enjoyed more than one massage a day.

Doing some back-of-the-envelope math, my friend said, "I think you and Pele spend about $7,000 a year on massages."

Plenty of us have friends who are supposed to be good with money. But if we dig into their financial lives, you'll often find something that doesn't make sense. In our case, it was massages. My friend's calculations were right.

Paula Pant has a fabulous blog and podcast called *Afford Anything* (thanks for the steal on this chapter title, Paula). Her premise is that you can afford anything, but not everything.

Here's what Paula means: If you prioritize your spending, you can afford something that might otherwise look like a ridiculous luxury, as long as you're careful with your money in other areas. Perhaps you absolutely must have a five-star vacation every year. Fair enough. But if you're going to do that, unless you earn buckets of money, you should ruthlessly cut costs in several other places.

In my case, those massages could have been better if I had fewer of them. For example, in *Happy Money*, Elizabeth Dunn and Michael Norton say we appreciate luxuries more when they're a treat. Instead of getting at least one massage a week, I might have enjoyed them more if I had just one a month.

Opportunity Costs and Gains

Those massages also cost far more money than initially meets the eye. "Opportunity cost" is the difference in cost between making one decision over another. An opportunity cost isn't always financial. But in my case, those massages might have cost us more than $770,000.

Confused? Check this out:

We spent about $150 a week on massages during an eleven-year period (2003–2014).

That's $85,800 over eleven years.

Over that time, our investment portfolio averaged 8.34 percent per year.

If we had invested the money we spent on massages, we would have had an extra $143,239 in our investment account by 2014.

That's a lot of money. But I'm not done yet.

We left Singapore in 2014 (when I was forty-four). Assume we let that $143,239 grow in a portfolio that continued to average 8.34 percent per year. Without adding another penny to it, that money would grow to $770,241 by the time I am sixty-five years old.

That's the long-term opportunity cost of spending $150 a week on massages for just eleven years.

I can argue that my multiple weekly massages allowed me to keep running pain-free. They might have helped me sleep better, strengthening my immune system to better cope with pesky cancer cells. They might have helped my wife ward off her constant back pain. They gave us something to look forward to midweek. Perhaps, just maybe, those massages were worth $770,241.

Whether you agree or not doesn't matter. My point is that our teaching salaries weren't enough for us to enjoy those massages, and five-star holidays, and a new car, and weekly meals out, and a fancy wardrobe. We were able to afford anything (in this case, those massages), but not everything. Unless you earn a seven-figure income while also saving huge sums, the same should apply to you.

Your Income Doesn't Determine Your Wealth

As teachers at a private school, most of my friends won't qualify for a state pension. Some, because they worked overseas for their entire careers, won't receive US Social Security payments or defined benefit pension income.

When Pele and I left our Singapore-based teaching jobs in 2014, I began delivering more investment talks. Sometimes I spoke at companies. Other times I spoke at international schools. I still remember chatting with an older teaching couple from my former school in Singapore. They had worked at the same jobs for more than twenty-five years. They raised two children and paid their college fees. This couple wanted to show me their financial statements. They hadn't received a dime of inheritance money, and yet they had amassed a surprising amount of wealth.

Their circumstances were similar to, but at the same time very different from, the circumstances of another couple I knew. This second couple also spent their career teaching at that school. Like the first couple, they had children who were now in their twenties. They bought similar investment products. But when they explained their financial situation, it couldn't have been more different. This second couple had a fraction of what the first couple had.

Both of these couples were my friends. From my perspective, they lived similar lifestyles. They enjoyed traveling and dining out. But just a few subtle differences in choices explained the difference in their wealth. One couple spent slightly more than the other couple on vacations and cars. Both couples enjoyed eating out, but the couple who grew wealthier preferred lower-priced hawker food (if you ever visit Singapore, these eateries are great). My friends' lifestyles didn't differ much. But after more than twenty-five years, one couple had become millionaires because they were able to invest more money. They understood how opportunity costs worked.

Not everybody spends $150 a week on massages, of course. But many of us could cut back on expenses that don't enhance our lives.

A few simple decisions could be worth a million dollars. For example, at AssetBuilder.com, I published two stories about car purchases: "Why Buying New Cars Over Used Is a Million Dollar Decision"[1] and "Leasing Cars Instead of Buying Used Could Be a $1 Million Decision."[2] If someone chooses to buy a new car every five years, the opportunity cost of that decision could exceed a million dollars, compared to owning well-maintained used cars and investing what they saved. In most cases, consistently leasing cars also carries a seven-figure opportunity cost.

The benefits of lower-cost cars (or not having a car at all) coupled with a cheaper cell phone plan and a penchant for entertaining guests at home instead of always dining out can add up to a lot. When you use an opportunity cost model, it's easy to see how two couples can earn similar lifetime incomes but end up with dramatically different levels of wealth.

What Losing Weight and Spending Money Have in Common

Nobody should tell you how to spend your money, least of all a guy whose massages might knock $770,241 off his net worth. Your decisions are personal. You probably can afford almost anything if you prioritize it. My friend John, for example, spends more money on vacations than almost anyone I know. But he scrimps on everything else. For years, he refused to buy a car. He took buses everywhere. To him, those high-cost vacations were worth the sacrifice.

He travels with a friend who doesn't scrimp on anything. She regularly joins him on African safaris and at five-star luxury resorts, flying first class or business class. She and John worked at the same place. They earned similar salaries for a really long time. That's where the similarities end. Unlike John, his friend always put her travels on a credit card that she never fully paid off, and she continues to do so. Now in her seventies, she'll have to work forever. That wouldn't be so bad if she had a job she enjoyed, but she doesn't.

However, she didn't prioritize her spending the way John did, so she doesn't have a choice.

Prioritizing your spending means cutting back on things that don't enhance your life. To figure out what those things are, start by tracking what you spend and earn.

Several expense tracking apps are available online—for example, Goodbudget, Mint, and Pocket Expense. Plenty of people say you should create a monthly budget, but I'm not one of them. Your spending can fluctuate wildly month to month. If you take a big trip or you have a surprise home repair, that could blow your budget and make you feel like a schmuck. To me, budgets are like diets. Sometimes they work. . . but they usually don't.

For example, one study published in the *American Journal of Preventive Medicine* suggests that when people want to lose weight, documenting their food intake in a food diary is one of the most important things they can do.[3] I guess once they had documented their sixth jelly donut of the week, they might realize how much sugar they were consuming. The thought of entering one more jelly donut might make them pause and ask themselves, "Do I really need this? I've already had six this week."

When we record what we eat and spend, it increases our accountability. This helps us eat better and spend less money. After one of my friends began to track his expenses, he said, "I had no idea how much I spent on tech gadgets I rarely used." Now that he's committed to tracking what he spends, he spends a lot less.

My wife and I have been tracking what we spend for years. Every time we buy something, we add the expense in our app. Some people might say, "I don't need to do that. My credit card tallies everything." But that won't have the same effect. When you use an app to track your spending, you can see how much you're paying in each category. You can even customize the categories. My wife, for example, created one just for alcohol. Somehow, it helped her find even cheaper wines (that she claims she likes just as much).

Before long, you'll see some patterns. You might, for example, be surprised at how much you spend on dining out. You might be surprised at how much you spend on gourmet coffees or even—cough, cough—massages.

Track your income and your spending for the rest of your life. It only takes a few seconds after every purchase. And it allows you to think of your household income and expenses as a business. If a business didn't track its income and expenses, it would risk bankruptcy.

When you see where your money goes, confirm that it aligns with your pleasures. For example, if you're grabbing a gourmet coffee and drinking it while driving through rush hour traffic, are you getting the most from that coffee? Even if you were the world's greatest coffee lover, the answer would be no. Instead of savoring your coffee, you would be thinking about other things: Am I going to be late for work? Do I smell something bad in the back seat? Is that jogger wearing pink underwear on his head? Why did that driver just cut me off?

In this case, it usually makes more sense to make coffee at home, put it in a travel mug, and bring it with you. After all, you likely won't savor the full richness of the gourmet coffee on the run. And the opportunity cost of an expensive cup of coffee might be more than a million dollars over your working lifetime if you invested what you could have saved.

Here's an example. Assume someone spends $5.50 a day for expensive coffee on the run, including taxes and a tip, seven days a week. Assume they kept that up from age twenty-two to sixty-five. A cup of home-brewed coffee might cost 50 cents a day, making that a $5 daily difference. No, that isn't much, until we work out the long-term opportunity cost.

From 1972 until 2020, despite the market's ups and downs, a diversified portfolio comprising 60 percent in a US stock index and 40 percent in a bond market index earned a compound annual return of 9.47 percent. (I'll explain more about investing in chapters 8 and 9.)

Let's assume the same portfolio earned that return over the next forty-three years. If someone invested the difference between a daily cup of gourmet coffee and a cup of coffee at home, they would be investing the equivalent of $5 a day. That's $1,825 a year (not including the extra cup during each leap year). If they averaged 9.47 percent per year, from age twenty-two until age sixty-five, that money would grow to $1,011,422 after forty-three years.

Let's assume stocks and bonds don't perform as well over the next forty-three years as they did from 1972 until 2020. I'm not saying they won't. Nobody knows. But let's assume they don't. If instead of averaging 9.47 percent the portfolio averaged 7 percent, the opportunity cost of the gourmet coffee would be $483,845, compared to making that coffee at home. That's still almost half a million dollars.

A critical eye might say, "Wait, this is misleading! Half a million dollars (or $483,845) won't have the same buying power in the future that it has today." That would be true, based on inflation. Everything from a box of cereal to haircuts will cost more in the future. But a gourmet cup of coffee will cost more too. As a result, the daily savings between drinking a daily gourmet coffee and brewing the stuff at home wouldn't remain at $5 a day. It might be $6 a day five years from now, $10 a day fifteen years from now, and $20 a day twenty years from now. As a result, the actual savings would be far higher than $483,845 (assuming your money averaged 7 percent). But that higher dollar figure would provide about the same buying power that $483,845 would today.

No matter how you slice it, seemingly small savings can have big impacts. That's why one couple might retire with a million dollars while their similarly paid colleagues end up with nothing. So yes, expensive coffee on the run could be a $483,845 decision. Or it could be a million-dollar decision if the markets in the future match the returns of the past (more on this in chapter 6).

Once again, I'm not saying you should eliminate gourmet coffee on the run. That's up to you. I'm saying, track your income and expenses. Then cut costs on things that don't enhance your life satisfaction. If something truly turns your crank, don't cut back on it.

But be honest with yourself—and ruthlessly slash costs on what doesn't enhance your life. By doing so, and investing the savings, you'll have far more money. And you could spend that money on experiences and causes that could enhance your life and the lives of others.

Remember all choices have a long-term opportunity cost. It doesn't mean you need to eliminate all the fun from your life. But make smart choices. Remember, you can afford anything—just not everything.

A Few Tips for Living Well

- Never take a financial cost at face value. Always consider how that money could grow if it were invested.

- Start by tracking what you spend with an app that allows you to record expenses in categories.

- Think of your household as a business. A business that doesn't track expenses is likely to go bankrupt.

- Ask yourself if you could eliminate or cut back on specific expenses. Would it reduce your life satisfaction? If it would, don't cut back. But if it wouldn't, slash those costs.

- Run an opportunity cost scenario, much as I did for this chapter's massage and coffee examples. You'll see an added benefit of slashing those costs.

6

BATHROOMS AND THE MARKETS
Daily Routines That Help You Make Money

I F YOU LIVE in a car, like my friend Casey Coleman, you won't need much money to retire. But if you choose an RV over a Subaru, you might require a bit more than Casey does. Others might spend their golden years in a condominium or a mountain chalet. Location matters—a lot. The costs of living in different towns, cities, and countries range from cheap to ridiculously expensive.

But unless we're endowed with a gold-plated pension or a trust fund, most of us require investments to fund our retirement.

As a schoolteacher, and eventually a finance writer, I haven't had mind-blowing incomes. But I started to invest in the stock market when I was young, and that helped a lot. That doesn't mean your hopes are dashed if you start investing later in life, but money breeds like rabbits when it has time to grow.

Contrary to what many talking heads on YouTube, on TV, or in financial magazines may lead you to believe, you don't need to follow the economy or know how to choose the best stocks to buy. You could spend an hour a year on your investments (often less than that) and beat the returns of most professional stock market traders. Do

I sound like an infomercial promising cures for baldness and wrinkles? If you're skeptical, I'm glad. Verify my sources. When it comes to money, don't believe what anyone says. That includes the folks in banks, insurance companies, and investment firms. In many cases, these industries are filled with legally sanctioned crooks (and sometimes kind, naïve people).

Using peer-reviewed economic science instead of a banker's promise, I added monthly sums to my investments when I was young. My account crossed $1 million two decades before I reached traditional retirement age. No skill required. That's a good thing, because I'm not that smart. Nor did it take time away from my day-to-day activities. That's also good, because I put friends, family, exercise, and lifestyle first. I didn't borrow to invest, because I'm too squeamish to use debt. But I did what works. And it could work for you too.

Make Money When Your Friends Go to the Loo

When John wakes up each morning, he grabs his iPhone from his bedside table and heads to the bathroom. Yes, he poops with his phone. At least one of your family members probably does the same. John does his business, wipes, and flushes the toilet. Then (thank God) he washes his hands with soap. Before John leaves the bathroom, he's made people money.

For example, he uses AT&T for his telephone plan. I own a small slice of AT&T, so he indirectly pays me for that service. He wipes his butt with paper made by Procter & Gamble. I own shares in that company too. Johnson & Johnson made his soap. I also own shares in J&J, so I applaud his hygiene.

John walks into his kitchen and turns on a light. I own shares in the hydro company that powered that light. For breakfast, John pours a bowl of Cheerios. That's made by General Mills. I own shares in General Mills.

From the moment John wakes up until he goes to bed, his actions fuel hundreds of business products or services I own a part of. They include transportation companies, food companies, energy companies, clothing companies, retail companies, restaurant and coffee companies, paper manufacturers, storage companies, elevator companies, air conditioning or heating companies, hygiene companies, insurance companies, drug companies, lumber companies, natural resource companies, farming companies, technology companies, beverage companies, waste management companies, recycling companies, solar companies. . . the list goes on. With as little as $100, you could own a sliver of thousands of different businesses. Your $100 could be split across every business sector.

It doesn't matter whether we're in an economic boom or a recession. It doesn't matter whether John is old or young. It doesn't matter whether John is single or a father of ten. He could be a vegan or a carnivore. He could be a Hare Krishna or just a hairy guy. Unless John lives in a cave, he will consume and use services supplied by hundreds of companies every day.

Sound far-fetched? I understand. You might be saying, "I don't contribute money to hundreds of companies every day!" But that isn't true. The simple act of wiping your bum has a broad business reach. Consider toilet paper. When John buys a new package, a toilet paper manufacturer like Procter & Gamble isn't the only company that wins. If he drives to the store, he uses fuel. That benefits oil and gas companies like ExxonMobil. You say he has a Tesla? The vast majority of that car's electric energy comes from fossil fuel or hydro businesses. (Environmental tip: no matter what car you drive, try to drive less.)

John might buy his toilet paper at Safeway, Costco, or Walmart. That adds revenue to their pots. Forestry companies, like Weyerhaeuser, own the timber from which the toilet paper originates. Firms like John Deere (Deer & Co.) sell equipment like skidders and feller bunchers to forestry companies to take down the trees. So when John wipes his bum, they rub their hands with glee. Railroad companies like

Union Pacific earn revenue through the transportation of wood, pulp, and paper. A business like Dow Chemical makes the toilet paper's plastic wrap. (Environmental tip: we should buy less of *everything*.)

It's hard to imagine, but just wiping our butts benefits hundreds of businesses. After all, each company I listed uses services supplied by other businesses to stay in operation.

The process of manufacturing, transporting, and selling everything from a cup of coffee to a tube of toothpaste involves a multitude of companies. Most of them trade on a stock market. You could own almost all of them through a product called an index fund or an ETF (exchange-traded fund). When you own a global stock market index, you own thousands of publicly traded businesses from around the world.

And when people use the products and services of those businesses, those companies earn profits. As an owner of those businesses (through that index fund or ETF) you will reap rewards.

Diversified Dividends: Perpetual Income Payments

Here's how you'll make money: Over time, most companies pay dividends to shareholders. Those are cash payments given to shareholders from a portion of the company's profits. Companies also increase dividend payouts as their corporate profits rise.

In Table 6.1, I list eight companies among the Dow Jones Industrials. This isn't a cherry-picked list. It represents the first eight companies on the Dow, in alphabetical order. Think of the Dow as a club of thirty American businesses that gained admission for being big and burly.

For example, 3M Company (first on the alphabetical list) makes a variety of products including adhesive tapes, dental and orthodontic products, car-care products, and consumer electronics components. They produce more than sixty thousand products under several brands. Unless you've been living off the land and off the grid, you've likely used this company's products this week (remember that toilet paper connection).

In 2007, 3M Company gave shareholders a dividend payout of $1.92 per share. The financial crisis of 2008 and 2009 didn't slow them down. The company continued to make more money and increase their dividend payouts. In 2020, they paid $6.16 in dividends per share. If you own a broad stock market index fund (once again, I'll get into detail about these later), these dividends were deposited into your account, or you automatically reinvested them to buy more units of your index fund.

The third company on the list of Dow Jones Industrials is Amgen, one of the world's largest biopharmaceutical companies. It didn't pay dividends until 2011. Instead, the company chose to reinvest its profits back into the business. Such reinvestments might not appear to benefit shareholders four times a year, like a cash dividend payout would. But when a company retains its profits instead of paying a dividend, it often leads to higher stock price appreciation, so investors benefit in the end. This was also the case with Apple, which didn't start paying dividends to shareholders until 2012.

Sometimes, when times are tough, a company might temporarily lower or maintain the same dividend payout. Take Chevron, for example. It increased its dividend payouts every year from 2007 to 2019. But COVID-19 contributed to a drop in oil prices, so the company reduced its dividend payout in 2020.

Over time, however, if you own the broadest selection of stocks possible—which you can buy through an index fund—you'll reap higher dividend payouts almost every year.

In Table 6.1, I averaged the dividend payouts for the first eight companies on the Dow. In 2007, they paid 95 cents a share. In 2009, they paid an average of $1.09 per share. That increased to $1.27 in 2011, $1.80 in 2013, $2.59 in 2015, and $3.44 in 2020. The same upward-dividend-paying trend exists with the market as a whole.

(To keep the table manageable for the purposes of this book I've limited myself to showing you every other year, with the exception of showing 2020 instead of 2019—but you'll get the picture.)

TABLE 6.1

Dividend Payments for the Dow's First Eight Stocks

Company	2007	2009	2011	2013	2015	2017	2020
3M Company	$1.92	$2.04	$2.20	$2.54	$4.10	$4.70	$5.88
American Express	$0.63	$0.72	$0.72	$0.86	$1.10	$1.31	$1.72
Amgen	$0	$0	$0.56	$1.88	$3.16	$4.60	$6.40
Apple	$0	$0	$0	$0.41	$0.50	$0.60	$0.80
Boeing	$1.45	$1.68	$1.68	$1.94	$3.64	$5.68	$2.06
Caterpillar	$1.38	$1.68	$1.82	$2.32	$3.01	$3.11	$4.12
Chevron	$2.26	$2.66	$3.09	$3.90	$4.28	$4.32	$5.16
Cisco Systems	$0	$0	$0.12	$0.62	$0.80	$1.10	$1.42
Dividend Payout Averages	**$0.95**	**$1.09**	**$1.27**	**$1.80**	**$2.59**	**$3.17**	**$3.44**

In alphabetical order. Source: Value Line Investment Survey[1]

When you own thousands of companies through an index fund or an ETF, you're putting your eggs in several baskets. Some of those companies will increase their dividends year over year. Others might stumble. But by owning them all, you'll increase the odds of receiving higher overall dividends every year, as seen from the sample above. That allows you to reinvest those dividends into more shares. And with more shares, investors receive an ever-increasing amount of dividends. What's more, those share prices often rise, giving the investor a two-part benefit.

Here's the power of that one-two punch: Assume one of your ancestors invested $100 in US stocks for your family in 1920. Your family could access that money a hundred years later. Its investment time period included the 1929 stock market crash, the Great

Depression, two world wars, a multitude of other US-led wars, the financial crashes of 1973–1974, the crashes of 2000–2002, the financial crisis of 2008–2009, and the mid-2020 COVID-related crash.

Imagine the $100 was divided into every stock in the US market. In other words, it earned the return of the US stock market from 1920 until 2020. Over those hundred years, the price appreciation of those stocks alone would have grown to $528,111. Cool. But if we included dividends, and reinvested them into the same stocks, that $100 would have grown to $2.37 million.

That's a good reason not to blow your dividends on too much ice cream.

The Power of Compound Interest

When I first started to invest, I was a university student who washed buses during the summers and worked at a grocery store on evenings and weekends. After I graduated from university, I became a teacher, so my income increased. That allowed me to invest an ever-increasing amount of money into several thousand businesses. You could do the same.

I began investing in 1989, when I was nineteen years old. Let's assume I invested $500 a month (just over $16 a day) from age nineteen until age fifty. When I first began my investment journey, I invested far less than that. But when I began to work full-time, I invested much more.

You might not be able to save $500 a month. And that might not matter. If you invest what you can, you'll still have far more money than you otherwise would have had.

A $500 per month investment in US stocks, starting in 1989, would have grown to about $1.23 million by January 2021, with dividends reinvested. That's a compound annual return of 9.85 percent per year. Some stocks beat that return. Others did worse. But if you owned a sliver of every publicly traded business in the United States, you would have earned that return. Every person you know would have helped. For example, every time John paid his cell phone bill; every time he ate; every time he turned on the heat; and every time he pooped, showered, or shaved, he would have used products and services of companies you owned.

Why Didn't We Learn This in a High School Class?

The United States has been the highest-performing stock market over the past hundred years. But that doesn't mean it always will be. Nor does that mean it has won every decade. Asian stocks, for example, beat US stocks from 2000 until 2011. Canadian, Australian, New Zealand, and several European country markets (to name a few examples) have also left US stocks behind during several measured time periods.

Nobody knows which stock markets will perform best in the future. That's why it's best to own them all. When you do that, there isn't a person on the planet (unless they live under a rock) who doesn't somehow contribute to your financial bottom line.

From 1920 until 2021, US stocks averaged a compound annual return of 10.67 percent per year, with dividends reinvested. I used the US stock market as an example because it provides the easiest source of historical information. But as I'll discuss later, you should invest globally in US and international stocks.

During some decades, US stocks performed better than 10.67 percent. Other decades, they lagged. In Table A1, in the Appendix, I listed rolling returns to show every ten-year period beginning in 1920. As shown, over the ten years between 1920 and 1930, US stocks averaged a compound annual return of 15.4 percent. That would have turned $10,000 into $41,884 after just ten years.

But from 1929 until 1939, US stocks dropped 1.34 percent per year. In other words, they earned a negative annual return. If someone invested $10,000 at the beginning of 1929, it would have been worth just $8,737 ten years later.

However, over the ten years from 2009 to 2019, US stocks averaged a compound annual return of 13.90 percent. That would have turned $10,000 into $36,748.

But from 1999 until 2009, US stocks recorded negative returns again. They dropped 1.89 percent per year. A $10,000 investment would have fallen to $8,262.

It looks like a crapshoot, right? Over ten years, it is. But time is relative. If you're a dragonfly, ten years is multiple generations. But we shouldn't think like insects. The longer the time horizon, the lower the overall risk.

Even if you're sixty years old, your investment duration is about thirty more years. That three-decade lens is the only one that counts. How stocks perform this week, this month, this year, or even this decade is completely irrelevant. No, I'm not expecting you to work until you're ninety. But for now, recognize that short-term returns (ten years is short-term) don't mean much. Later I'll explain how you could retire on the eve of a massive market crash, withdraw money every year, and your portfolio should still last at least thirty years. (This is why a sixty-year-old should think of a thirty-year investment duration.)

But let's get back to a bit of history. When we were in high school, many of us were tested on the periodic table of elements. I wish teachers tested students on rolling ten-year returns for stocks instead. If they did, more people would realize that ten-year returns are meaningless distractions in the face of a long-term plan.

Life Satisfaction and Expected Investment Returns

I didn't include that table to confirm I'm a geek. Understanding history helps to educate investors and temper expectations. Too often, investors hear that stocks average about 10 percent per year. But if they run into several down years in a row, or a decade that doesn't make them money (see that chart in the Appendix), they might believe this isn't normal. That might cause them to sell everything in disgust or stop adding fresh money. If, however, people saw rolling ten-year returns from the past, it might prevent them from throwing in the towel when stocks hit the skids. Multiple down years in a row is actually a very normal thing.

In 2014, University College London conducted a research study to predict levels of happiness based on different events. They used an app called The Great Brain Experiment and enrolled more than eighteen thousand people in their study. They found that personal expectations were the greatest predictor of our happiness. In other words, when we expect something fabulous and the outcome falls short of our expectations, we tend to be bummed out. If we expect something bad and things turn out better than we expect (even if they're still somewhat bad), we feel pretty good.[2]

Realistic expectations can also help you make money. Here's an example: A couple of years ago, one of my sister's friends emailed me in a tizzy. "Stocks are supposed to rise 10 percent a year," she said. "I'm in a diversified portfolio of index funds, as your book [*Million-aire Teacher*] suggests. But over the past two years I haven't averaged 10 percent." This woman knew that US stocks had averaged about 10 percent a year over the past hundred years. She also knew that global stocks had averaged about 10 percent a year over the previous fifty years. But her portfolio had only averaged about 6 percent over the previous two years, so she thought something was wrong. She didn't consider the fact that her portfolio contained stocks and bonds (I'll explain more about bonds soon). But she missed something else important: Ten years is a blip when it comes to investing.

She just knew that US stocks had averaged about 10 percent per year over the previous hundred years. Disillusioned with her growth, she stopped adding money. Long-term, this will cost her plenty. She'll have less money to give away, less money to spend on experiences, and, depending on her life circumstances, less money to buy food and keep a roof over her head. That's why expectations are so important. If she had seen the range of possible annual or decade-long outcomes, based on the past, she might not have given up.

When she sent me this email, she was forty years old. That meant she had about fifty more years to invest (if she sees her ninetieth birthday). While she's still working, she'll add money to her investments. And when she retires, she'll be selling portions every year. She'll have money invested for as long as she lives. That's why, if she lives to age ninety, her investment duration would be fifty more years. Too many investors think short-term. But single-year and single-decade returns don't mean much. Lifetime returns are the only ones that matter.

And when viewed through the long-term lens of time, stocks are far less risky than if you judge them through daily, weekly, monthly, annual, or even a single decade's term. Table 6.2 shows every rolling thirty-year return for US stocks, starting from January 1927 (measured in USD). It also includes every rolling thirty-year period for Canadian stocks (measured in CAD) from 1959, the earliest date from which I could find records. Morningstar Direct provides global stock market performances starting in 1971, so the table also includes twenty-two rolling thirty-year periods for global stocks (measured in USD).[3] The global stock market is a compilation of returns from almost every stock market in the world. It includes US, Canadian, European, Asian, South American, Australian, African, and New Zealand stocks.

Imagine if you had invested a $10,000 lump sum in US stocks at the beginning of 1929. That would have been a horrible time to invest a lump sum, right? After all, it marked the start of the biggest market crash in history. Your money would have languished during the years of the Great Depression. It would have faced the carnage of World War II and the Korean War. You might wonder what that

$10,000 would have been worth after thirty years. By January 1959, that $10,000 would have grown to $107,555. That was a compound annual return of 8.24 percent.

Nobody can predict the future. But diversification and a long-term perspective dramatically reduce risk.

TABLE 6.2

Rolling Thirty-Year Annual Returns

Starting and Ending Years	Duration	US Stocks*	Canadian Stocks**	Global Stocks*
1927–1956	30 years	10.02%		
1928–1957	30 years	8.50%		
1929–1958	30 years	8.24%		
1930–1959	30 years	9.08%		
1931–1960	30 years	10.0%		
1932–1961	30 years	13.17%		
1933–1962	30 years	13.02%		
1934–1963	30 years	12.08%		
1935–1964	30 years	12.98%		
1936–1965	30 years	11.78%		
1937–1966	30 years	10.40%		
1938–1967	30 years	12.55%		
1939–1968	30 years	12.49%		
1940–1969	30 years	11.90%		
1941–1970	30 years	12.36%		
1942–1971	30 years	13.20%		
1943–1972	30 years	13.21%		
1944–1973	30 years	11.71%		
1945–1974	30 years	9.93%		
1946–1975	30 years	9.90%		
1947–1976	30 years	11.12%		
1948–1977	30 years	10.78%		
1949–1978	30 years	10.72%		

Starting and Ending Years	Duration	US Stocks*	Canadian Stocks**	Global Stocks*
1950–1979	30 years	10.74%		
1951–1980	30 years	10.62%		
1952–1981	30 years	9.80%		
1953–1982	30 years	9.94%		
1954–1983	30 years	10.60%		
1955–1984	30 years	9.35%		
1956–1985	30 years	9.42%		
1957–1986	30 years	9.97%		
1958–1987	30 years	10.18%		
1959–1988	30 years	9.57%	10.95%	
1960–1989	30 years	10.27%	10.32%	
1961–1990	30 years	9.95%	10.87%	
1962–1991	30 years	10.04%	10.22%	
1963–1992	30 years	10.67%	9.90%	
1964–1993	30 years	10.31%	9.81%	
1965–1994	30 years	9.78%	10.31%	
1966–1995	30 years	10.57%	9.48%	
1967–1996	30 years	11.60%	9.74%	
1968–1997	30 years	12.08%	10.92%	
1969–1998	30 years	12.54%	10.82%	
1970–1999	30 years	13.62%	10.02%	
1971–2000	30 years	13.12%	11.06%	14.52%
1972–2001	30 years	12.11%	11.46%	13.85%
1973–2002	30 years	10.66%	10.68%	12.30%
1974–2003	30 years	12.07%	9.31%	10.67%
1975–2004	30 years	13.42%	10.16%	11.96%
1976–2005	30 years	12.43%	11.77%	12.79%
1977–2006	30 years	12.53%	11.98%	12.43%
1978–2007	30 years	13.11%	12.15%	13.34%
1979–2008	30 years	10.69%	12.12%	13.04%
1980–2009	30 years	11.07%	9.68%	10.05%

Starting and Ending Years	Duration	US Stocks*	Canadian Stocks**	Global Stocks*
1981–2010	30 years	10.70%	9.42%	10.70%
1982–2011	30 years	11.05%	9.06%	10.36%
1983–2012	30 years	10.65%	9.12%	10.00%
1984–2013	30 years	10.93%.	9.17%	10.38%
1985–2014	30 years	11.19%	8.52%	10.56%
1986–2015	30 years	10.40%	8.97%	10.34%
1987–2016	30 years	9.80%	7.85%	8.94%
1988–2017	30 years	10.59%	8.23%	7.92%
1989–2018	30 years	9.91%	8.33%	8.42%
1990–2019	30 years	10.0%	7.62%	8.14%
1991–2020	30 years	10.66%	7.66%	8.28%
1992–2021 (June)	30 years	10.05%	8.44%	8.44%

Sources: DQYDJ, S&P 500 Return Calculator,[4] Morningstar Direct
*US and global stock returns measured in USD
**Canadian stocks measured in CAD, using TSX Composite Index: Stingy Investor Asset Mixer[5]

Be an Owner with Stocks and a Lender with Bonds

On average, stocks increase in value roughly two out of every three calendar years. That means we have to expect calendar year declines, perhaps even a decade-long decline. But the odds of a decade-long decline drop dramatically when we diversify further and add some bonds.

When you own stocks, you're a business owner. With bonds, you're a lender. A bond is a loan you would make to a corporation or a government in exchange for a fixed rate of interest. Those interest rates are low. But when you own thousands of different bonds (which you could have with a broad bond market index fund or ETF), you have more stability. With bonds in your account, your money won't drop as far when stocks plunge.

Vanguard's research shows historical returns of diversified portfolios with stocks and bonds. You can see the range of returns in

Table 6.3. Note that portfolios with 100 percent invested in stocks earned higher long-term returns. But they also fell harder than portfolios of stocks and bonds when markets crashed. Few people have the strength to say, "I can invest 100 percent in stocks, even if I lose money for a decade." (See the decades 1929–1939, 1930–1940, 1999–2009, and 2000–2010 in Table A1, in the Appendix.) That's why diversified portfolios with stocks and bonds make much more sense. After all, most people overestimate their ability to emotionally tolerate market drops.

TABLE 6.3

Historical Investment Returns (1926–2020)

	100% Stocks	80% Stocks / 20% Bonds	70% Stocks / 30% Bonds	60% Stocks / 40% Bonds	50% Stocks / 50% Bonds
Average Annual Return	10.1%	9.4%	9.1%	8.6%	8.2%
Calendar Years with a Loss	26/93	24/93	23/93	22/93	18/93
Calendar Years with a Gain	67/93	69/93	70/93	71/93	75/93
Worst Year	-43.1% (1931)	-34.9% (1931)	-30.7% (1931)	-26.6% (1931)	-22.5% (1931)
Best Year	+54.2% (1933)	+45.4% (1933)	+41.1% (1933)	+36.7% (1933)	+32.3% (1933)

Source: vanguard.com[6]
Note: Figures calculated based on using US stocks and US intermediate government bonds

How Bonds Can Help You Stay the Course

Since 1926, four rolling ten-year returns for US stocks have been negative. But for investors with at least 20 percent in bonds, none of those decades recorded a loss. For example, the worst decade return for US stocks was negative 1.89 percent per year from 1999 until 2009. That would have turned a $10,000 investment into $8,262.90. However, if the investor had 80 percent stocks and

20 percent bonds, they would have averaged 0.34 percent per year. That would have turned a $10,000 investment into $10,345.25.

If the investor had 60 percent stocks and 40 percent bonds over the same time period (1999–2009), they would have averaged 1.90 percent per year. That would have turned $10,000 into $12,070.96.

Don't underestimate what a decade-long decline could do to your investment psyche. If it convinces you to sell or stop adding fresh money, it could cost you plenty. That's why it makes sense to include a bond allocation. If bonds collar your doppelganger, they could help boost your long-term profits.

Why Using Savings Accounts Is Riskier Than Investing

Plenty of people fear stock market drops, so they don't invest. They stuff money into savings accounts, money market funds, and certificates of deposits (CDs) instead. But such accounts are guaranteed to lose. I'm not saying you shouldn't keep money in such accounts. If you're saving money for a home down payment, for example, one of these accounts will work well. The same applies to emergency money (everyone should keep about six months of living expenses in such accessible cash accounts in case they lose their job). If the markets drop when you're ready to buy a house or you lose your job, you'll have to sell at a low to access your cash. Nobody wants that. However, when it comes to saving for retirement, savings accounts, money market funds, and CDs are far riskier than a diversified portfolio of stock and bond market index funds. My mother-in-law's story is a case in point.

My mother-in-law loves CDs despite their floor-scraping interest rates. Recently, she bought a one-year CD that will pay her 0.5 percent in interest. That's slightly better than the national average. According to Bankrate.com the average one-year CD at the time offered 0.45 percent for the year.[7] She has shoveled money into CDs and saving accounts for the past fifty years. That represents far more risk than anyone should take. My notion might sound counterintuitive, so let me explain: If you're saving money for a down payment on a house or you're keeping six months' worth of living expenses aside, CDs and savings accounts make a lot of sense—you won't lose any of your investment. But using them for a retirement account is like using a tennis racket to row a boat upstream. That's because inflation would continue to push you back. Here's an example:

Assume you had $1,200. You plan to spend that money in a single day. You want to buy:

- a case of toilet paper,

- a new pair of pants,

- a restaurant meal for your entire extended family, and

- new tires for your car.

But you decide to postpone the big day. You put $200 in a savings account and the remaining $1,000 in a CD that you decide to renew once a year.

Five years later, you withdraw the money from the savings account and the CD, including the interest you earned. Your money grew from $1,200 to $1,300, so you're feeling pretty good. You earned about 1.7 percent per year.

You buy the case of toilet paper. It costs more than you remember. You then buy the pants, which cost more too. At lunch, you treat your parents, your siblings, and your children to a meal at your favorite restaurant. But the meal costs more than you were anticipating. Then you take your remaining money and try to buy a set of tires for your car. No can do. You don't have enough.

What happened here? Five years previously, you could have paid for everything with $1,200. Now you need *more than $1,300*. The $1,000 in the CD would have barely kept pace with inflation, and the $200 in the savings account would have lost to inflation every month. Simply, the $1,200 you stuffed into "something safe" lost money in terms of buying power. That's why an after-inflation return is called a *real return*. It's the only thing that counts. It's the only thing that's real.

This might sound harsh, but it's worth repeating. Unless you twist the laws of mathematics, you can't make a *real* penny in a savings account or CD.

Does this make you yearn for the good old days? I still remember opening my first savings account in 1980. I was ten years old, and my mom took me down to TD Bank. That year, my money gained about 11 percent. You might have earned a similar amount. But according to the CPI (Consumer Price Index), inflation was 12.52 percent that year. The typical CD matched that rate. But savings accounts didn't. Much like today, savings accounts and CDs didn't make a *real* profit. Those good old days weren't *that* good.

Unfortunately, we can't hide from what's real. Consider the five-year period from January 2015 to January 2020. US inflation averaged 1.82 percent per year. If you didn't earn at least 1.82 percent per year, you lost money. Goods and services that cost $10,000 in 2015 would have cost about $10,943 at the beginning of 2020.

Conversely, if you had split your money equally between a US stock market index and an intermediate government bond market index over the same five-year period, you would have earned a *real* profit. You would have gained a compound annual pre-inflation return of about 6.83 percent. The *real return* would have been 5.01 percent per year (after inflation).

Between 1972 and 2020, there were forty-four rolling five-year periods: 1972–1976 was the first, 1973–1977 the second, 1974–1978 the third, 1975–1979 the fourth, and 2015–2019 was the forty-fourth. During all forty-four of these rolling five-year periods, money stuffed into savings accounts and CDs didn't earn a *real* penny.

In contrast, money split evenly between a US stock index and an intermediate government bond index would have earned a *real return* in forty of the forty-four five-year periods (see Table 6.4).

TABLE 6.4

Rolling Five-Year Periods
(January 1972–2020)

	Profit from CDs and Savings Accounts, Measured in Five-Year Periods	Profit from a Balanced Portfolio (50% stocks, 50% bonds), Measured in Five-Year Periods
44 Measured Time Periods	0/44	40/44

Source: portfoliovisualizer.com[8]

You might wonder how the investment portfolio of stocks and bonds performed during the four five-year periods when it didn't beat inflation. From 1972 until 1976 it averaged a compound annual return of 6.09 percent. From 1973 until 1977 it averaged 3.81 percent per year. From 1974 until 1978 it averaged 6.29 percent annually, and from 1977 until 1981 it averaged 7.57 percent annually. Table A2, in the Appendix, shows how each of the forty-four five-year periods stacked up against US inflation levels.

Portfolios with higher stock allocations beat the portfolio with 50 percent stocks and 50 percent bonds during most measured time periods. But portfolios with higher stock allocations are also more volatile. Whether you choose higher or lower stock allocations, however, isn't as important as the main point I want to make: CDs and savings accounts don't make money. Period.

They aren't designed to increase anyone's buying power. That's why, when you're saving for retirement, a diversified portfolio of stock and bond market index funds makes much more sense. Fortunately, it's easy to build such a portfolio. But don't walk into a bank or investment firm to ask a financial advisor to build you a portfolio of index funds or ETFs. The industry has a dirty little secret they don't want you to know. We'll get into that next.

A Few Tips for Living Well

- Owning a sliver of every business in a portfolio of index funds or ETFs increases your odds of investment success.

- Investing regular sums—regardless of the short-term performance of the market—can help you enjoy future financial security.

- Don't be afraid of short-term fluctuations. In the stock market, even ten years is a blip. Understand historical stock returns so you can have realistic expectations.

- If you're saving money for a home down payment or for an emergency fund, don't put that money in the stock market. Keep it easily accessible in a savings account or money market account.

7

DON'T LET A FINANCIAL ADVISOR POUR WATER IN YOUR TRUMPET

Hidden Fees Drown Out Returns

A FEW YEARS AGO, Marilyn Arsenault and her husband, Joey Pietraroia, learned the financial services industry's dirty little secret. When they first decided to save for their retirement, they booked an appointment with a financial advisor. Marilyn, a running coach, and Joey, a symphony orchestra conductor, expected the advisor to look after their interests.

And on the surface, that's what happened. The financial advisor asked the couple about their goals, much as Marilyn asks her athletes about their goals every year. Then the advisor outlined a plan, much as Joey does when he prepares an orchestra. But there were a couple of differences. Marilyn doesn't feed her athletes buckets of ice cream before every workout. Joey doesn't pour water into trumpets. Most financial advisors, however, do something similar to harm their clients' performances, often without realizing they're doing it. Marilyn and Joey's advisor was no exception. She stuffed their money in several actively managed mutual funds. Such funds charge hidden fees that obstruct a strong performance. Here's how they work.

Each fund is managed by a fund manager or a team of managers. Their job is to buy and sell stocks for the fund. For example, one of Marilyn and Joey's mutual funds focused on US stocks. In this case, a fund manager bought shares in more than a hundred American companies. The manager tried to buy what was hot and avoid what was not. Typically, active fund managers trade in and out of different shares every week, sometimes every day. Most of the stocks that are inside the fund at the beginning of the year (about 60 percent of them) are no longer in the fund at the end of the year.

At first blush, that sounds smart. If a manager expects a stock to do well, they'll buy it. If they believe one of their stocks might be ready to fall, they might trade it for another. But such trading rarely works. Besides, that isn't the fund company's top priority. The company's top priority is to make money for its firm. Investors are a distant second. The investment firm makes money by legally sifting money from their funds every year. In other words, they pull money from the funds that Marilyn and Joey owned. That's known as the fund's *expense ratio*. The mutual fund company uses that money to pay for the firm's expenses. Such costs include electricity, paper, advertising, building construction and maintenance, rental spaces, salaries, computers, trailing fees (commissions paid to advisors who recommend the funds), and... profits for the investment company owners.

Investors often ask, "What fees do I pay?" Some financial advisors say, "Nothing. You don't pay a fee." If you ever hear that, sprint for the door. Investors can find their fund's expense ratio fees listed on the fund company prospectus. But there's an additional cost that doesn't show up. It's the fee investors pay when the fund manager trades stocks.

For example, if a fund manager trades Coca-Cola shares for Netflix shares, a third-party brokerage charges a transaction fee for the trade. Unfortunately, the mutual fund company doesn't pay that fee on behalf of people like Marilyn and Joey. Instead, it's extracted from the value of the fund. In other words, people like Marilyn and Joey pay the fee.

According to a research paper by John C. Bogle, which he published in the *Financial Analysts Journal*, when combining expense ratio costs, commissions, cash in the fund that isn't invested, and internal trading transaction fees, the average actively managed US mutual fund costs investors about 2.27 percent per year. That might not sound like much. But it could hit harder than an 80 percent salary cut.[1]

Assume a mutual fund's stock holdings made 2.27 percent in a given year, before fees. After paying 2.27 percent in fees, the investors wouldn't make a penny. They would lose 100 percent of the pre-fee proceeds. If the fund earned 4.54 percent in a given year, before fees, the investor would lose 50 percent of the pre-fee proceeds if they paid 2.27 percent in total fees. If the fund made 9.08 percent before fees, the investor would lose 25 percent of the pre-fee proceeds.

Over long periods, such hemorrhaging results in a lot of blood loss. Below, I've shown how $10,000 would grow over fifty years, before and after fees. Assuming a 2.27 percent annual drag (including expense ratio charges, uninvested cash, commissions, and internal trading fees), $10,000 would grow to:

- $469,016 (at 8% before fees), and

- $162,148 (at 5.73% after fees and internal costs).

Why Buy Index Funds Instead?

If the stock market gains 8 percent in a given year, the aggregate return of actively managed mutual funds that invest in that market will earn that return minus fees. In other words, if investors paid 2.27 percent in fees, the average investor in actively managed funds would make about 5.73 percent. This calculation is based on research by William F. Sharpe, a Nobel Prize–winning economist.[2]

But it doesn't just apply to actively managed mutual funds. It applies to all active management: hedge funds, day traders, college endowment funds, and mutual funds. As a group, they represent the market's return. For example, assume the US stock market earned 1 percent next year. If we averaged how all mutual funds, hedge funds, college endowment funds, and day traders performed in US stocks that year, their average return would have been about 1 percent (before fees).

As a group, they can't earn a higher or lower return than the market, because they represent the market. This is why it's better to buy a low-cost index fund. A broad stock market index, for example, owns virtually every stock in a given market. If the stock market earned 1 percent in a given year, the index would earn 1 percent, minus its small fee. In most cases, that fee ranges between 0.03 percent and 0.15 percent per year. It's sometimes even lower. Fidelity Investments, for example, offers zero-fee index funds for Americans. And because an index fund doesn't have an active trader at the helm, nobody feverishly trades one stock for another. As a result, their internal trading fees are almost zero.

Why Would Fidelity Offer Index Funds without an Expense Ratio Fee?

When I worked in a supermarket, the store managers sometimes advertised bananas at prices that were lower than the store paid. In other words, during the sale, they lost money on bananas. I once asked the produce manager, "Why would you guys do that?" He replied, "It's called a loss leader. It gets people in the store. And while they're here, they usually don't just walk out with bananas. We make a profit from them when they buy other things." Fidelity's zero-fee index funds are much like that. They get investors in the door, people who might be tempted to add some of Fidelity's more expensive actively managed funds to their portfolio (especially if one of those funds posts a strong, recent performance).

If you want to beat the vast majority of professional investors (after fees), build a portfolio of low-cost index funds. Ensure that it includes US stocks and international stocks, as well as a bond index fund for diversification and stability. Once again, I'll show you exactly how to do that, or how to hire someone who can help you.

Index Funds Are an Ingredient for a Better Life

When I speak to groups of young people I often say, "If you become financially literate, you can choose a career you enjoy, even if it doesn't pay a lot of money." Index funds are part of that financial literacy. I've met plenty of young people who skipped their dream careers because they felt they wouldn't earn enough money. Some of them wanted to become teachers, writers, or brewmasters, but after researching salaries, they bypassed careers they would love for jobs that pay more.[3]

That's a pity, because, as I keep mentioning, time is the only nonrenewable resource we have. According to Our World in Data, we spend far more time working than doing anything (except sleeping— we sleep every night, but usually we don't work every day). So why would we spend most of our conscious time doing something we don't enjoy?[4]

Unfortunately, plenty of people trade quality of life for a higher income. Yet, as I mentioned in chapter 2, happiness doesn't increase beyond a certain income level. In fact, there's a high-income point at which happiness begins to decline. That's because high-paying jobs often come with greater responsibilities and greater time commitments. Such demands often reduce the time we can spend with friends and family and enjoying sports or hobbies.

People who earn more money also tend to spend more money. And as I referenced in chapter 1, research shows that most people who buy more expensive cars, upgrade their homes, or acquire more material goods don't report feeling better about their lives. Hedonic adaptation sees to that, as we get used to what we own.

With the right mindset and investment products, however, someone could embrace a career they love and reach retirement age with more money at their disposal than many higher-income earners. It starts with a person tracking their expenses and cutting back on the purchases that don't add much (if indeed any) value to their lives. Next, if that person understands opportunity costs (see chapter 5), they might be inspired to invest more money. And with index funds, their money will go further than with actively managed funds.

For example, if a portfolio of index funds beat a portfolio of actively managed funds by 2 percent per year, someone enjoying a middle-income job could invest far less than their neighbor (who's festering in a higher-paying job they hate) and retire with as much money.

Imagine someone investing $500 a month in a portfolio of index funds for forty years. Over their career, they would have invested a total of $240,000. If they averaged 8 percent per year, their money would grow to about $1,621,694 after forty years.

Now consider someone who invests almost 70 percent more. They sock away $840 a month for 40 years. Over their careers, they would have invested $403,200. But if they earned 2 percent less each year (thanks to higher mutual fund fees) they would end up with roughly $1,610,701. In other words, this person could invest almost 70 percent more money but still end up with less.

If you learn to invest effectively, you could enjoy your chosen career instead of selling your soul for a higher-paying position you hate.

Financial Advisors and Their Anti-Index Battle Plan

I used to think financial advisors who stuffed actively managed funds into their clients' accounts were either bad people, or good people with a particular vice. But now I know differently. When they're trained to become financial advisors, they don't learn whether index funds or actively managed funds produce better results for clients. They work for firms that want to pad their corporate bottom line, so they're encouraged to sell actively managed products. Such products pay high commissions and trailer fees to advisors and their firms. In contrast, low-cost index funds pay neither. That's why, if you ask a financial advisor to build you a portfolio of index funds, most of them will have an anti-index battle plan. Here's what they'll say: "An index fund will just give you an average return. Why settle for mediocrity?"

The famous American novelist Upton Sinclair once said, "It is difficult to get a man to understand something when his salary depends upon his not understanding it."

In fact, index funds produce above-average returns. Every year, SPIVA (Standard & Poor's Indices versus Active Management) records how actively managed funds perform compared to their benchmark indexes. Every year, without fail, active funds fall short. The longer the time period, the lower the odds that an actively managed fund will keep up with its benchmark index.

For example, over the ten years ending June 30, 2020, the US stock index beat 84.49 percent of actively managed US stock market funds.[5]

Actively managed funds are even worse in Canada, where mutual fund fees are higher. Among actively managed mutual funds in Canada that focus on US stocks, a whopping 95.24 percent underperformed the US stock index over those same ten years. Of the Canadian mutual funds that focus on Canadian stocks, almost 90 percent underperformed the Canadian stock market index over the ten years ending June 30, 2020.[6]

Most financial advisors, however, won't be daunted if you confront them with this data. They'll reply with "We only recommend funds that beat indexes. I'll show you the charts."

Roughly 20 percent of actively managed funds beat their benchmark indexes over a ten-year period. So, on the surface, it makes sense to just pick the winners. But actively managed funds that win over one measured time period usually disappoint the next.

Every six months, SPIVA publishes its Performance Persistence Scorecard. It determines how many actively managed funds were among the industry's top performers over a specific time period. It then calculates whether those funds maintained their winning ways.

For example, SPIVA looked at funds that were among the top 25 percent of performers from 2010 until 2014. It then looked at the industry's top performers from 2015 until 2020. The big question is: How many of the top-performing funds from 2010 until 2014 were still among the top 25 percent of performers from 2015 until 2020?

If you believed in performance persistence, you might say, "Well, a fund that beats most of its peers during a five-year period will likely do so over the next five years." And why wouldn't we believe that? After all, that would be the case with most professional endeavors. Most teachers, dentists, or surgeons, for example, who are among the top 25 percent of performers in their field would remain among the top 25 percent for at least another five years.

But that isn't the case with fund managers. Largely, strong results are based on luck. That's why only 21 percent of the top quartile performers between 2010 and 2014 were still among the top quartile from 2015 until 2020. That means 79 percent of these former winning funds slipped to mediocrity, or worse. That's why, if a financial advisor says, "Let's pick these great performing funds," we need to understand the long odds of their continuing to do well.[7]

Sometimes, fund companies will advertise their index-beating record with data from the past. But they won't want you to look too closely. Such was the case with a company called American Funds.

In 2019, Capital Group, the company that owns American Funds, asked a question on its website: "Can I find [actively managed] funds that have beaten the index? I can."

They compared the returns of the S&P 500 Index to five actively managed Capital Group American Funds since 1976. The actively managed funds looked great. But their strong historical results failed the performance persistence test. By 2020, the S&P 500 Index had beaten the aggregate returns of these American Funds champions over the previous one-year, three-year, five-year, ten-year, and fifteen-year periods.

In a taxable account, the performance gap between these actively managed funds and index funds would be even wider. After all, American Funds has active traders at its helm. Those traders buy and sell stocks every year. When they sell at a profit, their investors (in taxable accounts) have to pay the tax. It's often a short-term capital gains tax, which penalizes investors more than the long-term capital gains tax rate.

By comparison, index funds rarely trade stocks. As a result, investors pay almost nothing in capital gains taxes until the day they sell. And when they do sell, it's at the lower, long-term capital gains tax rate.

If you show this to a financial advisor, it should make them sweat. But financial salespeople can be tougher to shake than toenail fungus. You might hear this next: "Index funds are dangerous when the stock market falls. Active fund managers can pull money into cash when they think stocks will drop. But an index fund is linked 100 percent to the stock market's return."

I call this the "financial advisor's horror card." If you're game for some fun, ask, "What year was the biggest stock market decline during your lifetime?" Unless your advisor is more than a hundred years old—and remembers 1931—they should say, "It was 2008. That was a horrific year. The US stock market index fell about 38 percent."

At this point, most advisors will start to rub their hands. This is your cue to then ask, "Did most US actively managed stock market funds beat the US stock index in 2008?"

Most advisors will reply, "Yes." But that's not the case. In 2008, 64.23 percent of US actively managed stock market funds lost to the US index.[8] That means their active managers didn't know stocks would fall.

But here's what's more important: Smart investors don't buy a single stock market index fund. Instead, they include exposure to global stocks and bonds. In some cases (as I'll describe in chapter 8) they buy all-in-one portfolios of index funds. These include stock and bond market indexes. That's important to remember. After all, diversified portfolios with stocks and bonds don't fall as far when the markets drop. If the advisor hasn't stormed out of the room in frustration by this point, you might hear this next: "Our research teams can tell us where to move your money. If we think bonds, US stocks, emerging market stocks, or gold are about to take a run, we can position your money accordingly. You can't do that with a portfolio of index funds."

Nobody can predict, with any degree of consistency, which asset classes will rise or fall during any given year. Financial experts and leading economists are always trying to forecast where stocks are headed. They look and sound impressive. But how often are they right? CXO Advisory put them to the test. The organization assessed 6,627 forecasts by sixty-eight leading financial experts over an eight-calendar-year period from 2005 until 2012. On average, the experts were right just 48 percent of the time.[9]

Had a five-year-old said stocks would rise every year over this period, they would have been right 87.5 percent of the time (only 2008 saw stocks decline). None of the experts came close to that level of accuracy.

Betting that stocks will rise every year might sound naïve. But historically, stocks gain ground roughly two out of every three years. Unfortunately, there's no actual pattern. Stocks might rise four years in a row and then drop for two years. They might rise six years in a row and only drop once. The economy itself provides misleading clues. For example, if you thought unemployment would hit a peak six months from now, would you sell stocks in anticipation of a crash?

In the United States, unemployment peaked at 14.8 percent in April 2020. Imagine finding a lamp in October 2019. You rub the lamp and a genie comes out. She says, "We're going to suffer a pandemic and US unemployment levels are going to peak in six months." Would you sell your investments after hearing the genie's prediction?

If you did, it would have cost you money. Between October 2019 and October 2020, US stocks gained 11.39 percent. And no, this isn't a one-off case. In Table 7.1, I've listed dates representing six months before every unemployment peak since 1932 and the twelve-month stock market returns that followed.

TABLE 7.1

Does Unemployment Predict a Market Drop?

Six Months before Unemployment Peaks	S&P 500 Returns Twelve Months Later
November 30, 1932	+57.7%
December 31, 1937	+33.2%
July 30, 1946	-3.4%
April 30, 1949	+31.3%
March 31, 1954	+42.3%
January 31, 1958	+37.9%
November 30, 1960	+32.3%
February 26, 1971	+13.6%
November 29, 1974	+36.2%
January 31, 1980	+19.5%
June 30, 1982	+61.2%
December 31, 1991	+7.6%
December 31, 2002	+28.7%
April 30, 2009	+38.8%
October 30, 2019	+11.39%

Sources: Ken Fisher, *Markets Never Forget*, and Trading Economics.[10]

This doesn't mean we should expect stocks to rise when soup kitchen lines grow. We're easily fooled by randomness. Nobody can reliably forecast where stocks are headed. But that doesn't stop leagues of people claiming otherwise.

In 2008, a group called Protégé Partners bet Warren Buffett they could pick a group of hedge funds that would beat the S&P 500 Index over a ten-year period. Protégé Partners picked hedge fund managers who appeared to have a knack for making accurate predictions. But past results meant nothing. Buffett's bet began in January 2008: the year of the biggest market crash since 1931.

Had the hedge fund managers seen that crash coming, they would have shorted the market. To "short the market" is to place bets that stocks will fall. Then, if stocks do fall, investors can profit from that bet. But the hedge fund managers didn't see the crash coming. And their tactical maneuvers over the following ten years were like a noodle in a swordfight, as they averaged just 2.2 percent per year. As a result, Buffett won the bet. The S&P 500 Index averaged 7.1 percent per year. It's worth noting that Buffett (arguably the world's greatest investor) has instructed that his estate be invested in a portfolio of index funds for his wife when he dies.

But what about the world's most famous hedge fund, Ray Dalio's Bridgewater Pure Alpha Fund? Between 1991 and 2011, it gained a whopping 1,258 percent.[11]

Plenty of new investors jumped aboard in 2012. They hoped for an exciting ride. Unfortunately for them, over the next eight years and eight months this famous fund just taxied along the runway. Between January 1, 2012, and August 30, 2020, it averaged just over 2 percent per year. In contrast, over the same time period, US stocks gained 14.46 percent per year. Global stocks gained 10.39 percent per year. Even US bonds beat the world's most famous hedge fund. They gained 3.31 percent per year. No matter how you slice it, a diversified portfolio of index funds left Dalio in the dust.

Some of the strongest evidence against trying to tactically move money around comes from the returns of tactical allocation funds. This is a specific type of mutual fund where the manager can bounce the money into whatever asset class they choose. This sets them apart from other actively managed mutual funds.

For example, a fund manager of a regular US stock market fund only buys US stocks. A fund manager for a US bond market fund buys only US bonds. A fund manager for a global stock market fund focuses on global stocks. But a tactical asset allocation manager could buy US stocks today and sell them tomorrow, placing the proceeds into bonds, emerging market stocks, developed market international stocks, or gold. They follow economic news, interest rates, political environments, trends, and corporate earnings projections. In some ways, they're like hedge funds. But unlike hedge funds, they must be more diversified by law and they cannot short the market.

According to Morningstar, in 2019, about 300 tactical asset allocation funds were available in the United States. But just 176 of them had five-year track records. Poor performers, as always, get buried, renamed, or closed.

Over the five-year period ending July 19, 2019, the surviving 176 tactical asset allocation funds averaged a compound annual return of just 2.94 percent. None of them beat the US stock market index, which averaged a compound annual return of 10.22 percent. Vanguard's Balanced Index (60 percent stocks, 40 percent bonds) also beat 174 of the 176 funds. As shown in Table 7.2, it wouldn't matter how you mixed a diversified portfolio of index funds. They beat most of these tactical asset allocation funds.[12]

TABLE 7.2

Tactical Asset Allocation Funds
(Five-year periods ending July 19, 2019)

Portfolios	Five-Year Average Return	$10,000 Grew to...
Tactical Asset Allocation Funds	2.94%	$11,559.01
100% US Stock Index	10.22%	$16,266.80
60% US Stock Index, 40% US Bond Index	7.51%	$14,362.97
33% US Stock Index, 33% International Stock Index, 33% US Bond Index	5.12%	$12,839.53
55% US Stock Index, 25% International Stock Index, 20% US Bond Index	7.01%	$14,033.21

Source: morningstar.com
Note: Morningstar's published performance data on tactical asset allocation funds doesn't exceed five years

At this point, your financial advisor should be ready to submit. But there's one final card they might try to pull: "Have you seen the movie *The Big Short*? That guy who predicted the market crash of 2008 now says index funds are dangerous."

Michael Burry set fire to investors' worries when he said index funds would cause the market to collapse. He compared indexes to the subprime mortgage bubble in 2008 when he made a fortune shorting mortgage securities.

I've been investing for thirty-two years. Doomsayers have been predicting stock market crashes every week of every year since before I was born. And they'll be predicting financial Armageddon long after you and I are dead. There's a saying that Wall Street analysts have predicted one hundred of the past three market crashes.

But Burry, who rose to fame through Michael Lewis's book *The Big Short*, has a louder voice than most because he predicted stocks would fall in 2008. That's why many people think he has a working crystal ball. Today, he manages $340 million in assets at Scion Asset

Management in Saratoga, California. In other words, he's an active fund manager who handpicks stocks. But he doesn't have a working crystal ball. In the first four years since his fund's inception (2016–2020) his fund averaged a compound annual return of 0.71 percent. That compares to 11.51 percent per year for the global stock market index and 13.95 percent per year for the US stock market index.[13]

As for Burry's assessment of index funds, in an interview with *Bloomberg*, he explained that the stock of a bad business could end up with a rising price if it were part of an index. He fears that when so many people buy index funds, the stocks of the businesses within the index will rise no matter what.[14]

Here's his rationale: When money goes into index funds (from investors), the index fund manager has to then buy stocks for the index. Buying stocks could push the prices up. After all, the stock market moves based on supply and demand. When there's more demand for shares, the prices rise. Burry says this could increase the price of a crappy business that's inside the index. He also fears the same thing in reverse: If index fund investors freak out and sell en masse, the stock of a company that's producing record business profits will fall hard too.

But rabid selling occurred long before index funds existed. It happened in 1929, 1930, and 1931. It happened in 1973–1974. When it happens again—and it will—index funds won't be to blame. After all, when the stock market crashed in 2008, index funds performed better than actively managed funds. This means index fund investors kept cooler heads than most people think. According to the 2008 SPIVA Scorecard, index funds beat their actively managed counterparts in twelve out of twelve stock market categories.[15] That wouldn't have happened if index fund investors had stampeded for the exit.

What's more, index fund investors don't represent most of the money in the market, so they shouldn't be blamed when the markets fall again. In a 2018 research paper, Vanguard says index funds comprise just a small amount of the investment universe.[16] Vanguard references Morningstar's data when reporting that 85 percent of the money in the US stock market and 90 percent of the money in the global stock market is actively managed.

This might sound reassuring. But how do we know it's true? To answer that, look no further than General Electric. It's part of the S&P 500. It has also disappointed active traders. As a result, its stock price dropped almost 50 percent between January 1, 2018, and August 31, 2019.

Over that same time period, the S&P 500 rose 12.9 percent.

If the flow of money into index funds controlled individual stock prices, GE's stock would have risen along with the S&P 500, despite the company's woes. But GE's stock price didn't rise with the market. Over long periods, individual stocks still rise or fall based on the profits (or losses) of each respective business's gains or losses. That means, if a stock's business earnings plummet over several years, that stock's share price (as with the example with GE above) will drop too, even if the broad stock market index has risen.

Why You Should Always Ignore Stock Market Forecasts

Plenty of people have made a lucky market call. But for most of them it's a one-off. Elaine M. Garzarelli famously predicted the stock market crash of 1987. But her crystal ball stopped working after that. On July 23, 1996, she said US stocks could fall 15–20 percent from their summer peak. But sixteen months later, they had gained almost 50 percent. In 1997, she said US stocks would fall again.[17] But they soared 88 percent over the next three years. In 2007, she told the *New York Sun*'s Dan Dorfman that stocks would soar in 2008. We know how that turned out.[18]

Gary Shilling, like Michael Burry, also said investors should sell their stocks. In 2009, he proclaimed the S&P 500 would fall to end the year between 500 and 600 points. But investors who listened to

Shilling (even a broken clock is right twice a day) were disappointed. The S&P 500 soared. It ended 2009 at 1,115 points.[19]

Meredith Whitney predicted the upcoming banking crisis in 2007.[20] This made her famous when the markets collapsed in 2008. But in 2010, she said there would be hundreds of billions of dollars of municipal bond defaults over the next twelve months. That didn't happen.

Every week of every year, an expert predicts that stocks will fall hard. When a crash does occur, people sift through predictions to see who was "right." But it's better to listen to Warren Buffett. He never jumps out of the market if someone claims to see the future. He always stays invested. He says, "Stock market forecasters exist to make fortune tellers look good."

You can test this yourself. Find someone who has made a successful market call. Then track every prediction they make. It won't take long. You'll learn that Warren Buffett was right. Stock market forecasters *really do* exist to make fortune tellers look good.

That's why your horoscope has more value than a financial advisor who touts actively managed funds. After all, their fees (coupled with their inability to see the future) could cost you plenty. Marilyn Arsenault and her husband, Joey, fired their financial advisor. They now invest in a diversified portfolio of low-cost index funds.

Most Financial Advisors Are Not Evil

Most financial advisors will try to fight you with the arguments above. And we've poked some fun at them. But are they evil people? Training to become a financial advisor—even a Certified Financial Planner (CFP)—does not take the same amount of time it would take you to become a doctor, lawyer, teacher, or mechanic. The course material doesn't include lessons on low-cost index funds versus actively managed funds. It doesn't warn about chasing past performance.

If advisors want to learn about these things, they must pursue this knowledge on their own.

Olivia Summerhill is a CFP and founder of Summerhill Wealth Management in Washington State. She says, "During the Certified Financial Planning extensive training, the focus is not on investment vehicles. A CFP candidate does not get any training in their program [about whether] actively or passively managed funds are better for clients."

Benjamin Felix, a Canadian financial planner with PWL Capital, says, "The CFP education program is designed to ensure that CFP professionals have a broad understanding of twelve topics core to the financial planning process; investments is one of those topics. . . but there is no requirement to fully understand the evidence in favor of buying and holding low-cost index funds."[21] Edward Goodfellow agrees. The CFP with PI Financial says, "If advisors understood, from an academic perspective, how markets actually worked, they would be much more suited to provide advice. The problem is, markets are noisy and the advisors, investors, and media get lost in the noise."

This is why most financial advisors put actively managed funds in their clients' accounts. But such advisors also eat their own cooking. . . typically after they burn it. On November 28, 2020, the finance researchers Juhani T. Linnainmaa, Brian T. Melzer, and Alessandro Previtero published "The Misguided Beliefs of Financial Advisors" in the *Journal of Finance*.[22]

They assessed data from 4,688 Canadian financial advisors and about 500,000 clients between 1999 and 2013. The two participating financial institutions provided personal trading and account information for the majority of the advisors. Of the 4,688 advisors, 3,282 had their personal portfolios with their firms. Most of those who didn't were just starting their careers.

Most of the advisors bought actively managed funds instead of index funds for their personal accounts. In other words, they bought the same things for themselves that they recommended to their clients. That doesn't reveal a lack of ethics, just a lack of knowledge.

When advisors put their clients in such funds, the advisors typically earn a commission or a trailer fee. When they put such funds in their own accounts, they receive a discount rebate on the fund. But despite these rebates, the researchers found that the advisors performed almost as badly as their clients. When comparing their performances to an equal-risk-adjusted portfolio of index funds or ETFs, the advisors underperformed by about 3 percent per year.

While the high fees of actively managed funds are part of the problem, they're not the whole problem. The advisors also chased past winners with their own money. If a fund was doing well, they jumped on board. And, as is usually the case, actively managed funds that perform well during one period often lag the next. That's why the advisors' personal money, and their clients' money, underperformed by 3 percent per year. That might not sound like much. But when compounded over the fifteen-year study, that totaled about 55 percent.

So the advisors punched themselves in the nose when they bought actively managed funds. Then they kicked their own shins by chasing past performance. And it all cost them a lot of money.

If you had (or have) an advisor who invested your money in actively managed funds, you might feel like tossing some punches of your own. But perhaps the Dalai Lama should have the final say: "A truly compassionate attitude toward others does not change even if they behave negatively or hurt you."

What Now?

If you have a tax-deferred account, such as an RRSP, RESP, or TFSA account for Canadians or an IRA or a 529 for Americans, you can transfer your actively managed holdings to a low-cost brokerage, robo-advisory firm, or full-service financial advisor who deals only with index funds or ETFs. (I'll provide examples in later chapters.) The money would remain under a tax-advantage umbrella, so selling the proceeds and investing them in low-cost index funds or ETFs won't attract a tax penalty.

If you also have actively managed funds in a taxable account, it might be best to sell them strategically, based on the most tax-advantaged circumstance. Always, however, confirm with an accountant or fee-based financial advisor to be sure. Then send your old advisor a thank-you card. After all, as I mentioned in chapter 3, kindness is also a key to a better life.

A Few Tips for Living Well

- When it comes to investing, put the odds in your favor. Evidence shows that the most effective way to beat the vast majority of professional investors is to build a diversified portfolio of low-cost index funds.

- Don't trust anyone offering financial advice. Always research and verify.

- Understand high fees and the long-term damage they can do.

- Chasing past winners is like pursuing last week's winning lottery numbers.

- Arm yourself with facts when a financial advisor wants to sell you actively managed funds.

- Remember, the less you pay in investment fees, the more money you will make over time.

- Not all advisors are evil. Most just don't know what they don't know.

8

SET IT AND FORGET IT

Hands-Off Investing Boosts Happiness and Profits

EBENEZER SCROOGE WOULD have been a lousy neighbor. He would have ignored you on the street and slammed the door on children selling Girl Scout Cookies.

In Charles Dickens's *A Christmas Carol*, Scrooge starts out as a crabby capitalist whose sole obsession is money. Fortunately, some ghostly visitors smarten him up. We don't need a university-based study to know that obsessing about money makes people less warm and cuddly. But recent studies show that just thinking about money can encourage Scrooge-like tendencies.

Kathleen D. Vohs could explain someone like Scrooge. The psychologist and behavioral economist has spent plenty of time studying the relationship between psychology and money.

In a 2015 issue of the *Journal of Experimental Psychology*, she says that research from more than 165 studies in eighteen countries confirms that, "compared to neutral primes, people reminded of money are less interpersonally attuned. They are not prosocial, caring, or warm. They eschew interdependence."[1]

Most of these experiments required the subjects to perform a task. Some of those tasks required them to think about money. That's called "priming." Researchers wanted to see whether subjects who were primed by money (encouraged to think about money beforehand) were more helpful or less helpful than subjects who weren't primed by money. In some cases, researchers staged opportunities for the subjects to help others. For example, actors pretended they were lost or they dropped a handful of items in front of test subjects.

It emerged that the people who were thinking about money were less helpful. They were also less likely to be pulled away from their tasks when tempted by social interactions. Instead of getting distracted and chatting, they preferred to stay on their money-thinking tasks much longer than control groups, who were given tasks that weren't money-minded. So far, nobody has researched how well ghosts could fix selfish tendencies.

Plenty of investors spend too much time thinking about the stock market. They wonder which direction stocks are headed. They might think about their next stock or bond purchase while they're walking to the grocery store, or sweat over which stock or fund to buy this month while sitting at their desk at work. They might even tune in to market-based radio, stock-based television shows, YouTube videos on investing, or even podcasts. When their children ask to play with them outside, they might be thinking about whether they should add fresh money to their account, in what quantities they should add it, and when they should rebalance their portfolios.

It's tough to escape money-related thoughts. But research suggests we should try to limit them. After all, according to the studies I mentioned earlier, we tend to be more social and helpful when we aren't thinking about money. We forge better friendships (just ask Scrooge), and by thinking less about money, we might even live longer. Harvard's eight-decade-long Study of Adult Development (see chapter 3) shows that strong human relationships, not money, have the strongest correlation with a happy life. And Marta Zaraska, author of *Growing Young,* presents reams of research supporting the notion that happier people live longer.

This chapter is about investing, so I can hear you thinking, "If I invest money in the stock market, I'll need to think about what I'm doing." Fortunately for your friendships, happiness, and longevity, that simply isn't true. And the less you think about your investments, the more money you'll likely make.

I might sound like a personal trainer saying, "Binge-watch Netflix and gorge on cake for the best body ever!" But when it comes to investing, the sloth beats almost everyone.

The Forgetful and the Dead Make the Best Investors

The mutual fund company Fidelity wanted to find out which of the firm's investors had the best performance. If you're like most people, you might think those who labored over their financial statements, read the economic news, traded in and out of hot funds, and did their best to "time" their purchases had the best results. But that wasn't true. The best investors were those who forgot they had accounts with Fidelity. Dead people performed just as well, but they weren't able to spend their profits.[2]

Investment portfolios are much like bars of soap. The more we mess with them, the smaller they get. That's why you should build a diversified portfolio of low-cost index funds and try to keep your hands and minds off the money. If you do that, you'll beat most day traders, most hedge funds, and most college endowment funds on an equal-risk-adjusted basis.[3]

What Does an Equal-Risk-Adjusted Basis Mean?

Nobody would compare an all-terrain vehicle to a Ferrari. They have different purposes. The ATV would crush the Ferrari on a desert run and the Ferrari would win on a regular track. In a similar vein, we shouldn't compare portfolios built for different purposes. Instead, to compare how well investments are performing, we make an equal-risk-adjusted comparison: like comparing a Ferrari to a Lamborghini or a Hummer to a Range Rover. For example, if a portfolio of actively managed funds comprises 100 percent global stocks, it should be compared with a global stock index. That's equal risk. If an actively managed portfolio has 70 percent global stocks and 30 percent bonds, it should be compared to a portfolio comprising 70 percent in a global stock index and 30 percent in a bond index. Again, that would represent equal risk.

Avoiding Paralysis by Analysis

There are almost as many index funds or ETFs as there are narcissists on Instagram. OK, I'm exaggerating. But there are a lot. For example, according to Statista, there are more than two thousand ETFs in the United States.[4] Morningstar reports almost a thousand ETFs trading on the Canadian stock exchange. So when I say, "Just build a portfolio of index funds or ETFs," it can trigger deer-in-the-headlights syndrome.

The American psychologist Barry Schwartz says that when we face too many choices, we suffer from paralysis. In his book *The Paradox of Choice*, he references a Vanguard retirement plan study. It found that employee participation in retirement plans was higher when employers offered them fewer investment choices. People dithered when they saw too many options. They feared making mistakes, so many didn't invest.

Furthermore, according to Schwartz, when we finally do make a decision, we often regret it. That isn't necessarily a result of the decision being bad. Instead, it's a result of too many initial choices. When, for example, we choose one fund out of one hundred on offer, we're often plagued by regret. We wonder if one of the other ninety-nine options would have been a better choice. Schwartz says this is what humans almost always do. And the more choices we have, the more miserable it can make us.[5]

So, instead of bombarding you with choices, I'll offer three solid options. In each case, they'll help keep your mind off your money. If the behavioral research is right, each of these choices should help you be more helpful, more social, live longer, and boost your odds of long-term investment success.

- Hire a financial advisor to build a diversified portfolio of low-cost index funds or ETFs.

- Open an account with a robo-advisor that will do the same thing, at a lower cost.

- Build your own portfolio with (preferably) an all-in-one portfolio fund of indexes or ETFs.

Full-Service Game-Changers Move toward the Future

When I wrote my book *Millionaire Teacher*, several readers asked, "Why would a full-service financial firm build portfolios of index funds for clients? After all, they can make more for themselves selling actively managed funds."

Let me share a story.

Several years ago, I received an email from a guy named Sam Instone. He's CEO of the investment firm AES International. "I would like to fly you to Dubai," he said, "so you can speak to my financial advisors." At first I wasn't keen. Most financial firms sell expensive products: actively managed funds or (even worse) insurance-linked investment schemes. His firm was no exception. His company website listed several actively managed funds.

I had never seen the desert in the United Arab Emirates. But I envisioned a scene from the original *Star Wars* movie. Early in the film, zombie-like Sand People tried to skewer Luke Skywalker with their sticks. As the index fund guy, I would be easier to bury than a future Jedi Knight.

Soon, however, I learned that AES was a business in transition. About eighteen months before he contacted me, Instone had asked his advisors to stop selling actively managed funds. He gathered his troops to say, "We're going to build portfolios of low-cost index funds instead. Anyone who's caught selling other funds will have to go."

He also encouraged every advisor at the firm to reach the highest level of professional certification, while providing materials to educate them on low-cost index funds. He tried to convince his advisors they would eventually make more money putting their clients' interests first. It sounds like a rousing speech. But nobody cheered. In fact, most of his advisors quit. They preferred making fast commissions with actively managed funds and insurance-linked schemes.

That's why Instone flew me to Dubai to speak to his small, surviving team. I didn't know whether his company would survive. In the end, it didn't just survive. It thrived. And this wasn't a one-off case. In his book *Give and Take*, the Wharton psychology professor Adam Grant describes some people and businesses as "givers" and others as "takers." Early on, "givers" are far less productive. They don't aggressively sell. They offer high levels of service but are often viewed as soft. However, over time, their tendency to focus on assisting with the needs of other people helps them develop solid reputations. As a result, new clients and customers begin to seek them out. According to Grant, they therefore gain momentum and leave most "takers" in the dust.[6]

This is why some firms say no to the quick money of commission-based actively managed funds and insurance-linked schemes. They understand that if they treat their clients well, it eventually works out better for everyone.

Fitness Guru Enjoys a Full-Service Index Investing Firm

Bob Connor invests with a client-focused firm. The sixty-eight-year-old doesn't look his age. In fact, he's fitter and stronger than most twenty-five-year-old men. The former PE teacher and school athletic director works out hard almost every day. He follows the latest nutritional research, sharing his knowledge through his health and fitness coaching business.

His lifestyle approach is based on science, much like his investments. Bob and his wife, Claire, invest in a portfolio of low-cost index funds. But they don't do it alone. They hired a full-service firm that only builds portfolios of index funds. Plenty of DIY investors might scoff at this idea because they could buy indexes on their own and pay lower fees. But Bob says his advisor's fees are worth it.

For starters, he pays far less than most people who invest in actively managed funds. He also receives a high level of service. Many full-service financial companies offer advice on taxes, wills, estate planning, insurance, children's education planning, and retirement income planning.

As Bob says, "They have been a huge help in consolidating and managing all aspects of our investment portfolio. They provide us with plenty of evidence and research. They also ask us the tough questions when necessary. As we approach our retirement years, they're assisting us in ensuring that we have enough to cover all expenses—especially when the time comes that both of us may not be working."

Despite paying higher fees than a DIY investor, evidence suggests that people like Bob and Claire might beat the investment performance of most people who invest in indexes on their own. When stocks go on multiyear upward runs, investing is emotionally easy. Such was the case from 2010 until 2020. But when the economy flails, when stocks fall, and when forecasters are predicting financial Armageddon, plenty of DIY investors start to wet the bed.

The ten-year period from 2005 until 2015 was a case in point. Stocks soared for the first three years; bed sheets stayed dry. But in 2008, things got messy. It was the biggest calendar year decline since 1931. The markets reached a low in March 2009 and then began to recover. At the time, many people wondered, "Is this recovery real or another dead cat's bounce?" Many investors sold when the markets plunged. They were also afraid to re-enter the market before it had recovered. As a result, they sold low and bought high. Many others, who normally invested every month, stopped their automatic deposits. They waited for the markets to "go back to normal" before they resumed investing. And others sat on the sidelines, holding tight to their cash. Instead of investing an inheritance or proceeds from a home or business sale, they decided to "wait it out." Unfortunately, market timing almost never works.

Vanguard's S&P 500 Index averaged 7.89 percent over the ten years ending March 31, 2015. This period included the crash and frenzied markets of 2008 and 2009. If investors had kept their heads, those who invested in the S&P 500 would have earned 7.89 percent annually over this ten-year period. But that didn't happen, because... people are human. Fear and greed lead to speculation. As a result, according to Morningstar, the average investor in Vanguard's S&P 500 Index averaged just 5.82 percent per year over this period. That means they turned $10,000 into $17,606. However, if someone invested in the S&P 500 Index over that same time period—and didn't speculate or panic—they would have turned $10,000 into $21,370.

That's why I suggest methods that help investors control fear and greed. Stock market volatility is normal. Over your lifetime, you'll see several market crashes. And if you're like most people, your behavior will almost certainly lead you to underperform the very funds you own. That's why every investor must channel their inner Buddha. And getting some help doesn't hurt.

Does This Fund Company Encourage Good Behavior?

Dimensional Fund Advisors (DFA) is a Texas-based fund company that offers its funds to a select group of financial advisors. These advisors must travel (on their own dime) to Santa Monica, California, or Austin, Texas, for special training before they can sell DFA funds. Dimensional teaches them not to mess around with clients' money. Remember that bar of soap?

The Dimensional trainers teach the financial advisors how to build portfolios of low-cost DFA index funds. And they emphasize the importance of staying the course. The firm provides ongoing educational support to the advisors, encouraging them to pass that knowledge on to clients. As a result, the clients end up far less skittish when stocks hit the skids.

For example, according to Morningstar, over the ten-year period ending March 31, 2015, DFA's US Large Cap Value [Index] Fund (DFLVX) averaged a compound annual return of 8.06 percent per year. Not all of the fund's investors had the courage to stay the course when the markets crashed in 2008/2009. But most of them did. Investors averaged 7.34 percent in that fund from March 31, 2005, to March 31, 2015. Because most of them kept their cool, the average investor in this fund underperformed the fund's return by an average of 0.72 percent per year.

In contrast, most of the investors in Vanguard's S&P 500 Index didn't stay the course. Over the same ten-year period, they underperformed the fund they owned by a whopping 2.07 percent per year. It's worth remembering that it's behaviorally easy to invest when stocks are rising. For example, stocks increased almost every year from 2010 until 2020. Investing then was an emotional piece of cake. That's why Morningstar reported small gaps between how funds performed and how investors performed over that decade. But stocks don't just rise, of course. And when they crash, we're tested.

The 2008/2009 financial crisis saw most fund investors fail. They removed money from their funds. Dimensional was one of the few companies with net-inflows. That means their investors deposited more money into their funds than they were taking out. The full-service financial advisors who worked with Dimensional's funds helped investors stay calm.

That doesn't mean everyone should invest with a full-service firm. For starters, many people can't. Advisors who work exclusively with index funds don't earn commissions, so they rely on smaller margins of profits for themselves. As a result, they usually require high entry points to make up for that. Most, for example, require that their clients have at least $100,000 to start. I've seen other entry points as high as $750,000.

To Hire or to Fire?

Not everybody wants (or needs) a full-service financial advisor. But if you do, here's a list of questions to ask before you commit to working with one.

1. Do you invest only with low-cost index funds or ETFs?

If the advisor says no, walk away. Some active funds do beat their benchmark indexes. But nobody can consistently pick such funds ahead of time. Looking for the funds that have done well in the past is a bad idea. Each year, S&P Dow Jones Indices publishes the Persistence Scorecard.[7] Their data shows that actively managed funds with strong track records rarely keep winning. Low costs are better predictors of strong fund returns. That's why index funds or ETFs give the best odds of success.

2. How do you earn your money?

Don't hire an advisor who gets paid commissions. They could be choosing investments based on how well the products help them make their Maserati payments. Instead, negotiate an annual fee (it could be a consistent dollar figure) or agree to pay a percentage of assets. Most fee-only advisors charge about 1 percent per year. They also typically reduce this percentage as investors' assets increase. That's fair. After all, it isn't tougher to manage $10 million than it is to manage $1 million.

3. Does your firm use research to forecast the economy or the market's direction?

If an advisor answers yes to this question, move on. Nobody knows whether stock markets will rise or fall this year or the next. If an advisor says they can forecast the market's direction, you're looking at a fool or a charlatan.

4. Can I see a model financial plan and portfolio?

There are two reasons you should ask for these things. First, when an advisor explains something, you need to understand it. If you can't, it's not your fault. It's the advisor's problem.

Second, what the advisor says about the sample portfolio is also important. They shouldn't try to wow you with past returns. Instead, they should show how risky and conservative portfolios have performed historically, based on different allocations of stocks and bonds. They should also help you determine your tolerance for risk before recommending a portfolio allocation.

5. What credentials do you have?

I've met people in banks who sell financial products after fewer than three weeks of financial training. Ensure that anyone you hire has robust qualifications. There are many financial advisory credentials. The Certified Financial Planner and Chartered Financial Planner designations (both known by the initials CFP) are the most rigorous. Not every CFP will exclusively build portfolios of index funds. In fact, most will sell higher-commission products. But a CFP is at least qualified to practice their craft. Most other three-letter designations at the bottom of an advisor's business cards are comparatively unimpressive.

6. Is it important for you to be on a "top advisor" list?

Each year, *Barron's* lists the year's "Top 100 Financial Advisors." Such lists largely base rankings on assets under management.[8] That's a lousy measuring stick for quality: silver-tongued sales teams and advertisements can snag a lot of clients. The best advisors should be rated on their credentials, levels of service, and evidence-based strategies. Financial advisors who sell actively managed funds shouldn't be on anyone's "top advisor" list.

7. Do you personally track your expenses and invest in index funds?

I wouldn't hire a 500-pound personal trainer who lives on beer and donuts. You likely wouldn't either. The same premise applies to financial advisors. Ask the advisor about their own financial journey. If they track their personal spending, set financial goals, and live within their means, they'll proudly tell you their story. But if they don't walk the walk, these questions might offend them. Do you want a financial train wreck giving you advice?

Once you're satisfied with the advisor's responses, complete one final step. Check their reputation through a governing body. In the United States, an advisor's Form ADV will tell you if an advisor is hiding anything inappropriate.[9] Also contact your state securities regulator to see if the advisor has a sordid history with any of the regulatory organizations that they belong to.[10] Canadians should check the Investment Industry Regulatory Organization of Canada (IIROC).[11] And British investors should check the Federal Conduct Authority (FCA) register, where they can find specific advisors and firms.[12]

I've included a list of links below to help you find a full-service advisor who uses Dimensional (DFA) funds. Such advisors typically build portfolios based on research conducted by two eminent economists: Eugene Fama, who won a Nobel Prize in economics for his studies on efficient market theory, and Kenneth French, the Roth Family Distinguished Professor of Finance at the Tuck School of Business, Dartmouth College. Fama and French found that by tilting index-like portfolios slightly toward lower-priced stocks and small-company shares, they could earn slightly better returns with a lower overall risk. To take advantage of this, they initially devised a three-factor model, which they've since extended to a five-factor model. It sounds fancy. But think of them as combinations of index funds that perform well in the long term.[13]

Just remember, however, that DFA isn't the only game in town. An advisor's decision to choose DFA index funds, traditional index funds, or ETFs won't make or break your retirement. But if you pick an advisor who handpicks individual stocks or who builds portfolios with actively managed funds, you might have to keep working much longer than you hoped.

If you're not sure where to find a full-service financial advisor who deals with DFA funds, here are a few suggestions:

· United States: us.dimensional.com/individuals/find-an-advisor-results

· Canada: ca.dimensional.com/en/individuals

· Europe: eu.dimensional.com/en/individuals

· Australia: au.dimensional.com/individuals

Hong Kong, Dubai, and Singapore have fewer fee-based advisors who build portfolios of index funds. Here are some resources you can look at:

- Hong Kong: private-capital.com.hk

- Dubai: aesinternational.com

- Singapore: providend.com/about and marcikelsconsulting.com

Robo-Advisors and Cyborgs

In the 1987 movie *RoboCop*, a gang of criminals murder police officer Alex Murphy. A corporation called Omni Consumer Products somehow revives him and builds him into a superhuman cyborg with no memory of his past. He lives on jars of baby food, so he shouldn't be that tough. But every villain fears him because he kicks ass. Over time, his human memories flood back. By regaining a sense of his humanity, he becomes even better at his law-enforcement duties.

The robo-advisory investment industry has plenty in common with RoboCop. In 2008, the world's first robo-advisor was born. It offered investors ready-made portfolios of low-cost ETFs. Investors just needed to sign up online, enter a few questions to assess their tolerance for risk, and the firm (like a robot) recommended a mix of ETFs. Compared to the actively managed portfolios offered by most financial advisors, these portfolios kicked butt. People could literally sign up with their phones and automatically transfer money from their bank accounts to their investment portfolios.

It was far cheaper than a full-service financial advisory firm. But the system wasn't perfect. Firms soon learned that people like the human touch. In time, robo-advisors began hiring financial advisors who could help clients over the phone. In many cases, investors can still open accounts with their phones, but by adding the ability to speak to a financial advisor, robo-advisors added a personal element that, like RoboCop, made them even better.

Chris Beingessner is a forty-three-year-old middle school vice principal. The Canadian is a father of two children, aged ten and twelve. Like many others, he began his investment journey with actively managed funds. "I soon realized they were too expensive," he says. "I then went to a full DIY model, buying my own ETFs. But the process stressed me out. I kept second-guessing my purchase decisions. And I kept looking at my account. No matter how much I tried, I couldn't shake the temptation to try to time the market."

In 2018, he opened an account with the robo-advisor CI Direct Investing (formerly WealthBar). "Fortunately, they don't make it easy for me to try to time the market," he says. "One of the company's advisors also helped me figure out how much I'll need for my retirement. Every few years, we plan to reassess that to see if we're on track." CI Direct charges Chris about 0.4 percent per year. That's less than half of what he would pay with most full-service financial advisors—but he also doesn't have access to the same level of wealth management services that some full-service advisors offer.

An Important Question for Any Robo-Advisor Firm

If you're considering investing with a robo-advisor, you'll find the following list, broken out by region, a helpful starting point. Just keep one thing in mind: Some robo-advisors claim they have special algorithms or an actively managed strategy designed to boost returns. That's like a health food store offering broccoli-sugared cupcakes.

Stick to the lowest-cost diversified portfolios they offer. Ask, "Would my portfolio maintain a consistent allocation, without any tactical maneuvers based on speculation?" If they answer, "Yes," that's good. But if they answer, "No, we have some tactical strategies based on blah, blah, blah. . . ," say no to that option. They make more money when you eat a cupcake diet.

1   United States:
· Betterment
· Wealthfront
· Ellevest
· SoFi Automated Investing
· Charles Schwab Intelligent Portfolios

2   Canada:
· CI Direct Investing
· Wealthsimple
· Nest Wealth
· BMO SmartFolio
· Justwealth

3   Australia:
· Raiz (formerly Acorns Australia)
· Stockspot
· Six Park

4   Mainland Europe and the UK:
· Feelcapital (Spain)
· Nutmeg (UK)
· Moneyfarm (Germany; UK)

5   Middle East/Asia
· Sarwa (UAE)

Robo-advisors charge lower fees than full-service investment firms. But for uber-cost-conscious investors, there's an even cheaper choice.

Back to the Beginning

Back in 1976, only Americans could buy index funds. Vanguard's
S&P 500 Index was their only choice. But more kept popping
up. Plenty of DIY investors focus on indexes or ETFs with the best
track record. But when they do so, they forget about reversion to
the mean. If a particular index beats another index during a desig-
nated period, it's likely that their roles will reverse. There's just one
problem. Without a working crystal ball, nobody knows when that
will happen.

That's why smart investors build globally diversified portfolios of
low-cost index funds or ETFs. This provides exposure to stocks not
only from the United States but also from around the world. Sometimes US stocks win. Other times, Australian, Canadian, European,
or emerging markets shine.

Nobody knows which market will next take center stage. That's
why it's best to own them all. There's a helpful science to investing
on your own. It doesn't take much time, but it might require putting
your ego to the side.

When Carlee Gold left the United States to work abroad she
took a huge risk: she could no longer contribute to America's Social
Security plan. When she retires, the US government therefore won't
provide her with the same retirement benefits as her friends in the
United States will enjoy. To make up for that deficit, the forty-three-
year-old knows she must save and invest well.

That's why she invested in one of Vanguard's target retirement
funds: a diversified portfolio of index funds rolled into one fund. In
other words, it includes US stocks, international stocks (including
emerging market stocks), and bonds. Carlee's fund costs her a paltry
0.14 percent per year. Vanguard rebalances the fund to maintain a
consistent allocation, and the firm increases the bond allocation as
Carlee grows older. It's the only investment she'll ever need.

Still, plenty of investors prefer to roll their own. If they build portfolios with several individual index funds or ETFs, they can get the same diversification and pay slightly lower fees. They might pay annual fees of 0.10 percent instead of 0.14 percent. But that's not a big difference. Complaining about 0.04 percent is like a marathoner whining about the weight of his eyebrows.

What's more, Carlee will beat most investors who build their own portfolios of index funds or ETFs. Here's why: Most investors (even index fund investors) chase past performance. They also speculate during elections, during market drops, during recessions, when market forecasts look grim, and when stocks hit all-time highs.

All-in-One Portfolios Help Investors Mind the Gap

Most investors say, "I would never do that! I know it's best to stay the course." But when push comes to shove, most eventually cave. They don't tend to mess up when stocks keep going up. But as Table 8.1 shows, when stocks jump around, most investors in individual funds eventually speculate.

The results were different for people like Carlee Gold. All-in-one portfolio funds calmed investors' nerves. In 2018, Morningstar's Jeffrey Ptak found that most people who buy all-in-one funds behave better than investors who build portfolios with individual funds.[14]

For starters, investors with all-in-one funds don't have to rebalance their portfolios. If, for example, they choose an all-in-one fund that has 70 percent stocks and 30 percent bonds, the fund company maintains that original allocation. DIY investors, however, must rebalance their own portfolios if they want to maintain consistency. And most carbon-based life forms screw up that rebalancing.

TABLE 8.1

Investor versus Fund Performance
(June 30, 2004–June 30, 2019)

Fund	Fund's Average Annual Performance	Investors' Average Annual Performance	Investors' Annual Underperformance or Outperformance
Vanguard's S&P 500 (VFINX)	8.62%	6.34%	**-2.28%**
Vanguard's Extended Market Index (VEXMX)	9.33%	8.65%	**-0.68%**
Vanguard's International Stock Market Index (VGTSX)	5.67%	4.47%	**-1.20%**
Vanguard European Stock Market Index (VEURX)	5.52%	0.93%	**-4.59%**
Vanguard Pacific Stock Market Index (VPACX)	5.05%	0.34%	**-4.71%**
Vanguard's Total Bond Market Index (VBMFX)	4.12%	3.61%	**-0.51%**

Source: morningstar.com

TABLE 8.2

Investors Behavior in All-in-One Funds
(June 30, 2004–June 30, 2019)

Fund	Fund's Average Annual Performance	Investors' Average Annual Performance	Investors' Annual Underperformance or Outperformance
Vanguard Target Retirement 2015 Fund	5.95%	5.63%	**-0.22%***
Vanguard Target Retirement 2025 Fund	6.53%	6.73%	**+0.20%**
Vanguard Target Retirement 2035 Fund	7.02%	7.53%	**+0.51%**
Vanguard Target Retirement 2045 Fund	7.38%	8.07%	**+0.69%**

Source: morningstar.com
*Investors in Vanguard's Target Retirement 2015 Fund were likely withdrawing money after 2015. That might be why such investors underperformed their fund. While the markets soared from 2015 until 2019, the investors were selling to cover their retirement costs.

The fifteen-year period from 2004 until 2019 was a behavioral litmus test. After all, it included exciting rising markets from 2004 until 2007, followed by a gut-wrenching decline during the financial crisis of 2008–2009, and another massive surge between 2010 and 2019. Vanguard has several all-in-one target retirement funds with fifteen-year track records. They each cater to different tolerances for risk. For example, some have much higher exposure to stocks. These offer odds of higher long-term returns. But they're much more volatile. Others include more bonds. These offer odds of lower long-term returns. But they're less volatile.

In most cases, investors added money to all-in-one funds every month. Perhaps these funds are self-selective. That is, maybe most of the people who choose them aren't interested in speculating. In many cases, they just keep adding the same amount monthly. They might not know or even care what's happening in the markets. After all, the best investors really are like Rip Van Winkle. They go to sleep for twenty years and wake up with juicy profits.

These investors' consistent deposits (which are often set up as automatic transfers) buy more fund units when prices drop and fewer fund units when prices rise. But I suspect most of the investors don't even know this is happening. As a result, instead of underperforming their funds over the fifteen years ending June 30, 2019, most of them outperformed their funds.

For example, Vanguard's all-in-one Target Retirement 2045 Fund averaged 7.38 percent annually over those fifteen years (see Table 8.2). But according to Morningstar, investors in the fund averaged 8.07 percent per year. Investors in all-in-one funds won't always beat the posted performances of their funds. But that's not important. What is important is that these investors speculate less. They have a hands-off approach. They allow the fund company to rebalance their funds and maintain a constant allocation. Consequently, the returns of such investors trounce the returns of most people who pick individual index funds and ETFs.

All-in-One Index Mutual Funds or All-in-One ETFs?

An ETF trades on a stock exchange. You need a brokerage account to buy one. Conversely, you buy mutual funds (including all-in-one portfolios of indexed mutual funds) from the fund companies that offer them.

Much depends on your nationality and country of residence. For example, only Americans can buy one of Vanguard's target retirement funds from Vanguard USA. But British investors can buy similar products from Vanguard UK. Canadian and Australian investors can't buy all-in-one portfolios of indexed mutual funds (Australians could in the past, but they're now closed to new investors). However, Canadians and Australians can buy all-in-one ETFs from one of their home country brokerages.

I believe investors behave much better in all-in-one portfolios of index mutual funds compared to investors in all-in-one ETFs. After all, with all-in-one index mutual funds, investors can set up automatic monthly deposits. This makes the process hands-free. Investors might even forget they're investing. This "minds-off-money" approach could boost our social ability (remember those social skills and money studies) and enhance our returns.

Nobody who invests in ETFs (even all-in-one ETFs) can forget they're investing. That's because they must log in to a brokerage account and manually make every single purchase. This adds a risk of speculative temptation—especially if they buy individual ETFs instead of all-in-one products. Investors in all-in-one portfolio ETFs don't have to choose which ETFs to buy in any given month. They don't have to worry about whether they should add money to their bond ETF, domestic stock ETF, or international stock ETF. Nor do they have to worry about rebalancing (it happens automatically). However, the act of logging in and making manual purchases could still tempt investors to try timing their deposits. If they try to "time the market," they might get lucky once or twice. But it would be much like visiting a casino. In the end, the house always wins.

Tables 8.3 to 8.7 list products for investors of different nationalities.

TABLE 8.3

For Americans: Vanguard Target Retirement Funds (All-in-One Index Mutual Funds)

Fund	Symbol	Approximate % in Stocks	Approximate % in Bonds	Annual Expense Ratio
Vanguard Target Retirement 2025	VTTVX	60%	40%	0.13%
Vanguard Target Retirement 2030	VTHRX	65%	35%	0.14%
Vanguard Target Retirement 2035	VTTHX	75%	25%	0.14%
Vanguard Target Retirement 2040	VFORX	80%	20%	0.14%
Vanguard Target Retirement 2045	VTIVX	90%	10%	0.15%
Vanguard Target Retirement 2050	VFIFX	90%	10%	0.15%
Vanguard Target Retirement 2055	VFFVX	90%	10%	0.15%

Source: Vanguard[15]

American investors can purchase any of these funds from Vanguard. Each of the target retirement funds in Table 8.3 increases its bond allocation over time. That makes each fund more stable as the investor grows older. Investors can buy similar all-in-one portfolios of index funds through Schwab and Fidelity. Choose a fund based on your risk tolerance.

Don't look at similar funds and make your selection based on past performance. For example, Vanguard's Target Retirement 2050 Fund has a similar portfolio construction to Schwab's Target 2050 Index (SWYMX) and Fidelity's Freedom Index 2050 (FIPFX). Over the three-year period ending November 10, 2020, Vanguard's Target

Retirement 2050 Fund averaged 8.70 percent per year, Fidelity's Freedom Index 2050 averaged 8.49 percent per year, and Schwab's Target 2050 Index averaged 9.35 percent per year. This doesn't mean Fidelity's is the worst of the three and Schwab's is the best. They are allocated similarly—but not identically. Over the next three-year period, Fidelity's target fund might edge out all three. That's why, if investors want a target retirement fund, they should just pick one, ignore past performance, and continue to add money for as long as they can.

TABLE 8.4

For Canadians: iShares All-in-One ETFs

Fund	Symbol	Approximate % in Stocks	Approximate % in Bonds	Annual Expense Ratio
iShares Core Conservative Balanced ETF Portfolio	XCNS	45%	55%	0.20%
iShares Core Balanced ETF Portfolio	XBAL	60%	40%	0.20%
iShares Core Growth ETF Portfolio	XGRO	80%	20%	0.20%
iShares Core Equity ETF Portfolio	XEQT	100%	0%	0.20%

Source: iShares/BlackRock Canada[16]

Canadians can buy the ETFs in Table 8.4 from any of Canada's brokerages. Each represents a complete portfolio rolled into one. They all include balanced exposure to Canadian stocks, US stocks, developed international stocks, and emerging market stocks. With the exception of the iShares Core Equity ETF, they also include bonds. iShares rebalances the portfolios to maintain the above allocations.

Several Canadian ETF providers, including Vanguard, BMO, and Horizons, offer similar all-in-one portfolio products. They are just as good as each other: no better, no worse. Don't make the natural and common mistake of comparing their past performances and making a decision based on what you find. Although they're similarly allocated, their indexed compositions aren't exactly the same. As a result, the iShares Core Balanced ETF (XBAL) might edge out Vanguard's Balanced ETF Portfolio (VBAL) over one period. But over the next period, the results could be reversed. Either way, the long-term differences would be far too small to sweat.

That's why you should pick a fund based on your risk tolerance. If you have a job, just keep adding money for as long as you can. You could choose the same fund for your tax-advantaged accounts (your RRSP and TFSA) as you do for your taxable account, if you have one. Just keep things simple. And respect the behavioral advantage that these funds offer.

Australians can buy any of the all-in-one portfolio ETFs in Table 8.5 from a brokerage account. Each fund includes exposure to Australian shares, US shares, developed international shares, and emerging market shares, as well as bonds. Each fund is regularly rebalanced to make sure it maintains the fund's target allocation between stocks and bonds.

British investors can buy funds in Table 8.6 directly from Vanguard UK. There's no fee to buy or sell them. Investors can also set up automatic deposits from their regular bank accounts into their LifeStrategy fund of choice, or into one of Vanguard UK's target retirement funds (which are similar to their US counterparts). Each fund includes exposure to British shares, US shares, developed international shares, and emerging market shares, as well as British bonds. Each fund is regularly rebalanced to make sure it maintains the fund's target allocation between stocks and bonds.

Europeans could choose a Vanguard all-in-one portfolio ETF trading on either the Italian or the German stock exchange. Each ETF, which is priced in euros, represents a globally diversified portfolio with bond allocations hedged to the euro to reduce currency risk (see Table 8.7).

TABLE 8.5

For Australians: Vanguard All-in-One ETFs

Fund	Symbol	% in Stocks	% in Bonds	Annual Expense Ratio
Vanguard Diversified Conservative Index	VDCO	30%	70%	0.27%
Vanguard Diversified Balanced Index	VDBA	50%	50%	0.27%
Vanguard Diversified Growth Index	VDGR	70%	30%	0.27%
Vanguard Diversified High Growth Index	VDHG	90%	10%	0.27%

Source: Vanguard Australia[17]

TABLE 8.6

For the British: Vanguard UK LifeStrategy Funds

Fund	Symbol	% in Stocks	% in Bonds	Annual Expense Ratio
Vanguard LifeStrategy 20% Equity	GB00B4NXY349	20%	80%	0.27%
Vanguard LifeStrategy 40% Equity	GB00B3ZHN960	40%	60%	0.27%
Vanguard LifeStrategy 60% Equity	GB00B3TYHH97	60%	40%	0.27%
Vanguard LifeStrategy 80% Equity	GB00B4PQW151	80%	20%	0.27%
Vanguard LifeStrategy 100% Equity	GB00B41XG308	100%	0%	0.27%

Source: Vanguard UK[18]

TABLE 8.7

For Europeans: Vanguard All-in One Portfolio ETFs

Fund	Symbol on Xetra*	% in Stocks**	% in Bonds	Annual Expense Ratio
Vanguard LifeStrategy 20% Equity UCITS	V20A	20%	80%	0.25%
Vanguard LifeStrategy 40% Equity UCITS	V40A	40%	60%	0.25%
Vanguard LifeStrategy 60% Equity UCITS	V60A	60%	40%	0.25%
Vanguard LifeStrategy 80% Equity UCITS	V80A	80%	20%	0.25%

Source: global.vanguard.com
*Xetra represents a Frankfurt stock exchange and is the commonly used exchange for this ETF.
**The stock market portion of these funds is roughly 60% US stocks and 40% international stocks.

Getting a Helping Hand

If you don't know how to open a brokerage account and make your first purchase, a few firms can help. Investors of any nationality could use the US-based firm PlanVision, for example. Unlike a robo-advisor or full-service advisory company, PlanVision doesn't invest your money. Instead, for about $200, they use a screen-share concept to guide people through the DIY process. The price includes help for one year, including financial planning for Americans and basic financial planning for other nationalities.

Canadian firms like You&Yours Financial are specialists in Canadian financial planning needs. They offer financial tutoring sessions, helping clients understand how much they're currently paying in fees, assisting them with a wealth management plan and suitable asset allocation strategies, and (when requested) showing investors how to open a brokerage account and purchase ETFs.[19] Plenty of people seeking a DIY approach might balk at paying a one-time fee for such a service. But most people's financial needs are more comprehensive than they think. In a conversation I had with founder Darryl Brown, he told me, "The pay-for-service element of financial planning is especially popular among higher income earners who seek a big financial picture and don't want to make mistakes."

Why Knowing Thyself Is So Darn Hard

Plenty of people overestimate their tolerance for volatility. They might choose a high stock market allocation because they know it leads to higher long-term returns compared to portfolios with lower stock allocations. I'm not talking about ten-year returns. That's short-term. Over thirty-year durations, portfolios with higher stock allocations have historically won.

But that doesn't mean *you* will do better with a higher stock allocation. Your personality and behavior matter. You might believe you can emotionally handle high volatility, but knowing how you'll respond in a crisis is so darn hard. You might sell when things get hairy. You might keep money on the sidelines instead of investing as soon as you have it, waiting for a time that you think might be better.

If you have a pulse, these are real risks.

You might be thinking, "I can emotionally handle 90 percent or 100 percent stocks." And you might be right. But most people can't. That's why, before you choose your allocation of stocks and bonds, I suggest you read the ghost story in the next chapter.

A Few Tips for Living Well

- Choose your investment service based on your personality. Full-service advisors can temper emotions. But only use financial advisors who exclusively use index funds (or ETFs).

- If you would prefer some service but want to pay less, consider a robo-advisor.

- The less time you spend thinking about your investments, the more money you'll likely make—and the happier you'll be.

- If you plan to be a DIY investor, all-in-one portfolios of index funds or all-in-one portfolios of ETFs make the process easier and help to collar your inner speculator. PlanVision can show you how to purchase such products for about $200 a year.

9

HOW WELL DO
YOU KNOW YOURSELF?

The Challenge of Picking a Portfolio
Allocation That Will Keep You on Track

I F YOU MET me on the street and asked, "Do you believe in ghosts?"
I would likely reply, "No." But under certain circumstances, my
behavior might betray me. Several years ago, I took twenty high
school students to a remote Indonesian island. We stayed in a village
with dirt walking paths. There wasn't a single paved road. The families who hosted us lived on bamboo platforms perched over the sea.
They didn't have electricity or running water. Their outhouses were
holes in the wooden decking over the sea. They lived much as their
ancestors had.

We hired an American tour group who had built an educational retreat on a nearby island. Their leader's name was Mike.
We boarded several of their tiny motorboats and followed a river
upstream, deep into the jungle. When the tide receded, the river
became too shallow for the boats, so Mike led us on foot up a jungle
trail. We then walked up a dry riverbed, scrambling over boulders.
The students loved it, but it was hot and exhausting. When Mike
eventually found our camping spot, we hung our hammocks, cooked
and ate dinner, then headed off to sleep.

I woke up in the middle of the night to find a short woman in rags standing next to my hammock. Her long black hair obscured most of her face. "I told you not to come," she said.

"I'm really sorry," I replied. "Nobody told us not to come."

"You have no respect," she said. "So I'm going to kill everyone. You will have to watch."

I begged this woman to spare us, swearing to leave in the morning and never come back. Then I woke up. We were on the equator. But I was shivering from the cold. It was the most terrifying dream I have ever had.

Shifting in my hammock, I looked slowly to my left. And there she was again! "We will never return here," I whimpered. "Please don't hurt anyone." She replied, "If you promise never to come back, I will let you live."

Then I woke up for real, freezing cold and covered with sweat.

The next day, I hiked beside Mike down that empty riverbed while describing my terrifying double dream. And for an eerie length of time, this normally chatty guy didn't say a word. Then, with a touch of fear in his voice, he said, "We had a hard time getting a permit to camp at that spot. The nearby villagers said it was haunted. During World War II, Japanese troops slaughtered an entire village where we camped." Mike still lives a short boat ride away. But to my knowledge, he hasn't gone back to that site.

If you asked, "Do you believe in ghosts?" I would likely say "no." But if you had the power to transport me, *Star Trek*-style, to that spot at night, I think my bowels would release and I would crash through that jungle like a man who had lost his mind. Yet, I say I don't believe in ghosts? My behavior might be a more accurate barometer of my beliefs than my word.

Investors suffer from similar dissonance. They might say, "Yes, I can handle a portfolio with 90 percent stocks and just 10 percent bonds." But when they face a prolonged period of horrible market returns, many of these self-proclaimed stoics will soil their own shorts. This reminds me of something former heavyweight boxing champion Mike Tyson once said: "Everybody has a plan until they get punched in the mouth."

There are so many things we don't really know about ourselves. That's why we should temper our perceived tolerance for investment risk. When choosing an allocation between stocks and bonds, some people might look at a table such as the one to follow and select a mix that they believe suits their tolerance for risk. But most people don't know what they don't know. They might select a high allocation of stocks, believing they can stay the course, but then a prolonged down market (and the economic news, which can freak people out) might chip away at the person's courage. Wise investors respect what they don't know about themselves.

TABLE 9.1

Historical Investment Returns (1926–2020)

	100% Stocks	80% Stocks / 20% Bonds	70% Stocks / 30% Bonds	60% Stocks / 40% Bonds	50% Stocks / 50% Bonds
Average Annual Return	10.1%	9.4%	9.1%	8.6%	8.2%
Calendar Years with a Loss	26/93	24/93	23/93	22/93	18/93
Calendar Years with a Gain	67/93	69/93	70/93	71/93	75/93
Worst Year	-43.1% (1931)	-34.9% (1931)	-30.7% (1931)	-26.6% (1931)	-22.5% (1931)
Best Year	+54.2% (1933)	+45.4% (1933)	+41.1% (1933)	+36.7% (1933)	+32.3% (1933)

Source: vanguard.com (using US stocks and US intermediate government bonds)[1]

Which Target Allocation Should You Choose?

If, after looking at the historical returns in Table 9.1, you believe you could handle a portfolio of 100 percent stocks, consider a portfolio with 80 percent stocks and 20 percent bonds instead. This portfolio won't fall as far when the markets crash. And that subtle bond cushion might prevent you from freaking out when stocks crash or languish for years.

If, however, your gut says you could handle 80 percent stocks and 20 percent bonds, consider 70 percent stocks and 30 percent bonds.

After all, we don't know what we don't know. I won't even ask if you believe in ghosts.

Can We Retrain Our Lizard Brains?

Nathalie Legrée is a great saver. Motivated by the FIRE (Financial Independence, Retire Early) movement, she wants to become financially free at an early age.[2] The thirty-four-year-old is one of a growing number of millennials who live frugally and sock away large percentages of their incomes every year. When I first connected with Nathalie she had $50,000 in a portfolio of ETFs and was adding $2,000 a month.

Eighteen months after she began her investment journey, stocks fell about 10 percent. "The market's drop has me wondering if I've made the right decision," she told me.

Ironically, it would be better if Nathalie never knew whether stocks had risen or fallen during any given day, week, or decade. That might prevent her from freaking out and selling low. It might also help her maintain her life satisfaction. After all, happiness is largely based on our expectations. If Nathalie expects her portfolio to rise and instead it drops, the change could affect her daily moods (and her investment performance, if she chooses to react).

Unfortunately, the financial media is an investor's Anti-Christ. Its headlines are designed to scare and provoke because they send this backward message to people like Nathalie:

Rising stocks = Good

Falling stocks = Bad

Instead, anyone who plans to add money to the markets for at least the next five years should prefer falling prices. I still do. And young people, like Nathalie, should hold a massive block party when stocks fall hard.

William Bernstein, the former neurologist turned financial advisor, says young investors should "pray for a long, awful [down]market." In his booklet *If You Can*, he says that when stocks drop, investors pay less money for a greater number of shares.[3] When people invest consistent sums every month (dollar cost averaging) they can stockpile assets when they're cheap. When the markets recover, those asset values soar.

Warren Buffett says much the same thing in his 1997 chairman's letter to Berkshire Hathaway shareholders:

> If you will be a net saver over the next five years, should you hope for a higher or lower stock market during that time period? Many investors get this one wrong. Even though they are going to be net buyers of stocks for many years to come, they are elated when stock prices rise and depressed when they fall... This reaction makes no sense. Only those who will be sellers of equities [stock market investments] in the near future should be happy at seeing stocks rise. Prospective purchasers should much prefer sinking prices.[4]

I explained this to Nathalie, but she wasn't convinced. So I asked, "If you could manipulate the future, which of these two scenarios would you pick?" In Scenario 1, the stock market soars for three straight years. Over twenty years, it gains a compound annual return of 9.75 percent. In Scenario 2, the stock market slumps for three straight years. Over twenty years, it gains a compound annual return of 5.94 percent (see Table 9.2).

TABLE 9.2

A Tale of Two Scenarios

Scenario 1		Scenario 2	
Year	Stock Market Return	Year	Stock Market Return
1	+37.58%	1	-9.1%
2	+22.96%	2	-11.89%
3	+33.36%	3	-22.10%
20-Year Average	+9.75%*	20-Year Average	+5.94%*

*The average compound annual return for each respective time period

Nathalie said, "I would absolutely prefer Scenario 1. Seeing your stocks rise on a yearly basis is always more reassuring. Those look like strong numbers that promote trust in the market."

But for Nathalie, Scenario 2 would be better. Yes, it starts with three bad years and records a lower average twenty-year return. But if a young investor added the same amount of money every month, that money would have purchased more units when the market dropped. That would juice her returns when stocks recover. It's especially mind-bending to hear that Nathalie could make more money during a twenty-year period when stocks averaged 5.94 percent per year than during a twenty-year period when stocks average 9.75 percent per year.

This wouldn't always be the case. But it can happen if the first three years see a horrific market drop. I didn't make this up. Here are real-world examples with Scenario 1 and Scenario 2, using different historical twenty-year returns for the S&P 500 (see Table 9.3).

Scenario 1 shows the S&P 500 Index's actual twenty-year returns from January 1, 1995, to December 31, 2014. Stocks soared in 1995, 1996, and 1997, gaining 37.58 percent, 22.96 percent, and 33.36 percent, respectively. A lump sum investment in the S&P 500 would have earned a compound annual return of 9.75 percent over these twenty years. This was the scenario Nathalie says she would prefer.

Scenario 2 represents the actual twenty-year returns of the S&P 500 from January 1, 2000, to December 31, 2019. Stocks dropped right out of the gate, losing 9.1 percent in 2000, 11.89 percent in 2001, and 22.10 percent in 2002. A lump sum investment in the S&P 500 would have earned a compound annual return of 5.94 percent over this twenty-year period. This was the scenario Nathalie didn't like.

TABLE 9.3

Actual Returns of the S&P 500

Scenario 1		Scenario 2	
Year	S&P 500 Stock Market Return	Year	S&P 500 Stock Market Return
1995	+37.58%	2000	-9.1%
1996	+22.96%	2001	-11.89%
1997	+33.36%	2002	-22.10%
1995–2014	+9.75%*	2000–2019	+5.94%*

*The average compound annual return for each respective time period

At first glance, Nathalie's choice of Scenario 1 looks better. But that ignores what William Bernstein and Warren Buffett are trying to teach investors.

Let's start with Scenario 1.

Assume Nathalie had $50,000 in a portfolio of low-cost index funds in January 1995. If she had invested an additional $2,000 a month into the S&P 500 from January 1, 1995, until December 31, 2014, her money would have grown to $1,443,726 over these twenty years.

Now consider Scenario 2.

Assume Nathalie had $50,000 in a portfolio of low-cost index funds in January 1, 2000. If she had added $2,000 per month into the S&P 500 from January 1, 2000, until December 31, 2019, her money would have grown to $1,544,560. That's $100,834 more than she would have earned in Scenario 1 (see Table 9.4).

In other words, experiencing three huge calendar year losses early in her investment journey would have looked scary. But it would ultimately have boosted her returns. By adding the same amount of money every month, her consistent monthly purchases would have bought a greater number of stock market units when prices were low and fewer stock market units when prices went up. As a result, she would have paid a lower-than-average price over time. That's how she would have earned a compound annual return of 8.93 percent, despite the fact that the market averaged a compound annual return of just 5.94 percent over that same period.

Unfortunately, plenty of investors lose faith when they see markets drop. They don't keep adding money through good and bad markets. But young investors, like Nathalie, should try to conquer their emotions and hope for falling markets.

It would be even better, of course, if they never saw their portfolio balances or heard investment news. Remember that Fidelity study? The best investors forgot they had accounts—or were dead. Human actions and reactions kick future progress in the groin.

Market Timing Is Market Timing

Whether stocks are flying or declining, pundits always say, "This time it's different." And they're right. Every time is different. But time after time, one truth holds: Nobody can consistently predict how stocks will perform. Most of the time, professionals—including hedge fund managers, college endowment fund managers, and tactical asset allocation managers—who make predictions fall flat on their faces.

Statistically, the best odds of success come from investing as soon as you have the money. Don't wait for a decline, or for the results of an election, or for a pandemic to end, or for extraterrestrials to leave Moscow after an invasion.

TABLE 9.4

Scenarios 1 and 2

(With a $50,000 starting value, and investing $2,000 per month in Vanguard's S&P 500 Index)

SCENARIO 1			SCENARIO 2		
Year	Portfolio Return	Portfolio Balance	Year	Portfolio Return	Portfolio Balance
1995	37.45%	$96,263	2000	-9.06%	$67,658
1996	22.88%	$144,988	2001	-12.02%	$83,278
1997	33.19%	$220,107	2002	-22.15%	$86,616
1998	28.62%	$310,550	2003	28.50%	$139,308
1999	21.07%	$402,701	2004	10.74%	$180,136
2000	-9.06%	$388,717	2005	4.77%	$213,757
2001	-12.02%	$365,472	2006	15.64%	$273,268
2002	-22.15%	$306,318	2007	5.39%	$312,058
2003	28.50%	$421,629	2008	-37.02%	$215,040
2004	10.74%	$492,779	2009	26.49%	$300,991
2005	4.77%	$541,328	2010	14.91%	$372,899
2006	15.64%	$652,076	2011	-9.06%	$404,079
2007	5.39%	$711,270	2012	15.82%	$492,988
2008	-37.02%	$466,462	2013	32.18%	$678,819
2009	26.49%	$619,003	2014	13.51%	$776,209
2010	14.91%	$738,339	2015	1.25%	$830,299
2011	1.97%	$776,703	2016	11.82%	$954,232
2012	15.82%	$924,579	2017	21.67%	$1,187,309
2013	32.18%	$1,249,277	2018	-4.52%	$1,115,791
2014	13.51%	$1,443,726	2019	31.33%	$1,544,560
Compound Annual Rate of Return for the S&P 500 (What a lump sum would have averaged)	9.75%		Compound Annual Rate of Return for the S&P 500 (What a lump sum would have averaged)	5.94%	
Compound Annual Rate of Return (Consistent dollar cost averaging each month)	8.41%		Compound Annual Rate of Return (Consistent dollar cost averaging each month)	8.93%	

Source: portfoliovisualizer.com

Yes, this is easier said than done. I've been writing personal finance articles for more than twenty years. I've given seminars around the world, and I've tried to help people who ask investment-related questions online. But even many self-declared stay-the-course devotees try to time the market when inner greed or fear pull them by their private parts.

Often, I'll get messages that say, "Andrew, I have a lump sum to invest. I know I should invest it right away, but there's something happening right now that's never occurred before. I'm going to wait until. . ."

That's trying to time the market.

If you're afraid that stocks are at an all-time high and you decide to wait for a pullback before you invest, well. . .

That's trying to time the market.

If markets have dropped hard, but instead of investing you're waiting for a bigger drop. . .

That's trying to time the market.

If you've retired on the eve of a market crash and you've decided to put everything (or even some of your money) into cash. . .

That's trying to time the market.

Instead, we have to collar our inner fears. We have to expunge deluded thoughts that we (or someone on TV) can predict the future. Market timing doesn't work. If you try to time the market and you guess correctly, that's like winning during a romp in a casino. You'll almost certainly try it again, but over time, the house won't only win, it will kick your butt. Hard.

If you're questioning the wisdom of this, please re-read chapter 7. Hedge fund managers and tactical asset allocation fund managers try, and almost always fail, to time the market. They're also professionals. And that's why you shouldn't even try to time it. After all, according to the former hedge fund manager Chelsea Brennan, many hedge fund managers don't put their money in the hedge funds they manage. They dispassionately add to their portfolios of index funds instead of messing around with their personal bars of soap.[5]

Retirees, Don't Shoot Yourself in the Foot

Young people should prefer to see stocks crash. After all, they're collecting market assets. But retirees are selling. That's why older people fear market crashes more than their youthful counterparts do. However, the biggest threat to their retirement isn't the market itself. Instead, it's the person they face in the mirror each day.

Here's an example: Fidelity Investments reported that almost one third of the firm's investors over the age of sixty-five shifted some of their stock market investments out of stocks and into non-stock market–related investments between February 20 and May 15, 2020. In other words, they panicked or speculated during COVID-19's stock market plunge and sold when stocks were low. Unfortunately for them, over the ten months after April 1, 2020, US stocks gained 49.44 percent and global stocks gained 52.27 percent.

Unlike the kneejerk reactions of those who sold stocks during the market plunge, fund managers of all-in-one portfolios of index funds or ETFs (see chapter 8) actually added to their stock positions when the markets were low. They didn't do so to speculate. They were simply maintaining a consistent allocation of stocks and bonds. As a result, when US and global stocks soared over the ten months after April 1, 2020, the investors reaped handsome rewards.[6]

Instead of worrying about the markets, retirees should focus on just one thing: their inflation-adjusted 4 percent withdrawals. Everything else is simply a distraction.

For example, assume you retired with $100,000 in a diversified portfolio with 60 percent in stock indexes and 40 percent in bond indexes. Back-tested studies suggest that retirees with such a portfolio should be able to withdraw an inflation-adjusted 4 percent per year. That means a retiree with $100,000 can withdraw $4,000 in the first year of retirement. That's 4 percent of $100,000. And each year after that (no matter what happens to the stock market) they should be able to give themselves a raise to match inflation. If the cost of living increased by 2 percent in the second year of their retirement, they would withdraw 2 percent more than $4,000 that year. In this case, that would be $4,080 (2 percent more than $4,000 is $4,080).

Each year, they would withdraw an ever-increasing amount to cover the rising cost of living (unless a period of deflation resulted in withdrawing less).

The 4 percent rule was back-tested to 1926. That means a portfolio of 60 percent stocks and 40 percent bonds would have lasted at least thirty years if someone had withdrawn an inflation-adjusted 4 percent. In other words, even if someone retired in 1929 (on the eve of the Great Depression), they could have withdrawn an inflation-adjusted 4 percent per year and their money would have lasted at least three more decades.

This practice, however, requires Buddha-like Zen. That's why the retiree's biggest risk isn't the market itself. Instead, it's their behavior. And if stocks crash on the eve of an investor's retirement, their behavior will be tested. Consider someone who retired in January 2000. That would have been one of history's worst years to retire. They would have faced three terrifying crashes in just the first two decades of their retirement: From January 1, 2000, to September 30, 2002, global stocks plunged 46 percent. From January 1, 2008, to February 28, 2009, global stocks cratered almost 52 percent. And from February 1, 2020, to March 31, 2020, global stocks dropped about 21 percent.

The year 2000 was also the beginning of the so-called lost decade for US stocks (the largest component of a global stock index). Let me explain what that means: If someone invested $10,000 in Vanguard's S&P 500 Index on January 1, 2000, and didn't withdraw a penny, their investment would have been worth just $9,016 ten years later, with all dividends reinvested. If the same $10,000 were invested in a global stock index over the same time duration, it would have been worth just $10,639. Without a doubt, retiring in 2000 would have tested the strength of any retiree's ticker.

Assume the retiree had the nerve to stay the course. They retired with $100,000 in January 2000: 60 percent in a global stock index and 40 percent in a global bond index. Assume they withdrew an inflation-adjusted 4 percent per year. Twenty-one years after retiring at one of history's worst possible times, they would have withdrawn a total of $112,764 from their initial $100,000 portfolio—and they would still have money left.

According to Portfolio Visualizer, despite these withdrawals, the investor would have $117,375 remaining by January 1, 2021. You might wonder, though, if this $117,375 could last another nine years, bringing the retirement duration to a total of thirty years. After all, the investor would need to withdraw more than $6,185 at the beginning of 2022. I base this assessment on the 4 percent inflation-adjusted withdrawals, which you can see in Table 9.5.

We don't know if the remaining money would last another nine years. But Vanguard's Nest Egg [Monte Carlo] calculator determines the odds are high.[7] A Monte Carlo simulation assumes anything that happened in the past could happen again—in any order! For example, stocks could fall 86 percent, as they did from 1929 to 1932. That market drop wasn't coupled with inflation. But what if the high inflation levels of the late seventies and early eighties happened at the same time as the 1929–1932 stock market crash?

The Monte Carlo simulator tosses 100,000 such historical variables into the mix.

Based on Vanguard's calculations, the $117,375 that remained after twenty-one years would have a 100 percent chance of lasting another nine years, a 98 percent chance of lasting another fifteen years, and a 93 percent chance of lasting another twenty years.

Sadly, plenty of retirees will sabotage their rides. It's easy to say, "The 4 percent rule works." But retirees would need to do two tough things to benefit from that rule:

· Ignore the stock market.
· Ignore their portfolio's value.

TABLE 9.5

4% Inflation-Adjusted Annual Withdrawals

Year ·	Amount Withdrawn at the Beginning of Each Year	Portfolio Value at the End of Each Year (after withdrawals)
	Starting Value	$ 100,000
2000	$4,000	$91,839
2001	$4,135	$83,298
2002	$4,200	$72,939
2003	$4,299	$85,198
2004	$4,380	$91,067
2005	$4,523	$93,832
2006	$4,677	$101,691
2007	$4,796	$104,834
2008	$4,992	$73,555
2009	$4,997	$87,184
2010	$5,132	$92,484
2011	$5,209	$86,957
2012	$5,364	$93,741
2013	$5,457	$102,022
2014	$5,539	$103,418
2015	$5,581	$96,674
2016	$5,622	$98,534
2017	$5,738	$108,511
2018	$5,859	$96,225
2019	$5,971	$108,020
2020	$6,108	$115,689
2021	$6,185	$117,375

Total withdrawn over 21 years: $112,764.

Source: portfoliovisualizer.com (60% global stock index, 40% global bond index)

If you're a retiree, you shouldn't watch the stock market or the level of your portfolio. You have better things to do. Just continue to withdraw more money every year (based on the initial 4 percent rule). If that makes you squeamish, and you have to "do something," commit to not giving yourself an inflation-adjusted raise in any years when stocks fall. This would further the odds that your retirement money will last at least thirty years.

Most importantly, however, never speculate. Ever. Market volatility frightens men and women. But men pose the biggest risk. That's why, if there's a man in your life, you might want to lock him in the basement the next time stocks crash. Give him food, water (maybe beer), and handy access to a toilet. When it comes to smart investing (in other words, not doing anything dumb), men are the weaker sex.

Do Men Have Bigger Lizard Brains?

When I ask married couples, "Who is in charge of your investments?" most say it's the man. But couples should work together. After all, women appear better at steering investment boats. I would be fascinated to see research on same-sex female couples. I suspect their investment performances might beat most same-sex male couples' performances. Guys, I know I'm being tough on us. But the research is solid. On average, women are better investors than men.

I first suspected this after giving several financial seminars about investing in low-cost index funds or ETFs. I often returned to speak to the same people years later. When I asked specific couples, "How are things going?" some said they had managed to stay on track. But plenty didn't. Those who deviated from the plan often started chasing hot stocks, jumping into cryptocurrencies, or trying to time the market. More often than not, the results were disastrous. When I asked heterosexual couples, "Whose idea was it to stray from the plan?" I learned that most of the time it was the man's.

Couples should work as a team when making investment decisions. But based on my observations, usually the men take charge. That's a shame, because women are better investors.

A University of California, Berkeley, study researched brokerage account performances for men and women. They found that single women beat single men. And married men beat single men.[8] That's why married men should work with the woman in their home if they want strong results.

"I believe that testosterone affects men's decisions," I say, when giving investment talks. "Men's overconfidence pushes them to gamble and break smart investment rules." At this point, some of the women jab their husbands. Most of the men just smile and nod good-naturedly.

In a Vanguard study conducted between 2005 and 2010, female investors beat their male counterparts by about 5 percent. Women hold higher bond allocations, so that might be expected. After all, bonds beat stocks from 2005 to 2010.

But women beat men when stocks soar too. Brad Barber and Terrance Odean, both finance researchers, studied 35,000 household brokerage accounts between 1991 and 1997.[9] Despite the soaring market—where higher risks can mean higher rewards—women beat men by nearly 3 percent per year on a risk-adjusted basis. This means that when women and men took the same amount of risk (in other words, when they had the same allocations of stocks and bonds), the women beat the men by 3 percent per year.

Fidelity tracked performance for 8 million of its clients in 2016 and found that women beat men by 0.4 percent.[10] If Fidelity had conducted an equal-risk-adjusted comparison, the women would have won by more. Wells Fargo also found that women beat men when it compared investment performances between 2010 and 2015. When it compared portfolios of equal risk, women pulled even further ahead.[11]

A thirty-six-month-long UK-based study by Warwick Business School came to the same conclusion after examining 2,800 investment accounts. Women beat men by almost 1.8 percent per year.[12]

Another Wells Fargo study says men fall behind because they trade more often and are more likely to break investment rules. The study found men were six times as likely to jump from 100 percent stocks to 100 percent bonds. In other words, they try to time the market more.[13]

The fact that men have more testosterone than women might lead to overconfidence and their own poor returns. The finance researchers Yan Lu and Melvyn Teo published fascinating findings via the University of Central Florida and Singapore Management University. They looked at 3,228 male hedge fund managers between January 1994 and December 2015.[14]

But saying that they "looked at them" is a serious understatement. The researchers literally measured the widths of their faces. Men with wider faces tend to have higher testosterone levels. The researchers found that the hedge fund managers with narrower faces beat their higher-testosterone, wider-faced counterparts by 5.8 percent per year on a risk-adjusted basis.

Lu and Teo wrote, "In the context of the ultra-competitive and male-dominated hedge fund industry, where masculine traits such as aggression, competitiveness, and drive are encouraged, expected, and even celebrated, our results on the underperformance of high-testosterone fund managers are indeed surprising. Investors will do well to go against conventional wisdom and eschew masculine fund managers."

This brings me back to married heterosexual couples. Most often, men take the investment reins, leaving the women on the sidelines. But couples should establish a solid plan, stick to it, and not let fear, greed, or machismo send them off track.

Plenty of us believe we know how we would respond to tragedies: getting cancer, losing a loved one, etc. But the truth is, we don't know until it happens. That's why, when determining your asset allocation, it's better to err on the side of caution than excessive courage.

A Few Tips for Living Well

- Consider an asset allocation that you believe you could tolerate if stocks collapsed. Then settle on something slightly more cautious and stick to it. This could help you stay the course when the smelly stuff hits the fan.

- Young investors should rewire their thinking about the markets. Falling markets are good. Economic uncertainty (for their investments) beats a cheery economic consensus.

- Nobody can predict how stock markets will perform. When it comes to investing, consistency is best. If you can, add money every month. Maintain your allocation. Do not speculate.

- Always remember that market timing does not work. Anyone who guesses correctly once will run the risk of going back into the casino. In the end, the house always wins.

- Retirees should ignore their portfolio's value and all forecasts. Instead, they should stick to an inflation-adjusted 4 percent withdrawal plan. Even if they retire on the eve of a market crash, their money should still last at least thirty years (especially if they don't give themselves an inflation-adjusted "raise" during years when stocks decline).

- Whenever possible, couples should ensure that women do their share (or more) of the investment lifting. In the long run, most men will be happy that they did.

10

HAPPY PLANET, HAPPY PEOPLE

Socially Responsible Investing and Spending Can Help Save the Planet

MERCEDES MARTIN INHALED more than her share of crappy air when she lived in Beijing, China. Factories pumped out visible toxic fog, which created safety hazards, especially for people who exercised outdoors. Actually, even the indoor air quality is poor. When I last visited Beijing, several of my friends had air purifiers in their homes.

Mercedes often drove into the country for work projects. "I had to travel to remote locations to negotiate land deals to develop wind farms," she says. "It was almost impossible to get away from the smog, even when we were driving hundreds of miles from the city." She saw firsthand the importance of wind-driven sustainable energy projects. "Working in the renewables industry with people so passionate about the environment inspired me to contribute to change the world in this direction."

These days the forty-two-year-old mother of three works in Singapore as a sustainability communications specialist. When she and her husband decided to invest some money, they chose socially responsible ETFs. "I just could not invest in an ETF that contained companies that were involved in businesses such as fossil fuels or tobacco. Those are companies I don't respect."

Socially responsible investment (SRI) funds include higher exposure to companies with smaller carbon footprints. Typically, they also shun businesses that manufacture weapons, cigarettes, or alcohol. They don't include stocks connected to pornography or gambling either.

I'm excited by the growing demand for these funds. Others are too. Samuel M. Hartzmark and Abigail B. Sussman are associate professors at the University of Chicago Booth School of Business. In 2019, they published a report suggesting that SRI funds are becoming magnets for investors.[1]

In 2016, Morningstar ranked more than twenty thousand funds, based on their holdings. They gave mutual funds with low global sustainability a one "globe" score. Funds that included stocks that Morningstar figured were better for the environment were given up to five globe scores.

Hartzmark and Sussman drew on Morningstar's ranking system to see where Americans were investing their money. They found that Americans had added more money to funds with higher globe rankings than to funds with lower globe rankings. Before the introduction of Morningstar's sustainability rating system, all the funds were similarly popular, as measured by relative inflows. But eleven months after the globe scores were assigned, Morningstar learned that investors had added more money to the funds with the highest sustainability scores and withdrew money from funds with low sustainability scores. This is great news for two reasons. It shows people care. And as a result, index fund providers have introduced several SRI funds to meet this demand.

Critics of SRI funds, however, say such funds (whether they're indexed or not) don't perform as well as regular stock market indexes. They also argue that they don't really help the environment.

How Do Socially Responsible Funds Perform?

Most SRI indexed mutual funds and ETFs charge slightly higher fees than their traditional indexed counterparts. But their returns don't suffer. Some studies say they beat traditional indexes. Other studies show they slightly lag. Much depends on the time periods measured. Michael Schröder of the Leibniz Centre for European Economic Research compared indexes for twenty-nine different stock markets. He found that SRI index funds were able to keep pace with non-SRI index funds. He says, "SRI stock indices do not exhibit a different level of risk-adjusted return than conventional benchmarks."[2]

Schröder published his research in 2007. That year, iShares Canada launched its first socially responsible ETF: the Jantzi Social Index ETF (XEN) of Canadian stocks. It charges more than most ETFs, 0.55 percent per year. But that hasn't hurt investors. Some years, it beats a traditional Canadian stock market index. Other years, of course, it doesn't. But its performance reflects Schröder's findings. From its 2007 inception, it has battled toe-to-toe with the broader stock market index.

In the United States, Vanguard's oldest SRI index of US stocks has also performed similarly to the S&P 500 Index since its inception in 2000. And over the ten-year period ending November 30, 2020 (the date Vanguard gave me this information), it beat the S&P 500, averaging 15.35 percent per year compared to 14.05 percent for the broader index. That doesn't mean it will continue to win. But over long time periods it should put up a respectable fight.

Do Socially Responsible Funds Really Help the Environment?

Investment companies market the heck out of SRI funds, as if buying them were equal to planting trees and saving whales. I'm a huge fan of SRI funds but they aren't as noble as the marketing suggests. For example, Vanguard's FTSE Social Index Fund is the most popular

SRI fund in the United States, based on assets under management. It tracks a collection of stocks called the FTSE4Good US Select Index. The fund's seven largest "companies for good" include Apple, Microsoft, Amazon, Alphabet (Google), Facebook, Procter & Gamble, and Visa. I doubt Mother Teresa would have prayed, "Please, God, bless these companies so they can continue to serve the planet." That's because they don't really help the environment.

There's something else you should know about stocks in general. When we invest in stocks that trade on the stock exchange (whether through an index or purchasing individual shares) our money doesn't directly support those businesses. For example, if you invested in a windmill manufacturer trading on the stock exchange, your money wouldn't go toward building more windmills. If you invested in an oil company, your money wouldn't go toward extracting icky black stuff. You would just own a piece of that windmill manufacturer or oil company on the open market. In other words, you would profit or lose based on how that company performed (long-term, a stock price rises or falls in correlation with its business earnings).

Mercedes Martin knows this. But she still doesn't want to own regular index funds, because they include companies that fly in the face of her values. "I believe it is important to hold companies accountable for more than just profits," she says. "The businesses that are working to positively impact the planet will be the ones that succeed in the future. They'll provide the greatest returns. So I think investing in SRI funds not only aligns more closely with my personal beliefs, these funds will also earn the best future returns."

If you're comfortable earning profits from the entire economic sector, including oil and gas companies, then you could pick traditional index funds or ETFs, such as I mentioned in chapter 8. If, however, you would rather earn profits from companies with higher sustainability ratings, then SRI funds are for you.

SRI Investing with Full-Service Financial Advisors

If you hire a full-service financial advisor, they can build you a portfolio of SRI indexed mutual funds or ETFs. But make sure the advisor meets the standards I describe in chapter 8. Don't deviate from those criteria. Stay clear of actively managed products and the silver tongues that sell them.

SRI Investing with Robo-Advisors

In chapter 8, I listed some robo-advisory firms for investors in different countries. Most of those firms offer portfolios of socially responsible funds as well as their traditional index or ETF counterparts. If you want SRI funds, you have to ask for them specifically, though.

SRI Investing on Your Own

It's even cheaper to buy your own socially responsible indexed mutual funds or ETFs. But as of this writing, the only all-in-one SRI portfolio solutions are available as ETFs on the Toronto Stock Exchange.

That doesn't mean Americans and other nationalities can't build their own indexed portfolios of SRI funds. They'll just have to use more than one fund.

SRI Index Fund Portfolio Models by Nationality

Americans

In Table 10.1, I've listed sample building blocks for a diversified SRI portfolio for Americans: four allocations based on different tolerances for volatility. Investors would need to set up an account with Fidelity (as of this writing, Vanguard doesn't yet offer a full selection of SRI funds). Investors could then set up automatic deposits into each fund to keep the process hands-free. In other words, if some-body wants to invest $100 a month into a balanced SRI portfolio, they could assign $30 to Fidelity's US Sustainability Index (FITLX), $30 to Fidelity's International Sustainability Index (FNIDX), and $40 to Fidelity's Sustainability Bond Index (FNDSX). Fidelity doesn't charge commissions for the purchases and there are no monthly minimums. The total expense ratio charges for these portfolios would be less than 0.17 percent per year.

TABLE 10.1

For Americans: SRI Index Mutual Fund Portfolios

Fund	Fund Code	Cautious	Balanced	Assertive	Aggressive
Fidelity US Sustainability Index	FITLX	25%	30%	40%	50%
Fidelity International Sustainability Index	FNIDX	20%	30%	35%	50%
Fidelity Sustainability Bond Index	FNDSX	55%	40%	25%	0%

Source: Fidelity USA[3]

Canadians

Canadians can buy socially responsible all-in-one portfolio ETFs. I've listed the iShares funds in Table 10.2.

TABLE 10.2

For Canadians: SRI All-in-One ETF Portfolios

Fund	Symbol	Approximate % in Stocks	Approximate % in Bonds	Annual Expense Ratio
iShares ESG Conservative Balanced	GCNS	40%	60%	0.27%*
iShares ESG Balanced	GBAL	60%	40%	0.27%*
iShares ESG Growth	GGRO	80%	20%	0.27%*
iShares ESG Equity	GEQT	100%	0%	0.27%*

Source: iShares/BlackRock Canada[4]
*These posted fees are estimates. iShares charges 0.22% per year for each fund, but as of this writing, the funds are less than twelve months old. Total estimated costs (including internal trading costs for rebalancing) will likely be about 0.27% per year.

British

As of 2021, no British investment firm offered all-in-one socially responsible portfolios of ETFs or indexed mutual funds. But British investors could build such portfolios on their own with a selection of SRI ETFs through any number of UK-based brokerage accounts. In Table 10.3, I've provided sample portfolios with different tolerances for risk. Each fund trades on the London Stock Exchange.

TABLE 10.3

For the British: SRI ETF Portfolios

Fund	Fund Code	Invests In	Cautious	Balanced	Assertive	Aggressive
UBS MSCI United Kingdom IMI Socially Responsible UCITS	UKSR	UK Stocks	20%	30%	35%	50%
iShares MSCI World SRI UCITS	SGWS*	Global Stocks	25%	30%	40%	50%
Vanguard UK Gilt	VGOV**	British Government Bonds	55%	40%	25%	0%

Sources: Morningstar UK, Vanguard UK, and iShares UK
*SGWS is currency-hedged to the British pound (sterling). There's a hidden, internal cost to such hedging. Studies show it could cost investors as much as 1% per year. If investors want a non-currency-hedged version, they could purchase SUWS. It's the same as SGWS, but it's priced in USD.[5]
**VGOV is a government bond index, but it isn't considered an SRI indexed bond fund. As of 2021, no such ETF traded on the London Stock Exchange.

Australians

As of 2021, no Australian investment firm offered all-in-one socially responsible portfolios of ETFs or indexed mutual funds. But Australian investors can build such portfolios on their own with a selection of SRI ETFs through a brokerage account. In Table 10.4, I've provided sample portfolios with different tolerances for risk. Each fund trades on the Australian Stock Exchange. Investment fees for these portfolios average about 0.20 percent per year.

TABLE 10.4

For Australians: SRI ETF Portfolios

Fund	Fund Code	Invests In	Cautious	Balanced	Assertive	Aggressive
Vanguard Ethically Conscious Australian Shares	VETH	Australian shares	20%	30%	35%	50%
Vanguard Ethically Conscious International Shares	VESG	Global shares	25%	30%	40%	50%
Vanguard Ethically Conscious Global Aggregate Bond Index	VEFI	Global bonds	55%	40%	25%	0%

Source: Vanguard Australia[6]

Helping the Planet While Juicing Happiness

Kirk Warren Brown and Tim Kasser are two American psychology professors who say that trying to help the planet boosts our social well-being. They assessed middle school and high school students from two Midwestern schools in the United States. To test the students' subjective well-being, they asked, "How would you say you're feeling these days?" The students measured their responses on a five-point scale, ranging from 1, "very unhappy," to 5, "very happy." They compared the results against the students' ecological responsibility. For example, they asked the students if they turned off lights after they left a room, recycled, reused plastic bags, and conserved water.

Overall, the students with higher environmentally conscious scores reported being happier. Brown and Kasser found the same results with adults. You might wonder whether happier people are more environmentally conscious or whether environmental consciousness makes people happier. The research isn't clear on that point. But coupling this research with some of his earlier findings, Kasser believes that when we're motivated to help others, or the environment, we achieve far more satisfaction than we do when we seek fulfillment through the acquisition of stuff.[7]

What Are the World's Best Environmental Investments?

Early in 2020, my wife and I spent five weeks cycling around Costa Rica on our tandem. We saw much of the country, not through the lens of tourists at a resort but as travelers who wanted to learn. A couple of things struck us as unique. First of all, Pele and I have traveled to more than seventy different countries. In our subjective opinion, Costa Ricans seemed among the happiest and most helpful people we had ever encountered.

We learned that others agree. According to the World Happiness Report, Costa Ricans are among the happiest people on the planet.[8] At one point, while we were cycling along a remote dirt road, Pele's jacket fell off the back of the tandem. But we didn't know this had happened until a young man caught up to us on his motorcycle. He saw the jacket fall as we went by his home. He climbed on his motorcycle, returned the jacket, and then went back home. This complete stranger was happy just to help.

We've pedaled our tandem in dozens of countries. Every country has friendly and unfriendly people. But none were more welcoming than Costa Ricans. We never had so many people ask, "Do you need somewhere to camp? You're welcome to pitch a tent in our yard. We have a bathroom you could use too."

Midway through our trip, I found the Happy Planet Index online. Each year, it publishes ratings on how efficiently people in different countries convert the consumption of natural resources into human well-being. They cross-reference the Gallup World Poll data on overall life satisfaction with life expectancy, equality levels, and the ecological footprint of each resident, as determined by the Global Footprint Network.

Out of 140 countries ranked, Costa Rica was #1. While cycling around the country, we marveled at its cleanliness. Outside the capital city of San José, it appeared to be about as clean as Canada. We saw several signs in Spanish that read "Garbage doesn't go away on its own." The locals have an expression that seems to combine their happy-go-lucky culture with their care for their environment: *pura vida*. It means "simple life" or "pure life."

We pedaled into the town of La Fortuna, at the base of the Arenal Volcano. After wheeling our tandem into a family-run hotel lobby, we checked in. I then peppered the woman behind the counter with questions about her country's cleanliness. With a huge smile, forty-year-old Ivette López said, "It's part of pura vida. Our schools teach us to look after the environment. We learn not to litter and we learn about recycling."

I was impressed, but a bit confused. Costa Ricans, from what I noticed, used the term pura vida for just about everything. When you pass them on the street, they say, "Pura vida." Instead of saying, "Goodbye," they often say, "Pura vida." Ask them how they're feeling and they might say, "Pura vida." Ivette laughed when I brought this up. "Even to us, pura vida is a mystery," she said.

This simple, happy term truly is part of Costa Rican culture. Even the government is on board with it. In 1994, Costa Ricans amended their constitution to focus on a healthy environment for its people. A few years later, they initiated a carbon tax which helped to finance reforestation and environmental projects. No country is perfect, of course. Not even Costa Rica. It still has a long way to go, but in 2021, 80 percent of the country's power came from hydroelectricity. No form of energy creation has zero impact. Hydro dams, windmills, and solar panels all require mined materials. And their construction, maintenance, and in some cases disposal and replacement aren't ecofriendly. But hydroelectricity is a renewable energy source, and with 80 percent of Costa Rica's power coming from hydro, they're beating most of the rest of the world. Costa Rica also plans to be the world's first country to ban single-use plastic.

Carlos Alvarado Quesada became president of Costa Rica in 2018, when he was just thirty-eight years old. He says the climate crisis is "the greatest task of our generation." Costa Rica is one of the world's only countries to have more tree and plant life today than it did thirty years ago. It has doubled its tree coverage over just three decades.[9] The former environment minister, Carlos Manuel Rodríguez, says the country's long-term goal is to be emissions-free by 2050. Some people say that's overly ambitious. But as Quesada said, "We have to inspire people. . . we can be that example."[10]

One of the biggest impacts we can make is at the governmental level. In democracies, we vote for people who represent ideas. We can also tell them what we want. For example, according to one poll, more than 70 percent of Americans say they want "aggressive action to stop climate change."[11]

In that case, they should vote for policies that push for action. As Costa Rica has shown, when people vote for leaders who commit to help the environment, change can happen. Governments can ban single-use plastics and introduce regulations to get toxic chemicals out of products. And voters can buy less crap.

The Story of Stuff

In Annie Leonard's short video "The Story of Stuff," the environmental researcher says, "We use too much. Too much of it is toxic and we don't share it very well. But that's not the way things have to be. Together, we can build a society based on better, not more, sharing not selfishness, community not division."[12]

One of the reasons Costa Ricans rank #1 in the Happy Planet Index is that they are less obsessed about buying stuff than people in most developed world countries. That suggests that even if our country's leader doesn't prioritize the planet, we can impact the world in other ways.

Step 1 is keeping our wallets closed more. Sure, the stock market might progress at lower-than-historical rates if everyone bought less crap. But that shouldn't matter. In the face of a healthy planet, shopping shouldn't be considered patriotic. President George W. Bush urged Americans to go shopping after 9/11, and I believe he meant well. But that's destructive. It echoes what American retail analyst Victor Lebow is reported to have said in 1955: "Our enormously productive economy demands that we make consumption our way of life, that we convert the buying and use of goods into rituals, that we seek our spiritual satisfaction and our ego satisfaction in consumption. We need things consumed, burned up, worn out, replaced and discarded at an ever-increasing rate."[13]

Unfortunately, Lebow's mandate gained traction. Mass consumerism became ingrained in our culture. Meanwhile, as we saw earlier, having more stuff doesn't make us happier. In fact, the opposite is true. We can help our planet and boost our happiness by purchasing less and sharing more. And if our purchasing habits change, we won't need as much in retirement because we'll be accustomed to living on less.

Less Is Best

My most environmentally conscious friends are Don and Anita Gillmore. They have always recycled, they compost, and, more importantly, they don't buy what they don't need. Almost twenty years ago, they bought a home in Shawnigan Lake, British Columbia. At the time, the house cost slightly more than the average Canadian home. Yet their frugal living helped them pay off their mortgage after just six years. That's quite a feat considering they never earned a combined income of more than $80,000 a year before taxes.

Now in their mid-fifties, they earn a total pre-tax household income of about $45,000 a year. Don is semiretired and Anita works as a groundskeeper at a private school. They have a few egg-laying ducks, they grow seasonal food, and their entire family commutes mostly by foot and bicycle. Don has a custom-built bicycle trailer that he uses to haul everything from groceries to buckets of manure.

"Cars have a huge environmental impact," he says. "And when you aren't operating a motor vehicle, it costs so much less. Most people don't consider how much their vehicles cost when they count the purchase price, fuel, insurance, depreciation, maintenance, and loan payments." For several months at a time, Don and Anita let their car insurance run out. During that time, they walk and cycle everywhere. That helps them save money and it's better for the environment.

Don and Anita also have more money than most people their age because they differentiated early on between their "wants" and their "needs." As a result, they invested more money. And when they retire, they'll need less than the average person because their lifestyle is simple. They don't eat at restaurants or drink coffee at cafés. They still don't make unnecessary purchases. Anita is a former bronze medalist at Canada's National Cycling Championships and Don once ranked second in the country as a cycling sprinter, but these former athletes don't pay money on gym memberships—they're both extremely fit from spending so much time outdoors and in their home gym.

You might say to yourself, "These people sound far too frugal to be happy." But they smile and laugh with an ease that suggests otherwise. What's more, according to a research study from the University of Arizona, people who buy fewer things (like Don and Anita) tend to be happier than those who engage in pro-environmental consumer behavior. In other words, the less we purchase (of anything) the happier we might be.[14]

I'm not saying everyone should live like Don and Anita; restaurant meals can be rather nice, after all. But if we embrace just a part of their lifestyle, we might be happier and our air quality, rivers, oceans, and lakes would be so much cleaner. It really is that simple.

According to the Global Footprint Network, humanity is consuming nature 1.75 times faster than it can regenerate.[15] Yes, we're farming fish and planting new trees. But we're also depleting fish and trees faster than we can replace them. This goes for other natural resources too—and many aren't renewable.

We're also polluting many natural resources. Much of what we buy is made from plastic and then wrapped in more plastic before being transported, usually by air or ground transport, to stores and warehouses. The people making our stuff are often located in low-income countries. They're exposed to toxic chemicals all day and they earn very low wages for their trouble. The manufacturing process pumps toxic chemicals into these factory workers and into the air. We all breathe that air. According to one study published by the *International Journal of Environmental Research and Public Health*, plastic production contributes to respiratory and cardiovascular diseases.[16] Ethylene oxide, a basic building block for plastic production, also has strong links to cancer, according to the National Cancer Institute.[17]

Those toxins also work their way into our water systems, affecting our fish, crops, and wildlife. When we consume the fish, crops, and wildlife, we're also consuming the toxins. There's no escape from them.

Recycling Is Good, but It's Not the Solution

Recycling sounds like an answer. And it helps. But it's only one answer and it doesn't solve the bigger problem. If we focus on recycling, we might feel like we're doing something great. As a result, we might consume even more single-use products, comforting ourselves that they'll be recycled. But recycling takes energy. The production of that energy has an environmental impact. Recycling is good. We should recycle. But buying fewer things would be even better.

We throw out much of what we buy not long after purchasing it. That includes children's toys, tubes of toothpaste, plastic soap dispensers, shoes, clothing. . . the list goes on.

That's a lot of waste. Some of it gets tossed directly into landfills. Other stuff gets incinerated before it's dumped. This burning emits dioxins, one of the most toxic chemicals known to humanity.[18]

In a Penn State Public Broadcasting interview, Patty Satalia asked Annie Leonard what she personally does to share with others and reduce consumption. Leonard doesn't live in a commune but her neighbors share what they own. She says that among twelve local families, one person has a pickup truck, somebody else has a barbecue, and one family has a hot tub. There's also only one ladder, one wheelbarrow, and one pair of heavy-duty garden shears. Everybody shares. She says this helps them save money—and it brings her community together.[19]

Planet-Friendly Buying

Leonard wisely notes that we can't buy a solution to overconsumption at a store. But unless we're living off the grid and off the land, we still need to spend to survive. That's why it's good to ask how our purchases can least affect the environment. Here are a few things you could try at home. Many of them are mentioned in Dr. Tara Shine's book *How to Save Your Planet One Object at a Time*.[20]

Buy local
Whenever possible, buy locally produced food and products. They might cost you more than the equivalent at a big box store but you'll help the environment. Goods shipped from afar require more packaging. Creating that packaging emits toxins. The shipping also increases carbon pollution levels (think planes, trains, boats, and automobiles). And when goods are more heavily packaged, we have

more waste in the landfill or more energy used to recycle the packaging. Local foods are also heathier because they're fresher. Fruits and vegetables lose their nutritional punch soon after they've been picked, so the time spent in shipping and storage reduces not only their freshness but also their nutritional value.

It's also relatively easy to confirm if producers of locally grown food are following sustainable farming practices. It's tougher to trace your Mexican strawberries from Walmart back to their source.

Another option is to buy as little processed food as possible. Processed foods require more wrapping. And reduce your meat intake as well. Agriculture consumes about 70 percent of the world's fresh water withdrawals each year and is responsible for about 78 percent of global and fresh water pollution. According to a report on NPR (National Public Radio), the UN's Intergovernmental Panel on Climate Change reports that about half of the world's vegetated land is used for agriculture and about 30 percent of the world's cropland is used to grow grain for the meat production industry. As a result, meat production is a leading cause of deforestation. If we eat less meat, we could see a great deal of reforestation in return.[21]

When drinking tea and coffee

Tea and coffee are staples in most Western homes. They're also environmentally problematic.

For example, most tea bags take a long time to recycle. Few are compostable because they include polypropylene, a plastic that takes years to break down. Fairtrade International and Rainforest Alliance loose-leaf teas, however, use less packaging. They're also certified organic, so they're free from synthetic fertilizers, pesticides, and herbicides, which is better for everyone, including the growers and pickers. And the Fairtrade and Rainforest Alliance certification means that those who work to produce the tea are provided fair wages. Yes, it's more expensive than cheap, bagged tea. But if you're buying such products, your money is directly supporting the enterprise that's making it. And that's worth the extra cost.

One such brand is Teapigs, the first tea brand awarded the Plastic Free Trust Mark.[22] Teapigs are plastic-free tea bags made from biodegradable corn starch. The bags (known as temples) are heat-sealed, so there's no plastic glue involved. Their cartons are made from FSC-certified cardboard, which is fully recyclable. The inner wrapping looks like plastic, but it's actually a wood pulp material called NatureFlex.

Much of the world is obsessed by coffee. Each year, we drink more. In 2018/2019, we consumed a record 165.35 million 132-pound (60-kilogram) bags of coffee.[23] According to a 2017 Fairtrade research study, 100 percent of Kenyan coffee farmers, 25 percent of Indian farmers, and 35–50 percent of Indonesian farmers don't earn a living wage from growing coffee.[24] When we buy coffee that isn't Fairtrade, chances are we're exploiting those people. That's why it's worth paying a bit more to only buy Fairtrade coffee. If you don't believe you can afford the higher price, consider buying it anyway but drink it less frequently or in smaller amounts. This would also make coffee more of a treat. And you know what that means: you'll enjoy it more.

To reduce your environmental footprint, it's also better to drink coffee at home than in a coffee shop where they use paper cups. Even if the paper cups are compostable, they take a lot of energy to mass produce. If, however, your local café uses real reusable cups, support that business and socialize there with friends.

Say no to plastic water bottles

There are two reasons the Chinese drink more bottled water than anyone in the world: First, they have a massive population, so a bigger consumer base. Second, even in futuristic-looking cities like Beijing or Shanghai, you can't safely drink water out of household taps. If Costa Ricans can safely drink water from their taps (and they can!), the government of China should be able to make the same thing happen.

Several other countries have a high per capita consumption of bottled water. And in many of them, such as Mexico and Thailand, the tap water isn't safe either. But in countries like the United States, Italy, France, and Germany, residents can safely drink tap water. So why is the per capita consumption of bottled water in the United States, Italy, France, and Germany among the highest in the world?[25] It's called manufactured demand.[26] Marketers have tricked us into buying bottled water. Yet the University of Glasgow professor Paul Younger, author of *Water: All That Matters*, says bottled water isn't safer than tap water.[27]

Plenty of people believe they prefer the taste of bottled water. But in blind taste tests, such as one facilitated by researchers at Dalhousie University in Halifax, Canada, tap water generally comes out on top.[28] In a 2010 study published in the *Journal of Sensory Studies* the researchers revealed that most of the subjects couldn't tell the difference between six different bottled mineral waters and six municipal tap waters when the tap water was chlorine-free.[29]

In "The Story of Bottled Water," Annie Leonard says Americans buy enough single-use plastic water bottles every week to circle the planet five times if they were placed end to end.[30] And that's just one week! The production of those bottles requires oil, and that pollutes the atmosphere. Couple that with pollutants caused by shipping and we have a big problem. That problem compounds when we toss the bottles away. According to a 2019 article in *National Geographic*, only 9 percent of plastic bottles get recycled. And the energy required to recycle them plus the resultant pollutants created have their own devastating effect on the environment.[31]

To make the biggest impact, support movements to ban single-use water bottles in your country. If the Costa Ricans can do this, we can too. If you're traveling to a place where you can't safely drink tap water, bring stainless steel water bottles that you can refill from the 5-gallon reusable bottles that you'll see in most hotels.

Wear out what you buy

Like plastic bottles, our shoes and clothing fill landfills, line beaches around the world, and pollute the atmosphere when they're incinerated. That's why we should buy fewer shoes and clothes.

The shoe industry is responsible for 250 million tons (almost 227 tonnes) of carbon dioxide emissions every year. Researchers at MIT found that a single pair of running shoes generates 30 pounds (almost 14 kilograms) of emissions. Most of that comes from producing the shoe.[32] Yet, most of us buy far more shoes than we need. And no, we aren't always wearing them out. We're often throwing them out instead.

Here's what we can do: For starters, buy fewer shoes. If you get tired of what you own, swap pairs with someone you know who wears the same size. Buy used boots and shoes from a thrift store. To date, I've only done that twice, with a pair of boots and a pair of running shoes. But in both cases, I might have been the first person to wear them. Sometimes, you can find "used" products with their store labels still attached. If you do buy used shoes, always sanitize them before putting them on.

When you're buying new shoes, consider buying leather rather than synthetic shoes. Synthetic shoes are made from rubber and plastic, both of which are derived from oil and are non-biodegradable. Leather is biodegradable. And although it's an animal product, leather production makes fuller use of an animal that was raised for consumption.

Also consider manufacturers like soleRebels. Their Ethiopian-made shoes are made in accordance with Fairtrade practices. soleRebels also only uses recycled materials, pays its employees three times the industry average wage, and provides all its employees and their families with healthcare coverage. Buying soleRebels products puts money directly into a sustainable model with little environmental impact. And it helps other people.

Lowering our water consumption also helps others. That can mean buying fewer pairs of jeans—and washing them less frequently. Levi Strauss conducted a study on a pair of Levi 501s, estimating that a single pair uses approximately 999 gallons (3,781 liters) of water during its lifetime. Sixty-eight percent of that comes from growing the cotton required to make the jeans, and 23 percent comes from washing the jeans after we wear them.[33]

In fact, if we wash jeans only once for every ten times we wear them, we reduce the energy waste by 75 percent. It also takes a lot of energy to dry jeans, so air-dry them instead of putting them in a tumble dryer.

Recognize that fashion is a con

When I was a kid, we earned the rips in our jeans by snagging them on tree branches and fences. We wore out the knees playing soccer, football, and baseball. Then we tried to patch them (OK, our parents did that part).

Back in the day, I can't imagine someone saying, "We're going to make new jeans, rip them up, and sell them for more than a pair of Levi 501s." We would have laughed and said, "There's no way you can trick anyone into buying those." But trick people the marketers did. My seventeen-year-old niece says, "My ripped jeans, like, definitely don't last as long. The rips get bigger." That's a shame, considering how much water is required to manufacture a pair of jeans and how many pollutants are produced transporting them to consumers.

Fashion is a con, actively promoting blouses, shirts, purses, jackets, and shoes that are "in" one year and usually "out" the next. As an industry, it flips two middle fingers at the planet.

The United Nations estimates the fashion industry is responsible for using 24 percent of the world's insecticides and 11 percent of pesticides.[34] The UN Environment Programme has gone on record as saying fashion accounts for 8 to 10 percent of global carbon emissions. That's more than the combined total of all international flights and maritime shipping.[35] These emissions come from pumping water to irrigate crops like cotton, oil-based pesticides, machinery for harvesting, and emissions from transportation. And a McKinsey & Company sustainability study says clothing purchases increased by around 60 percent per person between 2000 and 2014. Unless we recognize fashion as a destructive industry that we can sidestep, those figures are only going to get worse.[36]

Take a journey from cradle to grave

Imagine going on a field trip to where clothing materials are produced and harvested. You apprentice with a family of crop-growers and crop-pickers. It's backbreaking work. You also measure the water required to grow the crops. You then apprentice for a week in a textile firm where you make jeans using an industrial sewing machine. Then you learn how to distress the jeans to create a fashionable look.

After that, you spend a week in a facility that makes packaging for the jeans. Scientists show you how to estimate the toxic emissions into the atmosphere. You then ride with the clothing to the stores. That ride might start with a truck, followed by a ship, train, or plane. These transport services emit more pollutants into the air. You then arrive at the store in another truck before someone purchases the jeans. Then, when the jeans get discarded, you follow them to landfills. Who would you bring on this field trip with you? Kim Kardashian, Victoria Beckham, or a posse of teenaged influencers? If everyone internalized the cradle-to-grave impact of the stuff we buy, I think we would all consume less.

Buy bars of soap, not plastic bottles and tubes

If you go to a local farmers' market, the odds you'll find someone selling soap are high. Find the scents you enjoy and then make the seller's day by buying enough to fill a small backpack. Local soaps don't require transcontinental shipping. Often, local bars of soap aren't wrapped in plastic either. If you can't find locally made soap, consider standard bars of soap from a store instead of the all-too-common plastic containers of liquid soap. For starters, bars of soap last longer. Second, they're less damaging to the environment (always remember the environmental impact of plastic production and disposal). Even when bars of soap are shipped from faraway lands, they tend to be lighter than plastic containers of liquid soap. That means they require less energy to transport.

You could also consider never buying another tube of toothpaste again. The American company Bite (to name one example) makes toothpaste and mouthwash tablets from natural ingredients. They come in glass jars, with no plastic. And if you're on an anti-plastic oral hygiene mission, you could buy bamboo toothbrushes, or even a mechanical one with a wind-up motor such as the "Be. Brush" by Goodwell. The wind-up brushes are made from 90 percent recycled plastic and the heads (which require replacing every couple of months) are made of starch and bamboo.

Flying and Driving

In 2020, the Australian airline Qantas figured out a way to make fast money. It offered a "flight to nowhere" while COVID-19 travel restrictions were in play. The flight lasted about eight hours, giving passengers the feeling of traveling despite departing from and landing at the same Sydney airport. It was the most popular flight in the airline's history, selling out less than ten minutes after tickets were made available.[37]

The bean counters at Qantas must have rubbed their hands. They saw how to recoup some of the lost revenue caused by the travel restrictions imposed in response to the pandemic. Singapore Airlines, among others, also decided to launch its own flights to nowhere. But environmental campaigners voiced strong disapproval. As a result, Singapore Airlines offered tickets for people in a grounded airplane to dine in its seats and watch movies on the little airline screens. Prices were based on whether diners sat in first class or economy seats, with meals in the first class cabin going for $496. No, I didn't make that up.[38]

Environmentalists opposed flights to nowhere for good reason. For example, taking a single flight from Europe to North America equates to about 20 percent of the average person's carbon footprint in a year.[39] It would be hypocritical of me to say that you shouldn't fly. But we should be mindful of how much pollution it creates. That goes for driving too.

The new car conundrum

Walking, riding bicycles, and taking public transit make the environment smile more than when we get behind the wheel of a car. Plenty of people, however, might ask, "But what about a new electric car?" Chris Jones is the national secretary of the Australian Electric Vehicle Association. He says, "Buying a new car is bad for the environment, whether it's electric, petrol or otherwise. All manufactured goods take energy and resources to make, and these aren't typically benign processes. Honestly if doing right by the atmosphere is your primary objective, just ride a bicycle. However if you must buy a new car, it might as well be an electric car."[40]

But constructing, powering, and disposing of even an electric car has a huge environmental impact. Jennifer Dunn, of Northwestern University's Center for Engineering Sustainability and Resilience, says, "The material that helps power the battery is produced from a number of different metals, things like nickel and cobalt and lithium."[41] Mining those materials, plus manufacturing the battery, pumps enormous carbon emissions into the atmosphere.

Is electricity super clean?

Unfortunately, the electricity that powers an electric car doesn't come without a cost. According to Our World in Data, most of the world's electricity still comes from burning fossil fuels.[42] Countries like Canada, France, Brazil, Sweden, Finland, and Norway produce much of their electricity through cleaner means. According to the Government of Canada, 60 percent of the country's electricity comes from hydroelectric dams.[43] But we should still use that energy as sparingly as we can, because even hydroelectricity comes at a cost.

Environment and Climate Change Canada says hydroelectric dams create "significant amounts of methane" from the decomposition of plants in flood areas. In addition to disrupting natural river flows, dams also damage fish stocks and increase the length of their natural migration. The increased bacteria in the areas of decaying vegetation change the mercury present in rocks. Mercury then ekes into the water, which can accumulate in the fish. The Canadian government says the added mercury "poses a health hazard to those who depend on these fish for food."[44]

As electrical demands increase, we have to burn more fossil fuels, mine more materials for windmills, mine more materials for solar panels, or build more hydro dams. Electricity of any kind comes at a cost.

Setting SMART Goals to Reduce Your Environmental Impact

When we think about the cradle-to-grave processes associated with what we buy, consume, and discard, it can be overwhelming. That's why we should make SMART goals. SMART is an acronym for Specific, Measurable, Attainable, Relevant, and Time-Based. In other words, we shouldn't just say, "I'm going to start driving less to work." Instead, we should make a specific, time-oriented goal. For example, we might normally drive to work five days a week. This week, we could make our goal to cycle, walk, or take public transit on two of those days instead. When we achieve a goal, it gives us a sense of accomplishment—and perhaps the motivation to set a new, more ambitious goal the following week. That goal might be finding bars of locally made organic soap and shampoo. We might buy enough for several months, limiting our future consumption of plastic-based products. No matter what goals we set, it helps to write them down and tell a friend about them. Research suggests doing so dramatically increases our odds of succeeding.[45]

A Few Tips for Living Well

- Consider investing in SRI funds.

- Vote for people who are pro-environment. They can help make a difference.

- Fly less frequently, drive less, buy local, say no to single-plastic water bottles, eat less meat, and reduce and reuse before you recycle.

- Consider cradle-to-grave impacts. Think about the full process of creating a product, from manufacturing, packaging, and shipping to consumption and disposal.

- Set SMART goals that positively impact the environment.

- Buy less of everything. This should improve your happiness, your financial bottom line, and your children's and grandchildren's future.

11

FROM LITTLE ACORNS. . .
Helping Your Children Succeed

"I DON'T GET PAID to do chores, so I'm not going to pay my daughter." That's what finance expert Kerry K. Taylor said when I asked if she paid her eight-year-old daughter to do household chores.

She and her husband, Carl, make child-rearing decisions with the help of evidence-based research. That doesn't mean Chloe won't turn into a credit card junkie who gambles online. Parents can't completely control how their kids turn out, no matter how much they might want to. But research says that if parents set the right wheels in motion, like Kerry and Carl are doing, there's a far higher chance their children will succeed, not just financially but in a holistic sense too.

Chores and Success

Amy Chua ruffled feathers when she wrote *Battle Hymn of the Tiger Mother*.[1] She said Asian kids have an edge over Western kids because Asian parents are stricter. As a Chinese American mom, she didn't let her children attend sleepovers, watch TV, play video games, or pick their own afterschool activities. They *had to* play the violin or the piano. They weren't allowed to act in any school plays. Fortunately, that recipe for success isn't based on science. If it were, more people might try this at home.

Research does say, however, that when children do household chores it makes a big impact. "Our daughter began doing chores when she was about four years old," says Kerry. "But we don't even call them chores. It's just about being a good human." Before Chloe entered kindergarten, Kerry encouraged her to help around the house by singing, "Clean up, clean up, everybody clean up!" Kerry and Carl modeled the family team effort. "Chloe [at eight years old] cleans her room and helps fold laundry. She also helps with cooking, baking, and cleaning up afterward. She helps us create grocery lists. And she helps us shop for groceries. We've taught her to look carefully at the cost of the food we buy."

Chores teach children responsibility, a sense of teamwork, and a sense of community that extends into adulthood. But ironically, far fewer kids do household chores today than they did in the past. In a Braun Research poll of 1,001 parents, 82 percent of the parents who were surveyed said they routinely did chores when they were children. But, perhaps in a quest to make life easier for their kids, just 28 percent of those same parents said their children do chores. That's like a parent saying, "I exercise to stay strong and healthy. But I don't want my kids going through that effort."

Yet, according to a twenty-year University of Minnesota study, chores are the best predictor of success in young adults.[2] The study determined success by career paths, level of education, and personal relationships. The best results came when children began to do chores by age three or four. A Harvard University study of inner-city males produced the same conclusions. Regular household chores beat "all other childhood variables in predicting adult mental health and capacity for interpersonal relationships."[3]

Julie Lythcott-Haims is former dean of Freshmen and Undergraduate Advising at Stanford University. She's also the author of *How to Raise an Adult*.[4] She says household chores help kids persevere and become responsible. Children should clean their bedrooms, make their beds, and do their personal laundry. But she also says those things aren't chores. In her opinion, chores are tasks that relate to taking care of the family, such as mowing the lawn, washing dishes, vacuuming, or doing poo patrol (for families with dogs and a yard).

She says, "When young people have been expected to roll up their sleeves and pitch in, and to ask how they can contribute to the household, it leads to a mind-set of pitching in in other settings, such as the workplace." She adds that parents who don't assign chores deprive their kids of certain life skills. And perhaps the most important life skill is the ability to be social.

Social Skills Are a Superpower

When I was in university, I met a guy named Dave Carlson. At the time, he wasn't focused on his studies, but he was miles ahead in something arguably more important: Dave was socially brilliant. He remembered and used people's names when he spoke to them. He also listened well, establishing great eye contact. Years later, when I read Dale Carnegie's book *How to Win Friends and Influence People*, I thought, "Dave Carlson doesn't need to read this. He does all these things naturally."

Twenty-five years after I last saw Dave, I tracked him down in Canmore, Alberta. He owns two sports stores. I wandered into one of his stores and struck up a casual conversation with one of his employees. The woman didn't know that I knew her boss, but she made it clear how much she respected him. Dave's other employees echoed her sentiments. He respects them as people, so they in turn respect him. I call this sociological math. When we show that we care about others, the returns are incredible. That's why social skills are so darn important. In fact, they're more important than any subject we could learn in school. The ability to communicate well (listening, demonstrating empathy, working with and motivating others) should be the skillset parents most covet for their kids.

But skills must be practiced. They must be honed over time. Let's assume we could measure social skills. Assume the average eighteen-year-old from the 1920s to the 1990s earned an 8 out of 10 for their interpersonal ability: the skill to read body language and facial expressions, look people in the eye, remember and use people's names, and carry out conversations with adults and people they might be romantically interested in. Sure, some teenagers today would score 10 out of 10 on such skills. But I'm guessing most would score lower than 6 out of 10.

When speaking to students I try to inspire them by saying, "Hey, if you develop what used to be an average level of human social skills, you're going to be a rock star among your peers." For at least the past decade, too many kids have buried themselves in rooms to play video games and text. It isn't enough to know that we should speak clearly, look people in the eye, and read facial and body language. If we don't practice these skills, we won't develop them.

One of the best ways for kids to build social skills is to limit the time they spend on screens so they can practice more face-to-face communication. Parents will find this tough, especially because most of them are glued to screens too. But if you can digitally detox your child (or better yet, never let them get addicted), they have far better odds of reaching their full potential.

Philip Zimbardo and Nikita Coulombe are the authors of *Man, Interrupted: Why Young Men Are Struggling & What We Can Do about It*.[5] Zimbardo is a psychologist and a professor emeritus at Stanford University. He says the excessive time that kids spend on social media and video games impedes the development of their social skills. He says the more time they spend in front of screens, the more difficult it will be for them to find jobs, maintain friendships, and develop healthy sexual relationships. Online porn consumption, especially among teen boys, is rampant, leaving many teens with a warped sense of sex.

In *The Common Sense Consensus: Media Use by Teens and Tweens*, US kids were reported to spend an average of nine hours a day using social media as a form of entertainment.[6] That includes time spent before school, on the way to school, and during classes. They also use social media for fun after school, in the bathroom, and at night when they should be sleeping.

For years, Daniel Goleman has been saying that emotional intelligence matters more than IQ. In his book *Social Intelligence* he says the ability to get along with others improves our health, wealth, happiness, and overall effectiveness.[7] A study published by the American Public Health Association even showed that a child's social skills in kindergarten were strong predictors of future success.[8]

Addiction to social media could guarantee that these skills don't fully develop. "Most parents today don't establish clear boundaries for social media use," says Jeff Devens, a school psychologist. "But they *must* establish boundaries."

Ironically, many of those who developed screen-based tools set far better boundaries than the average parent. What do they know that the rest of us don't? When the *New York Times* reporter Nick Bilton interviewed the late Steve Jobs about the iPad, Bilton expected Jobs's kids to be masters of the tech. "They haven't used it," Jobs said. "We limit how much technology they use at home." Bilton wrote, "Since then, I've met a number of technology chief executives and venture capitalists who say similar things: they strictly limit their children's screen time, often banning all gadgets on school nights and allocating ascetic time limits on weekends."[9]

Assigning regular chores and limiting social media won't guarantee success. But it does increase the odds. Success, after all, isn't hardwired—especially when it comes to money.

Your Child's Success Is Not Hardwired

We all battle a dark financial force. Nature loads it. The environment pulls the trigger. It's tempting to buy today, pay tomorrow. Retail marketers and credit card companies compel us to buy what we don't need. That's bad for the environment and our wealth.

That's why Dorothy Singer, a senior research scientist at Yale University, says kids should start to learn about money when they're barely out of diapers.[10]

Kerry K. Taylor has done that with her eight-year-old daughter. Kerry gives Chloe an allowance. And when Chloe wants something, she has to save her money. "This process teaches kids a lot," says Kerry. "They learn delayed gratification. When Chloe was five years old, she wanted a watch. But it wasn't near Christmas or her birthday, so she had to save her allowance, which was $5 a week. We try to teach her that if she wants something, she has to save for it." This leads me to one of the most comprehensive studies done on children's success, one that scares plenty of Type-A parents. It's popularly known as the Marshmallow Test.

Walter Mischel created the Marshmallow Test at Stanford University's Bing Nursery School in the 1960s. His research team offered preschool-aged children a treat of their choice. They could eat that treat right away. But if they had the willpower to wait twenty minutes, they could have two treats. Plenty of the children immediately gobbled up their treats. At the time, Mischel wanted to know at what age children could learn to defer gratification. The children in the first tests went to school with Mischel's daughter. As she grew older, she came home and talked about the kids in school. Her stories fascinated Mischel. He learned that most of the children who misbehaved were the same kids who had inhaled the treats the fastest during those early experiments.

He conducted similar experiments for years. By the time the former subjects were between the ages of twenty-seven and thirty-two, he found that those who had waited to receive a second treat when they were children were leaner as adults. They had a better sense of self-worth. They were more highly educated and were better able to deal with stress.

Years later, when his first subjects were in their fifties, he conducted MRI brain scans on several of them. The adults who delayed gratification while in preschool had higher activity in their prefrontal cortex area. This part of the brain helps people control impulsive behavior. In other words, the study participants with higher activity in this area were more likely to save money instead of spend it, avoid angry arguments, stay out of the casino, avoid consumer debt, and sidestep offers to join drug cartels.

One of Mischel's research colleagues had a young child. She wanted to know if her daughter would pass the Marshmallow Test, so she tested her at home. Much to her horror, her daughter devoured the treat right away. Distraught, the researcher feared her child would live life as a failure.

Most of the time, when people talk about Mischel's experiments, they assume discipline is much like an ovarian lottery ticket: We're either born to save, eat well, and exercise or we're not. But there's more to Mischel's research. The average preschool student gobbled up their treat after less than a minute of waiting. But then Mischel taught them strategies. For example, he asked the children to imagine that the treats weren't real. This gave them the strength to wait for an average of eighteen minutes. The children also waited longer when the researchers asked them to think about fun thoughts. Visualization worked. In his book *The Marshmallow Test: Mastering Self-Control*, Mischel says delayed gratification is a skill we can learn.[11]

Here's how parents can help their kids. If they ask for something (non-birthday- or non-Christmas-related), the parents shouldn't buy it. Children should learn how to save and wait for what they want. Parents could meet them partway, paying some of the cost. But the dark side wins if parents pay the whole thing.

Spend, Save, Share

Plenty of parents also help their children develop financial muscles by guiding their kids to spend, save, and share. When a child receives their allowance, or earns money from a part-time job, the child can spend one third of it on something they want. They save one third for something they want to buy later or put it aside for investment purposes. And they donate one third to a charity of their choice.

Amanda and Andrew Anderson have been doing this with their daughters, Aleena and Andee, for the past six years. They started when the girls were eight and five years old, respectively. "Every Sunday, we give them an allowance," says Amanda. "Our daughters each have three envelopes: for saving, spending, and donating. This teaches them to keep track of their money and encourages them to be responsible global citizens."

Amanda says they'll keep doing this until their girls graduate from high school. "We give them a weekly allowance that's equal to their age," says Amanda. "That way, they receive annual wage increases, much as they would in real life. Aleena is fourteen years old, so we give her $14 a week. Andee is eleven, so we give her $11."

Both girls also do household chores. They select charities based on their interests. Some of their money has gone toward spaying and neutering street dogs, for example. They've also donated to the American Cancer Society and to the Humane Society in the United States and the Bahamas. They've donated to a local group that's raising funds to build the Girls' Safe House in Addis Ababa, Ethiopia, and they've supported a local equestrian society. Aleena and Andee also support a school-sponsored global awareness plan that helps different people in need around the world.

Amanda says her daughters sometimes experience buyer's remorse because they're spending their own money. This occurs when they buy something they don't use much, such as stuffed toys and certain articles of clothing. "They're learning real-life consequences for their financial decisions," says Amanda.

As for their savings, Amanda and Andrew spoke to the girls about the benefits of short-term savings and long-term savings. Their short-term savings might include money they put aside for holiday spending. Long-term savings include money they're putting aside for college and for investments. When I asked about challenges, Amanda offered two key pieces of advice:

- Make the agreement early on that the system is for ALL their incoming money. The girls did not like it when we told them after we started that they had to split their birthday/holiday gift money into envelopes as well. They wanted all of that for spending.

- Talk about short-term savings (and what that could be for) versus long-term savings. Decide how long is "long-term" and what constitutes using money from your savings.

Boosting Children's Savings

Parents who choose the spend, save, share strategy often say convincing their children to invest is one of their biggest challenges. Their children might understand the concept of saving for an upcoming trip or for a new tech gadget. But investing? That requires a whole other approach. Tim and Bettina Woods found one that works for their three children.

Their nine-year-old son, Levi, loves investing his money. And their other son, seven-year-old Harper, figures that whatever his big brother does must be cool, so he invests his savings too. "We call it Dad Bank," says Tim. He offers his kids 6 percent monthly interest on their savings. "Levi has definitely become a better saver," says Tim. While we were chatting, Levi said, "I don't want to buy anything. I want to keep the deal going because the longer I save it, then I get more and more money." Their youngest child, four-year-old Reese, is still too young to understand the concept of investing. But in a few years, she'll be encouraged to follow in her older brothers' footsteps.

Tim says doing the math sometimes gets complicated when you're offering 6 percent per month. That's why some parents encourage their kids to save by doubling whatever their children deposit into the bank of mom or dad. This makes it real, like a corporate 401(k). When employees add money, the employer often provides a matching contribution. But parents should set clear rules about how long the money must remain "invested" before the children can access it.

Your Children Can Leverage Financial Gains with Time

If you didn't use a spend, save, share strategy with your children and they're now teenagers, you might wonder how you can convince them to open and contribute to real investment accounts. This may not be easy. They're exposed to flashy lifestyles of media-blown celebrities. They're living in a world where goods are delivered more than ever after a couple of taps on an iPhone. Their heroes on Netflix don't leap tall buildings in a single bound. These days, they drive flashy cars, live in lovely homes, and look drop-dead gorgeous (often artificially enhanced).

Responsible money lessons often fall flat against frivolous, unrealistic backdrops. But if you're a parent, here's something you could try. It isn't foolproof (what is?), but I've convinced plenty of high school students to spend less and invest—without telling them to do it.

Here's what I did. At the beginning of the year, I asked them to document their personal expenses, just as I believe everyone should. Most of them used an expense tracking app on their phone. If their family took a vacation, I asked them to record their flight or hotel costs. When a family member went grocery shopping, the student took the receipt and divided it by the number of family members. That gave them an idea of how much their food cost. They then entered that in their expense tracker. And when they went to a movie, met friends for lunch, bought clothing, or paid their cell phone bill (side note: parents should insist kids contribute to the data phone plan), they recorded the costs on their app. Your children could track their costs as soon as they're old enough for a phone.

To introduce the idea of opportunity costs (see chapter 5), I showed my students how to access historical stock market investment returns, using portfoliovisualizer.com.

Before long, I could walk into the classroom, give them some random dates, and ask them to determine how much $1,000 would have grown over those time periods. They learned that markets fluctuate. Sometimes I picked dates that didn't produce great results: 2006–2009, for example. Using portfoliovisualizer.com, they could see that a $1,000 investment in the US stock market in January 2006 would have shrunk to about $987 three years later.

But they also saw mouthwatering gains for those who were patient and invested long-term. If the same $1,000 were invested in the US stock market in 2006, and if it remained invested until the end of 2020, it would have quadrupled in value, to about $4,000.

I then gave students an Opportunity Cost Project where they created a few money-spending scenarios of their own. Some considered the cost of coffee and a muffin at Starbucks three times a week versus once every two weeks. Others wondered how much a family could save if they bought groceries in a low-cost supermarket instead of an expensive, hip one.

They then calculated how those savings could grow if they were invested in the stock market. The results shocked everyone, including me. For example, if one person spends $16 more per week at Starbucks than a second person, and if the $16 savings averaged 8 percent per year, it would grow to $103,900 over three decades. They worked this out using the compound interest calculator at moneychimp.com.

Here's how this might work with your own kids. Document your own spending and share the records. Ask them where they think you could cut costs. Using an online compound interest calculator, ask them to help you calculate how those savings might grow over time.

People who don't want to save won't save. But when they understand compound interest and opportunity costs, it can change their view. One year, 40 percent of my American students opened investment accounts with Vanguard—and I didn't overtly try to convince them.

Financial lessons are important. Life can be less stressful and empowering for your children if they start this part off right. That's why you should prioritize this at home. Model smart financial planning. Let them see you tracking the household expenses. Ask them to help. Talk about money and generosity. And do what you can to help them invest.

How American children can invest

Helping your children to invest doesn't mean giving them money. They'll build bigger financial muscles if they earn the money on their own. American children with taxable income could open a custodial or guardian IRA with a company like Vanguard or Schwab. But they must earn an income during the year they make the contribution. Roth IRAs make more sense than traditional IRAs because most kids don't earn enough money to benefit from the up-front tax deduction associated with traditional IRAs.[12]

And what about American children without a taxable income? If they want to invest their allowance or birthday money, they could open a custodial account under their state's *Uniform Gifts to Minors Act (UGMA)* or *Uniform Transfers to Minors Act (UTMA)*. There's no limit to how much money they can invest each year. And the child gains legal control of the account once they reach the age of majority. Depending on your state, that will be between the ages of eighteen and twenty-one.

That's what Chase Schachenman did. He was one of my personal finance students. Now twenty-four years old, the software engineer has been investing for eight years. "I'm glad I started early," he says. "My money will work hard for me, so I don't have to work as hard for money."

And if you would like a guide, PlanVision can help you set up an account for your children, using Vanguard, Schwab, Fidelity, or any brokerage of your choice. PlanVision charges a one-time fee of about $200 at the time of writing. That cost includes any follow-up questions you might have over the following twelve months.

How Canadian children can invest

Canadian children can't open retirement accounts like TFSAs or RRSPs until they reach at least eighteen or nineteen years of age, depending on which province or territory they live in. But they can open custodial accounts, much like Chase Schachenman did. Seventeen-year-old Canadian Taylor Howe works part-time at a restaurant. Like Chase, she opened a custodial (or in-trust) account. It's officially in her name and her mother's name. And when Taylor turns nineteen, the account ownership fully reverts to her.

In chapter 8, I listed some investment firms through which you could build a portfolio of index funds. Contact one of them. Ask them to help you set up a custodial or in-trust account for your children. "I don't think many parents consider using an in-trust investment for their kids," says David Dyck, head of Client Services at Canada's CI Direct Investing. "When parents think about 'trust accounts' they're more likely to think of an ultra-wealthy family setting up a trust fund instead of a typical family starting an investment with money saved from birthday gifts and allowance."

Taylor Howe adds $100 a month to her robo-advisor account at CI Direct Investing. "My main motivation for this is to be lazy," she says. "If I invest when I'm young, I won't have to work so hard and

I won't have to worry about money." Her mother, Samantha White, also helped her two other children, fifteen-year-old Sydney and thirteen-year-old Liam, set up in-trust accounts as well. Samantha insists they earn and invest their own money.

She and her husband, Jeff Howe, contribute money to their children's education accounts. But like many money-savvy parents, they won't foot the entire ride. As for the investment accounts that aren't earmarked for education, the couple won't contribute anything. Samantha says, "If I gave them money, it would probably make them weak, denying them feelings of pride and accomplishment."

How British children can invest

British parents can open tax-efficient accounts called Junior ISAs for their children. Any parent or legal guardian can set one up in a child's name. Friends and family can also gift money. There's a limit to how much money can be deposited into a Junior ISA each year (it was £9,000 for the 2020–2021 taxation year). And once children reach eighteen years of age, they gain full access to the account. British parents could set up accounts with any number of firms, including ultra-low-cost Vanguard UK. From there, they could invest the money in an all-in-one, fully diversified portfolio of index funds.

They could also select a Junior SIPP for their children. In this case, the child gains control of the investments at age eighteen but doesn't get access to the money until they're fifty-five. The UK government provides an incentive to contribute to a Junior SIPP. For example, in 2021, if a parent added £3,600 it would only cost £2,880 because the government would provide £720 in tax relief. Parents should be careful, though. They should ensure their children earn some of this money on their own, so they build financial muscles instead of a weak trust-funder's expectation.

The parent and child could add more money than a combined £3,600 in 2021, but doing so wouldn't provide further tax relief. That's why, if parents reach the maximum tax relief threshold but still want to add money (or even better, if the children earn money they want to add), they can do so through a Junior ISA.[13]

Opportunities are available in other countries too, so contact a brokerage or financial firm and ask how to do it.

Should Parents Pay for Their Children's College Education?

When I met Jacob Collums, he was a thirty-one-year-old engineer. We met in Oman, after his company sent him to the Middle East on a two-week assignment. Jacob works for a business that designs and manufactures flow and pressure control technologies for the oil and gas industry. One of the plants in Oman wasn't performing as well as expected. Jacob's job was to "fix the problem." I was intrigued. This fresh-faced engineer looked more like a college kid than the mastermind for a multimillion-dollar inefficiency problem. We met at Nomadic Desert Camp, a family-run tour company that offers desert camp excursions. One night, Jacob and I were lying on mats, staring up at the stars. That's when I began to ask questions.

I want to start by saying that I have few natural talents. I have no ability, for example, to recognize faces. I could meet you at a party. We might talk for hours. But I couldn't pick you out of a lineup the very next day. Nor can I remember what dresser drawers I put my clothing in. Before my wife put an end to it, I labeled drawers with masking tape: underwear drawer, t-shirt drawer, socks drawer. But there's one thing I'm getting good at: I can usually tell if a young person's parents paid their entire college bill.

My methods are hardly scientific. But as a personal finance teacher, global nomad, and, some might say, intrusively curious guy, I ask hundreds of young people similar sets of questions: How did you acquire money when you were a kid? Are you investing money? Do you own a car? If so, do you lease, did you buy a new one, or did you buy a second-hand car? How much do you pay for rent? Do you carry a credit card balance? What do you do for a living? Much to my mother-in-law's horror (she says nobody should ever talk about money), I eventually come round to asking all these questions— although never all at once. Perhaps that's why nobody has run so far.

Over time, I've learned that those who paid for some or all of their college costs appear to have better money management skills. They tend to be more frugal. Most earned their own money as kids. Many invest money. If they own a car, they bought a low-cost second-hand one. They pay low levels of rent and rarely carry outstanding credit card debt.

Jacob fit the bill. When he was a young child, he helped his family with their business. His role became a bigger one when he was old enough to drive. "As a sixteen-year-old, I woke up at 5:00 am, hooked a homemade trailer to my truck and hit the nicer neighborhood garage sales as soon as they opened. The early bird always gets the good cheap furniture. Then I would take the furniture back to my parents' store so they could sell it."

When we met, he was investing the maximum amount (for a matching contribution) into his company's 401(k). He rented a room for $400 a month in somebody else's house. Until recently, he drove a used pickup truck that he bought back in high school. "It finally died a few months ago," he said. "So I replaced it with a 2011 Toyota Tacoma truck."

While he was in college, he continued to work part-time, trying to limit the amount of money he had to borrow. By the time we met, he had just paid off his $65,000 student loan debt.

Even before I learned about his loan, I guessed Jacob's parents probably didn't pay the entire bill for his college education. They could have. But they chose not to. My observations might upset a few people, so let me add this: Many students who receive free college rides from their parents still do well. Many end up responsible and highly ambitious. But the right dose of financial adversity works much like Popeye's spinach. As Jacob looked up at the stars he said,

"If life were a financial race, it would be a marathon. I began behind the start line with student loan debt. But I've been training all my life. Most of those who were given a free ride to the 8-mile marker haven't trained to run. I'll catch most of them." His quiet confidence came from his sense of achievement. I have no doubt that he's right. The English writer and philosopher William Hazlitt summed it up best: "Prosperity is a great teacher; adversity is a greater."

Malcolm Gladwell, in his book *David and Goliath*, says the right amount of adversity is key to success. In an interview with Wharton management professor Adam Grant, Gladwell said, "We understand linear relationships. We understand diminishing marginal returns. We cannot understand the idea of the inverted U: The same thing that is positive at one level can turn negative at the other—with hugely deleterious consequences."[14]

In the case of college costs, too much can be crushing. CNBC's Susie Poppick reported that the average college graduate leaves school with nearly $30,000 in student loan debt. Many get crushed with two or three times more.[15] That's why, when it comes to paying for college, there has to be a sweet spot. Laura Hamilton, an associate professor of sociology at the University of California, Merced, compared the grades of students at four-year colleges. She found that the more money that parents paid toward their children's education, the lower their academic performance.[16] She feels that it detracted from their drive.

But those who didn't receive any financial help had lower odds of graduating. The realities of a growing debt proved too much. This mirrors Malcolm Gladwell's inverted U. Too little help can hurt. Too much can hinder. So how much should you pay toward your child's education? That's up to you as the parent. But a sweet spot might be half.

Would an Ivy League College
Help Your Kids Come Out Ahead?

I opened this book with a question I used to ask my students: "Why do you want to do well in school?" After getting over the initial shock, they echoed what they had likely heard from their parents: if they do well in school, they'll get into a good college. In their eyes, this would lead to success: a job that pays a lot of money. When I kept asking *why* they wanted that, they ultimately settled on responses suggesting that this would make them happy. That's a narrow definition of success, of course. But even the notion that a high-status school would bring them more wealth might be a flat-Earth fallacy. Plenty of my former students figured that out for themselves.

One of them was a boy named John. The Stanford-bound high school senior was a student in my personal finance class. He had just finished a series of calculations that blew apart what his parents (and society in general) believed about high-status colleges. That's why he looked liked a guy who just found hair in his favorite soup.

Ivy League colleges cost more than less prestigious schools, so I asked my students to figure out whether they were worth the extra cost. I posed the question as a lesson on "opportunity cost," and to be honest, I didn't know the answer. At the time, I just wanted the kids to understand the time value of money.

For example, if one student spends $220,000 on a Stanford degree and a second spends $86,980 for four years at Texas A&M University, what is the true cost of going to Stanford after loan interest payments? And what if the state college graduate invested what the Stanford graduate paid in interest-ballooned fees? Who comes out ahead?

John checked comparative college costs and median expected salaries for new graduates, as well as mid-career salaries at a variety of schools.[17]

He was certain that the Ivy League colleges would give him a leg up. But he was disappointed. And the vast majority of my students, running the numbers with a variety of different schools, came to the same conclusion.

Then one of the girls said, "None of us will pay for our college expenses, so it shouldn't matter. Our parents are paying." She was partly right. I was teaching at an expensive private school, where most of the parents could afford Harvard tuition for their kids.

But then I posed a different question: "What if your parents gave you the difference between an Ivy League college cost and a state college cost? And what if you invested it?" A twenty-two year-old with $134,000 in a portfolio of index funds would have $3.6 million at age sixty-five if she earned an 8 percent return. She would have $5.4 million if she earned 9 percent. My students concluded (in most cases) again that the Ivy Leaguer had virtually no chance of financially catching up.

You might disagree, suggesting that the Ivy League schools offer a greater number of connections. Their graduates' salaries are also much higher. But Alan Krueger and Stacy Berg Dale's studies, published by the National Bureau of Economic Research, says this ignores an important variable.[18]

In 1976, Krueger, a Princeton economist, and Dale, affiliated with the Andrew W. Mellon Foundation, began comparing students who entered Ivy League colleges with students who went to less prestigious schools. They found, for instance, that by 1995, Yale graduates were earning 30 percent more money than Tulane graduates. But that didn't isolate the variable they sought: whether Ivy League schools themselves added financial value.

To isolate the variable, they sought students who were smart enough to earn Ivy League acceptance but had declined their offer, choosing less prestigious schools instead. By their peak earning years, the isolated variable (the college) had no bearing on the graduates' salaries. Those who were smart and driven enough to gain Ivy League acceptance but chose to go elsewhere earned the same as their Ivy League contemporaries. Their financial net worths were about the same as well.

If Krueger and Dale calculated the opportunity costs of Ivy Leagues (loan interest costs coupled with future investment benefits), the stronger state school kids would run circles around the ivy patch. That's why, if you want your child to become an Ivy League grad for financial advantages (and not just bragging rights), that reasoning might be flawed.

If your child insists on an Ivy League education and you can't afford to pay the bill and there's no financial aid or scholarship available, don't discourage your child. Ask them to do an opportunity cost assessment. They can start by finding starting median salaries online for different college graduates. If they're smart enough to get into an Ivy League school, research suggests they will earn similar salaries to Ivy League grads, even if they go to less prestigious schools. But you might not have to bring that up. Use typical starting salaries for graduates of high-cost and lower-cost institutions. They can also find tuition and room-and-board costs. At that point, show them how to do a long-term opportunity cost assessment, much as I did with my massages in chapter 5. Students could start by using payscale.com for different reported salaries and college costs.[19]

This isn't to dissuade anyone from an Ivy League education (or higher education in general). But always determine the potential opportunity cost before making a decision.

Getting Real with Kids

If you aren't from a high-income family, here's something else you could try to develop financial awareness among your kids. I was one of four children. My father was a mechanic and my mom worked part-time at a retail store. She always wanted to be home when we finished school so we didn't get into trouble or destroy the house (brother-on-brother living room brawls often busted things).

We didn't have a lot of money. And as a teenaged boy, I didn't know anything about household income and expenses. One day, my mom brought me to the kitchen table and showed me how much money my dad made. I still remember. It was about $30,000 a year. She actually had one of his biweekly checks. At first, I thought it was a fortune. Then she showed me what they paid in income taxes, insurance, food costs, fuel for the car, mortgage fees, holiday costs for our summer camping trips, heat and water for the home, Christmas gifts, sports fees, and telephone and television cable costs. By the time we subtracted everything, I had a new respect. I was amazed to learn how hard they worked so we could live.

My mom's method might not work for high-income families. But if you're a parent in a low- to middle-income family, this is a golden lesson. My mom didn't do it to make me feel bad. Instead, she lovingly gave me one of the best educations I've ever had.

Children learn the best financial lessons when their parents model sound financial practices. So track your expenses and show your children. When you pay your credit balance in full at the end of the month, explain what you've done and why you aren't making minimum payments. If you have to make a minimum payment, explain why and talk about what that means.

When you donate money, talk to your children about it. When you invest, explain why. You might say, "This is so I don't have to sleep on your couch and eat your food when I get older." Explain how you invest. Children won't learn financial lessons by osmosis. And success and happiness won't come from a fancy school. Instead, they will come as a result of your children's grit, generosity, sense of community, relationships, health, and financial sense. Their education shouldn't begin or end at school. They'll get most of it at home. So, to raise successful kids, model everything you can.

A Few Tips for Living Well

- Encourage children to begin household chores at a young age and limit their screen time. Their social skills, discipline, and responsibility will improve as a result.

- Consider splitting money they earn, or are given, into thirds so they can spend, share (donate), and invest. Set clear ground rules ahead of time.

- Set up an investment account for your child, but ensure that they contribute their own money to it. To encourage them to save, consider matching a portion of what they save.

- If you have the financial means, help your child pay for their college fees. But even if you're wealthy, make sure they pay some of the costs themselves.

- Model sound financial practices at home (children learn more from what they see than from what you could ever say).

- Provide your children with opportunities to build their own financial muscles, responsibility, and personal pride.

12

RETHINK RETIREMENT
Boost Well-Being and Longevity
in Your Golden Years

I N 2005, I WAS teaching a high school English class when a student,
who obviously didn't want to talk about Shakespeare, dragged me
off topic. He asked, "Is there anything you wish you could do, but
haven't done yet?" I took the bait—much to his delight.

"I would like to meet Warren Buffett and Muhammad Ali," I said.
One of my students put up her hand and said, "Mr. Hallam, my mom
has a high-level position with JPMorgan Chase. She has always
wanted to meet Warren Buffett. But she hasn't been able to. If she
can't meet him, I don't think you will."

I wanted to respect that student while communicating an important lesson. I said, "We're often afraid to try new things. We fear
failure, so when we fail at something, we're often afraid to try again.
And sometimes, other people say we won't succeed at something
because they, or someone they know, tried the same thing and failed.
Listening to such advice can be like putting failures into your future."
Quoting the Hall of Fame hockey star Wayne Gretzky, I said, "You
miss 100 percent of the shots you don't take."

Then I had an idea. The students and I drafted a letter to Warren
Buffett. Of course, it wasn't part of the curriculum. But I figured it

related to life and (at least in part) an English class. We started with a catchy lead. We also used humor, while trying to avoid coming across as mentally unhinged (that last part is open to debate). "I would like to come to Berkshire Hathaway's annual general meeting," I wrote. "But there aren't any hostels in Omaha, and hotels are expensive, so I was wondering if I could sleep on your sofa or in your garage."

I once read that Buffett's wife bought bulk quantities of his favorite drink, Cherry Coke, at Costco, so I joked about slipping my camping mat in his garage between the stacks of Coke and his lawn mower.

When we finished the draft I copied it onto a postcard and mailed it to Buffett's business address in Omaha, Nebraska. Some of my students laughed and called me crazy. But I figured, "Why not try?" At the time, Buffett was seventy-five years old. I didn't know how much longer he would continue to work. If he retired, or were called to his Ultimate Reward, I might never meet him. I figured that even this long shot could be a decent lesson for the kids.

It turns out Buffett loved the postcard. He sent a copy to his friend at the *Wall Street Journal.* They published a story titled "Warren Buffett's Bed & Breakfast." CNBC interviewed me in Omaha. And although I didn't really sleep in Buffett's garage, I joked about the postcard in person with Buffett, Charlie Munger, and their good friend Bill Gates.

I was wrong, however, to think that Buffett would soon retire. Fifteen years later, at ninety years of age, he was still the chairman of Berkshire Hathaway. Plenty of people have a tough time making sense of this. After all, Buffett had several million dollars by his mid-thirties. By 2020, he had almost $90 billion. Why wouldn't he just retire and enjoy the life of Riley?

I'll admit, I wondered the same thing for years. But I've since learned that conventional retirement might be overrated. I'm not suggesting you die at your desk. That's bat-poop crazy, especially if you hate your job. But research suggests a flexible view of retirement might beat retiring early.

Could a Job Extend Your Life?

Shigeaki Hinohara, a Japanese physician, was chairman emeritus of St. Luke's International University and honorary president of St. Luke's International Hospital. He said it's healthier for people to work long past the age of sixty-five. Hinohara died when he was 105 years old. He was still working with patients just a few months before his death. In fact, his date book included five more years of appointments.[1]

Most people in Western cultures aspire to retire. But it's different in Japan. A 2017 survey revealed that 43 percent of Japanese workers plan to keep working after they reach traditional retirement age.[2]

And most of those people aren't doing it for the money. In Japan, an old man raking leaves in a park might be a multimillionaire. Part-time work keeps seniors moving. It keeps them engaged with younger people. There are even 1,600 employment agencies in Japan that are specifically for seniors. The work opportunities include outdoor and indoor jobs like cleaning up parks, weeding, managing bicycle parking lots, hanging posters, and doing office reception work or general building maintenance.[3]

Americans typically retire at a younger age. But they don't live as long as the Japanese. According to the US Department of Health and Human Services, American women live an average of 81.1 years and American men an average of 76.1 years.[4] Japanese longevity is legendary. On average, women live 87.45 years and men 81.41 years.[5]

In part, we could attribute Japanese people's longevity to their healthy diet. But the Japanese tendency to continue working longer might play a role as well. After all, older Americans who continue to work past traditional retirement age live longer too. In a study published in the *Journal of Epidemiology and Community Health*, researchers found that people who worked even just one year past traditional retirement age had between a 9 and 11 percent lower risk of dying over the eighteen-year study, regardless of their initial health status.[6]

Harvard Health references a study published in the CDC journal *Preventing Chronic Disease* that found that people who continued working past the age of sixty-five were three times more likely to be in good health than those who retired earlier.[7] And older people who continue working also have lower odds of developing dementia.[8]

Genetics play a role, of course. But our brains are like a muscle. We either use it or we lose it. That might be one of the reasons Warren Buffett remains so sharp. As mentioned earlier, he continues to run Berkshire Hathaway at ninety years of age. Even more extraordinary is that the company's co-chairman, Charlie Munger, is seven years older than Buffett. He turned ninety-seven on New Year's Day, 2021. Perhaps that's why Buffett adopted one of Munger's mantras: "All I want to know is where I'm going to die so I'll never go there."[9]

Retirement Numbers Can Be Fluid

Still, many people wonder how much money they'll need to retire, as if it's a magic number they can find online. But retirement is much like a fingerprint. No two people are the same. How much you might require in an investment portfolio depends on your mindset, your flexibility, and the cost of living where you plan to live. There's also a question of alternative income sources. Will you have a pension, a part-time job, or real estate income?

Plenty of investment firms have online retirement calculators. If you enter your savings rate, your desired annual retirement income, and your current portfolio size, they can spit out how much you need and suggest if you're on track. Wealthsimple, for example, has one for Canadians. SmartAsset has a good one for Americans that also calculates Social Security payments.

There's some sense behind their numbers. But many financial advisors overstate how much money people need. My wife and I have met plenty of North Americans and Europeans who happily spend far less than the typical retiree is supposed to spend. We've met them living in Canada, the United States, and low-cost countries like Portugal, Mexico, Thailand, Vietnam, Bali, Malaysia, and Costa Rica.

Part-Time Working Wonders

Many people work part-time after they retire from full-time work, no matter where they live. The socialization aspect of working can increase longevity. If the job requires some physical activity, it can also boost physical health. But perhaps most importantly, part-time employment gives them *ikigai*, a Japanese term that means a sense of purpose, a reason to be. Having purpose boosts happiness and fights mortality.

The money retirees earn from a part-time job can also reduce financial stress. Consider a part-time job that pays $15,000 a year. That's equal to an investment portfolio worth $375,000. After all, if a retiree withdrew an inflation-adjusted 4 percent per year from $375,000, that would equal $15,000 (see chapter 9).

Are Retirement Costs Smile-Shaped?

Most retirees and semi-retirees spend far less than they did when they were working full-time. In most cases, they no longer have a mortgage if they own their home (it's always a good idea to pay that off). They no longer have to save money for retirement or college expenses for their kids. And their adult children shouldn't be attached to their financial umbilical cords.

Retirees' transportation costs also plummet, as they don't have to go to their workplace every day. Their wardrobe costs drop as well, as they're no longer required to "look professional" or buy protective clothing. If they go bald (like me), they save money on haircuts too.

Plenty of people believe retirement costs tend to be smile-shaped. Spending is supposed to be higher during the first phase of retirement, when people often make the most of their free time by dining out more and traveling. Then their costs drop, only to rise again in their later years with increased medical costs. But research suggests that, for most retirees, costs continue to drop as they age, with only a small percentage paying higher medical costs during their final couple years of life.[9]

Why Defer a Pension with Part-Time Work?

Part-time work (or semi-retirement) obviously provides more flexibility than a full-time grind. In some cases, if you do it right, you can enjoy life as you did when you were a kid. You can tinker with projects that pay a bit of money. My uncle managed a bank, but after he retired he applied for a part-time job at a hardware store. My father did some consulting. My father's friend (a guy named Robin Hood, for real) got a part-time job at Costco. None of them needed the money. But it helped. And when they wanted time off for an adventure, they were able to quit or take an extended leave. For them, it's reminiscent of their younger days, before they had careers, mortgages, and kids.

Part-time work can also help people defer their pensions. For example, if someone were eligible to collect a pension at age sixty-two but they deferred those payments, they could earn a much higher income later. This might come in handy if they're among those who require money to cover higher medical or care facility costs.

The benefits of deferring pension withdrawals apply to most corporate defined benefit pensions. They also apply to most state-sponsored plans, such as the Canada Pension Plan (CPP), the UK state pension, and America's Social Security.

For example, two years ago, my friend Kathy Salvadore turned sixty-two. That meant she was old enough to qualify for US Social Security payments. But she said no, at least for now. Seniors with enough money, or those with part-time jobs, should consider doing the same.

That's based on research from Social Security experts Laurence Kotlikoff, William Reichenstein, and Russell Settle. Kotlikoff is the founder of MaximizeMySocialSecurity.com, Reichenstein co-authored *Social Security Strategies: How to Optimize Retirement Benefits,*[10] and Settle is the founder of SocialSecurityChoices.com.

At sixty-two years old, Kathy was still doing triathlons. Plenty of athletes half her age still wheeze in her wake. If she defers her Social Security payments until she's sixty-six, she'll get 33 percent more each month, plus a cost of living adjustment. If she suspends those payments until she's seventy, her monthly Social Security payments will be 76 percent higher than if she had started to take the money when she turned sixty-two.

Plenty of Americans wonder about a break-even point for Social Security. They wonder how long they would have to live for the waiting to make sense. It's about seventy-eight years of age.

Let's assume you took the monthly payments at age sixty-two and died just before your seventy-eighth birthday. In that case, you would have received more total income than if you had deferred taking payments until you were seventy.

But if you deferred payments until you were seventy years of age and lived until you were seventy-nine, you would have earned more total income compared to taking the money at age sixty-two. It sounds morbid, but some people look at life-expectancy charts to guess how long they might live. These numbers, however, are based on life expectancy at birth. If you're still healthy in your sixties, toss those figures out. For example, the average sixty-five-year-old American man lives until he's almost eighty-three. The average sixty-five-year-old American woman lives until she's almost eighty-six.[11]

It's also worth noting that Americans rank just 46th in the global life expectancy rankings.[12] So, if you're from another developed country, you might live even longer. That's another good reason to defer a pension if you can afford it. And, if you're among the few whose medical costs ramp up with age, you'll be in a better position to afford them.

Retirement Roads Less Traveled

In chapter 3, I introduced Amy Halloran-Steiner and her husband, Silas. They left their full-time grind to travel for several months with their two children in Costa Rica. It was much like a mini-retirement. They explored, volunteered, and broadened their horizons.

For several reasons, mini-retirements might be far more rewarding than a single big one. While traveling, I've met plenty of people who quit their jobs or took sabbaticals. Stefan Sagmeister, a designer in New York, does this every seven years. He says the average person spends twenty-five years learning, forty years working, and fifteen years in retirement. To mix things up, he "felt it might be helpful to cut out five of those retirement years and intersperse them with working years." He claims the sabbaticals enhance his creativity, which improves his work when he returns to employment.

Canadian James Dalziel worked as the head of the United World College in Singapore. As a recruiter, he sees similar benefits to taking extended time away from work. That's why he encouraged his international teaching staff to "boomerang." Boomeranging means quitting for at least a year to pursue personal interests. With luck, they'll eventually return to his school with new ideas and a fresh outlook.

A couple of years ago, Pele and I met an Australian couple on a mini-retirement with their two children. They were anchored off Juara Beach on Pulau Tioman, a picture-perfect Malaysian island in the South China Sea. The couple wasn't wealthy. But they had quit their jobs, bought a sailboat, and decided to homeschool their kids for two years.

Sabbaticals don't have to be expensive. Just pick the right country. Pele and I often spend less money traveling than we would if we stayed at home. And plenty of people spend a fraction of what we do. Creativity helps.

One of my friends loves WWOOFing. WWOOF is an international organization that offers volunteers room and board in exchange for working on organic, sustainable farms.[13] You could also try helpx.net. They list hosts around the world who are willing to trade food and accommodation in exchange for work on community projects and organic farms, at homestays, in backpacker hostels, and on sailing boats. Workaway.info offers similar opportunities for people around the world.

You could also house-sit. Trustedhousesitters.com is one of the most established sites for matching up house-sitters and houses. Other sites you could look at are nomador.com, mindmyhouse.com, and housecarers.com.

I had no idea how this worked until I met Kelly Hayes-Raitt. We met at a writers' group meeting in Mexico. After the meeting, she offered to drive me back to the home Pele and I were renting. "Do you want to see where I live?" she asked. "It's on the way." She turned onto a steep road that climbed above the town of San Antonio. We passed some of the region's biggest houses before Kelly stopped the car.

Kelly's home had three massive patios. Each provided a breathtaking view of Mexico's largest lake. She had a pool and a full-time gardener. "What do you pay for this place?" I asked. "Nothing," she replied. Kelly joked about being a "house-sitting diva." She spent four months a year staying in the same home, caring for a dog she grew to love, and the rest of the year house-sitting in other locations around the world. That's when it dawned on me. You might not need a pension, a large investment portfolio, or even a mortgage-free home to retire in luxury.

Kelly's book, *How to Become a Housesitter: Insider Tips from the HouseSit Diva*, offers tips on finding fabulous digs, whether you're looking for a short holiday abroad or seeking a new full-time lifestyle. The book's first few pages include a questionnaire: "Is Housesitting Right for Me?" After all, it won't suit everyone. Her third chapter, "The Bitch & The Chow," contains an honest account of how things can go sideways. Plenty of Kelly's tips explain her mistakes—so you don't have to make them.[14]

Perhaps you're thrilled by the thought of a mini-retirement but your life is too complicated, so you want to wait until you're old. That's a valid reason, but it's also worth remembering that old age isn't guaranteed. We all know people the Grim Reaper snatched early.

Retiring Where It's Cheap

When Pele and I quit our full-time teaching jobs in 2014, we spent six years traveling. Everything I thought I knew about financial planning went out the window—fast. Few financial advisors would ever say, "Jane, I know you love shoveling snow off your driveway every winter. But if you're willing to sacrifice frostbite to spend November to March near a tropical beach, you could quit that full-time job you hate five years ahead of schedule."

A few months after quitting our full-time teaching jobs, we flew to Guadalajara, Mexico. From there, we took a twenty-five-minute taxi ride to the lakeside town of Chapala. It's just 5 miles (8 kilometers) from what might be America's favorite retirement destination, the lakeside town of Ajijic. We had a fabulous view of Lake Chapala from the rooftop patio of the small home we rented which was about a two-minute walk from the bus station.

Each morning, I ran along the mountain paths high above the town. After breakfast, we usually took a local bus to Ajijic. I took Spanish language classes. Twice a week, we met up with a hiking group. I also joined a writers' club, where I met my housesitting friend, Kelly. Pele went to a yoga center owned by a Mexican/

Canadian couple. We lived on about $1,600 a month, enjoying restaurant meals at least three times a week.

Longtime resident Jim Cook told me the influx of retirees to Mexico has increased home prices and the cost of real estate rentals in Lake Chapala. But that hasn't deterred record numbers of new arrivals. "Plenty of things are more expensive than they used to be, such as gas prices," says Jim, "but with the peso near an all-time low, other things, such as restaurant meals, cost as little as they did when my wife and I moved to the region ten years ago."

Jim and his wife, Carole, live on a hill above the town of Ajijic. They eat in restaurants at least three days a week. They own their own home, so they don't have to pay rent. It costs them about $1,600 a month to live in Ajijic, including medical insurance. Plenty of American couples, if they don't spend foolishly, can live well there on their Social Security checks. Such is the case with two of my close friends. They don't have a single penny in a private retirement account, yet they can dine out, afford gym memberships, enjoy weekly massages, and rent a lovely bungalow in a small complex with a swimming pool.

In 1997, Dr. David Truly started Lake Chapala's most extensive retirement study. He surveys local retirees who have moved from other countries. My wife and I joined him for lunch, after he shared some of his research at an information session in Ajijic.

"American retirees have been coming for years," he said. "The region first attracted tourists in the early 1900s when the Mexican president encouraged international tourism. But the concept of retiring kicked in during the 1950s. Since then, Lake Chapala's popularity has ebbed and flowed."

Truly recently moved from Lake Chapala to Austin, Texas, so his young children could attend a US school. But he continues to research retirement in Mexico and has noted several changes: "Back in 1997, most of the retirees stayed for just a handful of years. But changes are taking place. People are staying longer."

Quality assisted-living programs in North America are getting more expensive. Truly says this might be why Mexico could be shifting "from a retirement place to a dying place." Some people call Lake Chapala "The Waiting Room." Low-cost nursing homes are popping up everywhere. Plenty are discrete. In 2019, Pele and I were enjoying a meal at a restaurant in Lake Chapala; two retired American women sat nearby. When the women finished their meals, they paid their bill and then walked to the house next door. From the outside, it looked like just another home. But it was the Mi Casita Nursing Home and Assisted Living Center.

It costs $1,500 to $2,000 per month depending on the care required. That's cheaper than apartment rental costs in some North American cities. It also contrasts sharply with assisted-living costs in the United States, where private rooms cost more than $8,000 a month according to the Genworth Cost of Care Survey.[15]

Mexico's affordability is attractive to a lot of people. Truly's earlier studies showed that 50 percent of the region's retirees reported coming to the area because they wanted to reduce their living costs. As US medical costs have risen, that number has increased to 80 percent.

Those flocking to the region have also made some fast decisions. According to Truly's surveys, people used to visit seven times before they decided to retire in Lake Chapala. "On average, people now visit just twice before they decide to move here," he says.

Mexico isn't the only choice, of course. While traveling, Pele and I met European and North American retirees who lived part-time or full-time in Thailand, Malaysia, Vietnam, Portugal, and Costa Rica. Each country is far cheaper than Australia, New Zealand, Canada, the UK, or the United States.

If you do decide to move to a low-cost destination, keep an open mind and embrace your new culture. You might be able to afford a better lifestyle on less, but get involved in the local community and learn what you can from them. As a result, your experience will be richer as you contribute to a new community.

Longevity in the Mind

Nobody knows how long they're going to live. We might look at life-expectancy tables. Or we might estimate our expiration dates based on lifestyle and age. Statistically, people who smoke or live unhealthy lifestyles don't live as long as those who eat well, exercise, and don't smoke.

But even young, fit people can kick the bucket anytime. We've all read stories about cancer (and any number of other nasty diseases) ending someone's party prematurely. There's a lot we can't control. But we can control our perception of time.

Think back to a vacation when you explored something new. I'm not referring to a holiday spent lying on a beach and drinking margaritas. Sand is sand. Water is water. Margaritas all look the same and pretty much taste the same. I'm referring to when you last explored.

Perhaps, after a week of such exploring, you recalled the day you arrived. You might have asked, "Was it just a week ago that we landed in this place?" That's how I feel when I visit somewhere different. Time seems to expand. My days and weeks stretch when I see new things, experience new cultures, learn bits of new languages, and try different foods. Variety stretches my perception of time.

Apparently, that isn't just my observation. Richard A. Friedman, a professor of clinical psychology at Weill Cornell Medical College, wrote in a *New York Times* article, "Attention and memory play a part in our perception of time. To accurately gauge the passage of time required to accomplish a given task, you have to be able to focus and remember a sequence of information."[16]

Think back to when you were a kid. Time crawled. When you're an adult, time appears to race. True, one year is a greater percentage of a ten-year-old's life than a fifty year-old's. But adults also experience fewer novel things. We get stuck in routines and the weeks fly by.

But if we keep learning, we can change that. We can learn a new language or a new instrument or challenge ourselves with a different job. Mini-retirements, especially if they involve travel to foreign lands add new experiences. That, in turn, expands our perception of time.

We get to live longer—without chronologically living longer.

This brings me back to my high school students and that story about Warren Buffett. Too many times, we place limits on ourselves. Far too often, we focus on why we can't do something instead of *how* we can. We might say mini-retirements are not practical. We might say we don't have time to keep learning. We might say nobody would hire us for a part-time job.

But it's best to shoot for a healthy, long life, filled with constant learning. Perhaps Henry Ford said it best: "Obstacles are those frightful things you see when you take your eyes off your goal."

A Few Tips for Living Well

- Early or conventional retirement is overrated. Finding the balance between work and play is the key to success.

- Research suggests you might enjoy a longer, happier, healthier life if you work part-time during your golden years.

- How much money you need to retire is as individual as your fingerprint. You have to consider location, passive income, and lifestyle.

- Don't allow other people's failure to influence your future. Focus on how you *can* do something instead of how or why you can't.

- Think outside the box. Mini-retirements could offer variety and stretch your perception of time.

- Consider living full-time or part-time in lower-cost destinations. Doing so could slash your overall costs. It could also increase your standard of living, while ensuring that you keep learning and expanding your perception of time.

CONCLUSION

EW PEOPLE WOULD look at my friend Casey Coleman and say, "Yeah, I want to live like that guy." After all, living in a car near the rim of the Grand Canyon would only appeal to an eccentric few. But there's much to learn from his happy, ascetic life. He doesn't feel the need to keep up with the spending habits of Mr. and Mrs. Jones. On his deathbed, he likely won't have the regrets that palliative care nurse Bronnie Ware documented among the dying. Casey lives the way he wants to. He's generous, he's kind, and he's the last person I know who would say, "Man, I've worked way too hard!"

We don't have to live like Casey. But we can be purposeful and kind and live in line with our values. In turn, that can boost our own life satisfaction and help us live longer. If we build wealth, that money can make us happier if we spend it on experiences and prosocial giving.

As with anything, balance is key. We need to focus on four quadrants of success:

- Having enough money
- Maintaining strong relationships (with yourself and with others)
- Maximizing your physical and emotional health
- Living with a sense of purpose

Unfortunately, far too often our culture seduces us into focusing more on the first quadrant. Television and online advertisements depict happy people with the latest fashionable traps:

More is better.

Newer is better.

Stuff will make you happy.

That's the madness of marketing. Most purchases don't boost life satisfaction. More often, they erode it, especially when people go into debt to acquire what they don't need. It's strange that we often buy stuff we don't need in a futile quest to impress people we don't know or care about.

The quest for more stuff is also environmentally destructive.

That's why, when it comes to stuff and money, the word "enough" is far healthier than the words "rich" and "more."

Having a lot more than we need won't make us happier. Nor will it make other people love us. Ironically, it could even make us jerks. Several studies show that people who are financially better off score lower on empathy. Perhaps the very focus required to make more money and buy better stuff makes people think less about others and the environment.[1]

None of us are happy all the time. Happiness is fleeting, fluctuating from day to day. But it's tough to be successful if we aren't generally happy. And it's hard to be happy without strong relationships. And we can't nurture strong relationships if we don't prioritize time with friends and family. And when we spend time with others, we should try to listen more than we talk. We can learn something from everyone if we ask questions. People will also care more about us if we show we care about them.

This reminds me of a t-shirt I once saw. It read, "Be yourself... but be your best self." I think we could all benefit from that reminder. After all, every single one of us is a work in progress. And that progress will help us live the best lives we can.

ACKNOWLEDGMENTS

WHEN I WAS twelve years old, my parents signed me up for an educational trip to England, Greece, Egypt, Israel, and Turkey. To pay for the trip, my mom took a part-time job at a retail store. She worked there while her four primates were in school (to be fair, my twin sisters were lesser primates because they fought less frequently and broke fewer windows).

When I think back, what I learned on that trip helped me write this book. It juiced my curiosity about other people and other places. That led me to read, learn, challenge my own beliefs, and, over the years, ask random strangers boatloads of questions. My father (who used to speak to mannequins to humiliate us kids) also set a great example. Thank you, Mom and Dad, for encouraging me to be curious. Without that curiosity, this book would not exist.

I would also like to thank my wife, Pele, for tolerating my bad, early manuscripts and offering suggestions and advice. She also informs me three out of every four mornings that my shirt is on either backward or inside out.

I would also like to acknowledge my fabulous siblings: Ian, Sally, and Sarah. For you, this is a test. If you read this sentence without one of your friends telling you to, I will give you $100. I feel my money is safe.

Thank you, also, to the incredible team at Page Two. This was our first journey together, and you have been fantastic. I recommend Page Two to anyone who wants to write their own nonfiction book. The entire team is beyond professional. More importantly, they're also great people. Thank you, Page Two!

APPENDIX

Technically, the s&p 500—formerly called the Composite Index—tracked just ninety stocks in 1926 and five hundred stocks, starting in 1957, so this data provides an estimate based on the performance of the largest us companies from 1920 until 1926.

TABLE A1

Rolling Ten-Year Returns for US Stocks

Decade	Avg. % per Year	Decade	Avg. % per Year	Decade	Avg. % per Year	Decade	Avg. % per Year	Decade	Avg. % per Year
1920–1930	+15.40%	1939–1949	+7.68%	1958–1968	+12.40%	1977–1987	+14.47%	1996–2006	+9.23%
1921–1931	+13.98%	1940–1950	+9.02%	1959–1969	+10.18%	1978–1988	+15.55%	1997–2007	+8.04%
1922–1932	+6.84%	1941–1951	+12.81%	1960–1970	+8.0%	1979–1989	+15.80%	1998–2008	+6.05%
1923–1933	+2.95%	1942–1952	+16.59%	1961–1971	+7.60%	1980–1990	+17.04%	1999–2009	-1.89%
1924–1934	+6.98%	1943–1953	+16.29%	1962–1972	+7.10%	1981–1991	+14.06%	2000–2010	-0.72%
1925–1935	+4.13%	1944–1954	+13.95%	1963–1973	+9.54%	1982–1992	+17.26%	2001–2011	+1.14%
1926–1936	+5.77%	1945–1955	+16.42%	1964–1974	+5.45%	1983–1993	+15.85%	2002–2012	+2.84%
1927–1937	+7.88%	1946–1956	+16.04%	1965–1975	+0.77%	1984–1994	+14.80%	2003–2013	+6.86%
1928–1938	+0.53%	1947–1957	+18.28%	1966–1976	+2.95%	1985–1995	+13.97%	2004–2014	+6.96%
1929–1939	-1.34%	1948–1958	+16.76%	1967–1977	+5.78%	1986–1996	+15.02%	2005–2015	+7.91%

Decade	Avg. % per Year	Decade	Avg. % per Year	Decade	Avg. % per Year	Decade	Avg. % per Year	Decade	Avg. % per Year
1930–1940	-0.15%	1949–1959	+19.49%	1968–1978	+3.52%	1987–1997	+14.31%	2006–2016	+7.09%
1931–1941	+1.42%	1950–1960	+19.11%	1969–1979	+3.25%	1988–1998	+17.82%	2007–2017	+6.93%
1932–1942	+6.36%	1951–1961	+15.55%	1970–1980	+5.95%	1989–1999	+18.56%	2008–2018	+9.15%
1933–1943	+8.77%	1952–1962	+16.31%	1971–1981	+8.02%	1990–2000	+18.41%	2009–2019	+12.97%
1934–1944	+6.49%	1953–1963	+13.53%	1972–1982	+6.33%	1991–2001	+17.81%	2010–2020	+13.40%
1935–1945	+9.38%	1954–1964	+15.50%	1973–1983	+6.45%	1992–2002	+12.99%	2011–2021	+13.72%
1936–1946	+8.12%	1955–1965	+12.85%	1974–1984	+10.68%	1993–2003	+9.62%		
1937–1947	+4.07%	1956–1966	+11.31%	1975–1985	+13.87%	1994–2004	+10.62%		
1938–1948	+8.70%	1957–1967	+9.60%	1976–1986	+13.21%	1995–2005	+11.46%		

Source: DQYDJ, S&P 500 Return Calculator with reinvested dividends[1]

TABLE A2

Portfolios of Stocks and Bonds Beat Inflation

5-Year Rolling Period	Average Annual Returns: 50% Stocks / 50% Bonds	5-Year Average Annual Inflation	5-Year Rolling Period	Average Annual Returns: 50% Stocks / 50% Bonds	5-Year Average Annual Inflation
1972–1976	+6.09%	+7.25%	1994–1998	+14.38%	+2.36%
1973–1977	+3.81%	+7.91%	1995–1999	+17.15%	+3.04%
1974–1978	+6.29%	+8.75%	1996–2000	+11.87%	+2.54%
1975–1979	+11.85%	+8.16%	1997–2001	+9.09%	+2.18%
1976–1980	+11.01%	+9.27%	1998–2002	+4.46%	+2.32%
1977–1981	+7.57%	+10.09%	1999–2003	+4.45%	+2.37%
1978–1982	+12.89%	+9.51%	2000–2004	+4.03%	+2.46%

5-Year Rolling Period	Average Annual Returns: 50% Stocks / 50% Bonds	5-Year Average Annual Inflation	5-Year Rolling Period	Average Annual Returns: 50% Stocks / 50% Bonds	5-Year Average Annual Inflation
1979–1983	+14.79%	+8.47%	2001–2005	+4.52%	+2.49%
1980–1984	+13.53%	+6.60%	2002–2006	+6.77%	+2.7%
1981–1985	+15.16%	+4.85%	2003–2007	+9.13%	+3.03%
1982–1986	+17.78%	+3.29%	2004–2008	+3.14%	+2.67%
1983–1987	+12.96%	+3.41%	2005–2009	+4.18%	+2.57%
1984–1988	+12.42%	+3.54%	2006–2010	+5.75%	+2.18%
1985–1989	+14.94%	+3.68%	2007–2011	+4.97%	+2.27%
1986–1990	+9.99%	+4.14%	2008–2012	+5.31%	+1.80%
1987–1991	+11.72%	+4.53%	2009–2013	+11.09%	+2.08%
1988–1992	+13.08%	+4.8%	2010–2014	+10.06%	+1.69%
1989–1993	+13.03%	+3.89%	2011–2015	+7.75%	+1.53%
1990–1994	+8.25%	+3.50%	2012–2016	+8.05%	+1.36%
1991–1995	+13.37%	+4.29%	2013–2017	+8.41%	+1.43%
1992–1996	+10.94%	+2.83%	2014–2018	+4.95%	+1.51%
1993–1997	+13.2%	+2.60%	2015–2019	+6.83%	+1.82%

Sources of returns and US inflation: portfoliovisualizer.com
Note: Returns measured in USD

NOTES

Chapter 1: The Grim Reaper Asks

1   Leaf Van Boven and Thomas Gilovich, "To Do or to Have? That Is the Question," *Journal of Personality and Social Psychology* 85, 6 (2003), doi.org/10.1037/0022-3514.85.6.1193.

2   Sarah Bridges and Richard Disney, *Debt and Depression*, Centre for Finance and Credit Markets, working paper 06/02, September 23, 2005, nottingham.ac.uk/cfcm/documents/papers/06-02.pdf.

3   Stefan Lembo Stolba, "U.S. Auto Debt Grows to Record High Despite Pandemic," Experian, April 12, 2021, experian.com/blogs/ask-experian/research/auto-loan-debt-study/.

4   Norbert Schwarz and Jing Xu, "Why Don't We Learn from Poor Choices? The Consistency of Expectation, Choice, and Memory Clouds the Lessons of Experience," *Journal of Consumer Psychology* 21, 2 (2011), doi.org/10.1016/j.jcps.2011.02.006.

5   Norbert Schwarz quoted in Bernie DeGroat, "Consumers Beware: In Reality, Luxury Cars Don't Make Us Feel Better," *Michigan News*, July 25, 2011, news.umich.edu/consumers-beware-in-reality-luxury-cars-dont-make-us-feel-better/.

6   Even most collector cars lose money when compared to inflation. For example, the 1965 Shelby Cobra sports car cost $7,500 when it was new. But in 2021, unless you could sell such a car for at least $62,622, the rising cost of living (inflation) would have outpaced the value of the car. See, for example, Terence W., "1965 Shelby Cobra 427 Roadster (Ultimate Guide)," SuperCars.net, supercars.net/blog/1965-shelby-cobra-427-roadster/#:~:text=races%20or%20shows.-,Pricing,1965%20was%20around%20%247%2C500%20USD.

7   Brittany Chang, "From Volkswagens to Paganis to the Humble Honda Accord, Here Are the Cars That 10 of the World's Wealthiest People Have Owned," *Business Insider*, August 2, 2019, businessinsider.com/cars-billionaires-drive-warren-buffett-elon-musk-mark-zuckerberg-2019-7#dustin-moskovitz-2.

8   Emmie Martin, "9 Billionaires Who Drive Cheap Hondas, Toyotas and Chevrolets," CNBC, August 21, 2018, cnbc.com/2018/08/21/9-billionaires-who-still-drive-cheap-hondas-toyotas-and-chevrolets.html.

9   The *Forbes* World's Billionaire's List is updated annually. You can find the most recent list here: forbes.com/billionaires/.

10   Sam Dogen, "The 1/10th Rule for Car Buying Everyone Must Follow," *Financial Samurai*, updated May 28, 2021, financialsamurai.com/the-110th-rule-for-car-buying-everyone-must-follow/.

11   Michelle Higgins, "Homeownership, the Key to Happiness?" *New York Times*, July 12, 2013, nytimes.com/2013/07/14/realestate/homeownership-the-key-to-happiness.html.

12   Jenny Olson and Scott Rick, "A Penny Saved Is a Partner Earned: The Romantic Appeal of Savers," *SSRN Electronic Journal*, 2013 (revised September 2017), doi.org/10.2139/ssrn.2281344.

Chapter 2: Would You Say No to a High-Paying Job?

1   See, for example, Marsha Richin and Scott Dawson, "A Consumer Values Orientation for Materialism and Its Measurement: Scale Development and Validation," *Journal of Consumer Research* 19, 3 (1992), doi.org/10.1086/209304; Jo-Ann Tsang et al., "Why Are Materialists Less Happy? The Role of Gratitude and Need Satisfaction in the Relationship between Materialism and Life Satisfaction," *Personality and Individual Differences* 64 (2014), doi.org/10.1016/j.paid.2014.02.009; and Sabrina Helm et al., "Materialist Values, Financial and Pro-environmental Behaviors, and Well-Being," *Young Consumers* 20, 4 (2019), doi.org/10.1108/YC-10-2018-0867.

2   Andrew T. Jebb et al., "Happiness, Income Satiation, and Turning Points around the World," *Nature Human Behaviour* 2, 1 (2018), doi.org/10.1038/s41562-017-0277-0.

3   See, for example, Glenn Firebaugh and Matthew B. Schroeder, "Does Your Neighbor's Income Affect Your Happiness?" *American Journal of Sociology* 115, 3 (2009), doi.org/10.1086/603534.

4   Michael Daly et al., "A Social Rank Explanation of How Money Influences Health," *Health Psychology* 34, 3 (2015), doi.org/10.1037/hea0000098.

5   See, for example, Sumit Agarwal et al., "Peers' Income and Financial Distress: Evidence from Lottery Winners and Neighboring Bankruptcies," *Review of Financial Studies* 33, 1 (2020), doi.org/10.1093/rfs/hhz047.

6   Sarah Hansen, "Warren Buffett Gives Another $2.9 Billion to Charity," *Forbes*, July 8, 2020, forbes.com/sites/sarahhansen/2020/07/08/warren-buffett-gives-another-29-billion-to-charity/?sh=4e1f09343544.

7   Erika Sandow, "Til Work Do Us Part: The Social Fallacy of Long-Distance Commuting," *Urban Studies* 51, 3 (2014), doi.org/10.1177/0042098013498280.

8   Annette Schaefer, "Commuting Takes Its Toll," *Scientific American*, October 1, 2005, doi.org/10.1038/scientificamericanmind1005-14.

Chapter 3: Your Real Superpower

1   Brené Brown, *Daring Greatly: How the Courage to Be Vulnerable Transforms the Way We Live, Love, Parent, and Lead* (New York: Gotham Books, 2012).

2   Liz Mineo, "Harvard Study, Almost 80 Years Old, Has Proved That Embracing Community Helps Us Live Longer, and Be Happier," *Harvard Gazette*, April 11, 2017, news.harvard.edu/gazette/story/2017/04/over-nearly-80-years-harvard-study-has-been-showing-how-to-live-a-healthy-and-happy-life/. See also the Harvard Study of Adult Development's website: adultdevelopmentstudy.org.

3   Research summarized in Jim Deegan, "How a Tiny Pennsylvania Town Held the Secrets to Long Life," *Lehigh Valley Live*, updated January 2, 2019, lehighvalleylive.com/slate-belt/2016/01/roseto_effect_carmen_ruggiero.html#:~:text=Stewart%20Wolf%2C%20studied%20the%20effect,of%20Roseto%20at%20the%20time.

4   Dan Buettner, "Power 9: Reverse Engineering Longevity," *Blue Zones* (blog), bluezones.com/2016/11/power-9/.

5   Brenda Egolf et al., "The Roseto Effect: A 50-Year Comparison of Mortality Rates," *American Journal of Public Health* 82, 2 (1992), doi.org/10.2105/ajph.82.8.1089.

6   "Blue Zones Project Results: Beach Cities, CA," *Blue Zones* (blog), bluezones.com/blue-zones-project-results-beach-cities-ca/#section-1. Learn more about Dan Buettner on his *Blue Zones* blog at bluezones.com/dan-buettner/. You can find information about his Blue Zones book series at bluezones.com/books/.

7   Bronnie Ware, *The Top Five Regrets of the Dying: A Life Transformed by the Dearly Departing* (Carlsbad, CA: Hay House, 2012).

8   David G. Blanchflower, "Is Happiness U-shaped Everywhere? Age and Subjective Well-Being in 132 Countries," National Bureau of Economic Research, working paper 26641, January 2020, doi.org/10.3386/w26641.

9   Hanna Krasnova et al., "Envy on Facebook: A Hidden Threat to Users' Life Satisfaction?" paper presented at the 11th International Conference on Wirtschaftsinformatik, Leipzig, Germany, February 2013, doi.org/10.7892/BORIS.47080.

10 Jonathan Rauch, *The Happiness Curve: Why Life Gets Better after 50* (New York: Thomas Dunne Books, 2018).

11   Lucy Rock, "Life Gets Better after 50: Why Age Tends to Work in Favour of Happiness," *The Guardian*, May 5, 2018, theguardian.com/lifeandstyle/2018/may/05/happiness-curve-life-gets-better-after-50-jonathan-rauch.

12   Tammy English and Laura L. Carstensen, "Selective Narrowing of Social Networks across Adulthood Is Associated With Improved Emotional Experience in Daily Life," *International Journal of Behavioral Development* 38, 2 (2014), doi.org/10.1177/0165025413515404.

13   Lara B. Aknin et al., "Does Spending Money on Others Promote Happiness? A Registered Replication Report," *Journal of Personality and Social Psychology* 119, 2 (2020), doi.org/10.1037/pspa0000191.

14   Lara B. Aknin et al., "Prosocial Spending and Well-Being: Cross-Cultural Evidence for a Psychological Universal," *Journal of Personality and Social Psychology* 104, 4 (2013), doi.org/10.1037/a0031578.

15   Elizabeth Dunn and Michael Norton, *Happy Money: The Science of Happier Spending* (New York: Simon & Schuster, 2013).

16   Elizabeth Dunn, "Helping Others Makes Us Happier—but It Matters How We Do It," TED2019, April 2019, 14:20, ted.com/talks/elizabeth_dunn_helping_others_makes_us_happier_but_it_matters_how_we_do_it?language=en.

17   Marta Zaraska, *Growing Young: How Friendship, Optimism, and Kindness Can Help You Live to 100* (Vancouver: Appetite by Penguin Random House, 2020).

18   Ashley V. Whillans et al., "Is Spending Money on Others Good for Your Heart?" *Health Psychology* 35, 6 (2016), doi.org/10.1037/hea0000332.

19   Zaraska, *Growing Young*.

20   David L. Roth et al., Family Caregiving and All-Cause Mortality: Findings from a Population-Based Propensity-Matched Analysis," *American Journal of Epidemiology* 178, 10 (2013), doi.org/10.1093/aje/kwt225.

21   Sonja Hilbrand et al., "Caregiving within and beyond the Family Is Associated With Lower Mortality for the Caregiver: A Prospective Study," *Evolution and Human Behavior* 38, 3 (2017), doi.org/10.1016/j.evolhumbehav.2016.11.010.

22   Kurt Gray, "Moral Transformation: Good and Evil Turn the Weak into the Mighty," *Social Psychological and Personality Science* 1, 3 (2010), doi.org/10.1177/1948550610367686.

Chapter 4: Who Are You Going to Follow?

1   Shawn Achor, *The Happiness Advantage: How a Positive Brain Fuels Success in Work and Life* (New York: Currency, 2010).

2   "Real Median Household Income in the United States," Economic Research, Federal Reserve Bank of St. Louis, fred.stlouisfed.org/series/MEHOINUSA672N.

3 US General Social Survey data summarized in Christopher Ingraham, "Americans Are Getting More Miserable and There's Data to Prove It,"*Washington Post*, March 22, 2019, washingtonpost.com/business/2019/03/22/americans-are-getting-more-miserable-theres-data-prove-it/.

4 Alexandria White, "Alaskans Carry the Highest Credit Card Balance—Here's the Average Credit Card Balance in Every State," CNBC, updated July 8, 2021, cnbc.com/select/average-credit-card-balance-by-state/#:~:text=On%20average%2C%20Americans%20carry%20%246%2C194,2019%20Experian%20consumer%20credit%20review.

5 Colin McClelland, "Canadians Racked Up $100 Billion in Credit Card Debt for First Time Ever and They're Not Done Adding to It," *Financial Post*, December 9, 2019, financialpost.com/news/economy/canadians-racked-up-100-billion-in-credit-card-debt-for-first-time-ever-and-theyre-not-done-adding-to-it.

6 Gordon Isfeld, "Canadians' Household Debt Climbs to Highest in G7 in World-Beating Borrowing Spree," *Financial Post*, updated March 16, 2018, financialpost.com/investing/outlook/canadians-household-debt-highest-in-g7-with-crunch-on-brink-of-historic-levels-pbo-warns.

7 Mark J. Perry, "New US Homes Today Are 1,000 Square Feet Larger Than in 1973 and Living Space Per Person Has Nearly Doubled," *AEIdeas*, American Enterprise Institute, June 5, 2016, aei.org/carpe-diem/new-us-homes-today-are-1000-square-feet-larger-than-in-1973-and-living-space-per-person-has-nearly-doubled/.

8 Alexandre Tanzi, "Millions of U.S. Homeowners Still Under Water on Mortgages," *Bloomberg*, May 29, 2018, bloomberg.com/news/articles/2018-05-29/millions-of-u-s-homeowners-still-under-water-on-mortgages.

9 Morgan Housel, *The Psychology of Money: Timeless Lessons on Wealth, Greed, and Happiness* (Petersfield, Hampshire, UK: Harriman House, 2020); Phil LeBeau, "Auto Loan Payments Soared to Yet Another Record in the First Quarter," CNBC, June 9, 2020, cnbc.com/2020/06/09/auto-loan-payments-soared-to-yet-another-record-in-the-first-quarter.html.

10 "Vancouver Real Estate Trends," Zolo, zolo.ca/vancouver-real-estate/trends.

11 *Survey of Financial Security, 2019*, Statistics Canada, released December 12, 2020, www150.statcan.gc.ca/n1/daily-quotidien/201222/dq201222b-eng.htm.

12 *Vancouver: City Social Indicators Profile 2020*, Social Policy and Projects, City of Vancouver, updated October 2, 2020, vancouver.ca/files/cov/social-indicators-profile-city-of-vancouver.pdf.

13 Thomas J. Stanley, *Stop Acting Rich: . . . And Start Living Like a Real Millionaire* (Hoboken, NJ: John Wiley & Sons, 2009).

14   Thomas J. Stanley and Sarah Stanley Fallaw, *The Next Millionaire Next Door: Enduring Strategies for Building Wealth* (Guilford, CT: Lyons Press, 2018).

15   Thomas J. Stanley as cited in Richard Buck, "Doctors Found to Be among the Biggest Spenders," *Seattle Times*, October 3, 1992, archive.seattletimes.com/archive/?date=19921003&slug=1516364.

16   Chris Dudley, "Money Lessons Learned from Pro Athletes' Financial Fouls," CNBC, updated May 15, 2018, cnbc.com/2018/05/14/money-lessons-learned-from-pro-athletes-financial-fouls.html.

17   Alec Fenn, "Why Do So Many Footballers End Up Broke? *FourFourTwo* Investigates..." *FourFourTwo*, September 18, 2017, fourfourtwo.com/features/why-do-so-many-footballers-end-broke-fourfourtwo-investigates.

18   See Summer Allen, *The Science of Gratitude*, white paper prepared for the John Templeton Foundation by the Greater Good Science Center at UC Berkeley, May 2018, ggsc.berkeley.edu/images/uploads/GGSC-JTF_White_Paper-Gratitude-FINAL.pdf?_ga=2.142441970.159432767.1620680622-458849061.1620680622.

19   Joshua Brown and Joel Wong, "How Gratitude Changes You and Your Brain," *Greater Good Magazine*, June 6, 2017, greatergood.berkeley.edu/article/item/how_gratitude_changes_you_and_your_brain. See also their study: Y. Joel Wong et al., "Does Gratitude Writing Improve the Mental Health of Psychotherapy Clients? Evidence from a Randomized Controlled Trial," *Psychotherapy Research* 28, 2 (2018), doi.org/10.1080/10503307.2016.1169332.

20   Jason Marsh, "Tips for Keeping a Gratitude Journal," *Greater Good Magazine*, November 17, 2011, greatergood.berkeley.edu/article/item/tips_for_keeping_a_gratitude_journal.

Chapter 5: Afford Anything, but Not Everything

1   Andrew Hallam, "Why Buying New Cars Over Used Is a Million Dollar Decision," AssetBuilder.com, September 12, 2019, assetbuilder.com/knowledge-center/articles/why-buying-new-cars-over-used-is-a-million-dollar-decision.

2   Andrew Hallam, "Leasing Cars Instead of Buying Used Could Be a $1 Million Decision," AssetBuilder.com, August 1, 2016, assetbuilder.com/knowledge-center/articles/leasing-cars-instead-of-buying-used-could-be-a-1-million-decision.

3   Jack F. Hollis et al., "Weight Loss during the Intensive Intervention Phase of the Weight-Loss Maintenance Trial," *American Journal of Preventive Medicine* 35, 2 (2008), doi.org/10.1016/j.amepre.2008.04.013.

Chapter 6: Bathrooms and the Markets

1   "Dow 30," Value Line Investment Survey, research.valueline.com/research#list= dow30&sec=list.

2   Robb B. Rutledge et al., "A Computational and Neural Model of Momentary Subjective Well-Being," *PNAS* 111, 33 (2014), doi.org/10.1073/pnas.1407535111.

3   Morningstar is a subscription-based service. All the data and information I cite comes via that service.

4   S&P 500 Return Calculator, with Dividend Reinvestment, DQYDJ:dqydj.com/ sp-500-return-calculator/.

5   Stingy Investor Asset Mixer: ndir.com/cgi-bin/downside_adv.cgi.

6   "Vanguard Portfolio Allocation Models," Vanguard, investor.vanguard.com/ investing/how-to-invest/model-portfolio-allocation.

7   Bankrate's "Current CD Rates" are continuously updated here: bankrate.com/ banking/cds/current-cd-interest-rates/.

8   Portfolio Visualizer is a subscription-based tool.

Chapter 7: Don't Let a Financial Advisor Pour Water in Your Trumpet

1   John C. Bogle, "The Arithmetic of 'All-In' Investment Expenses," *Financial Analysts Journal* 70, 1 (2014), doi.org/10.2469/faj.v70.n1.1.

2   William F. Sharpe, "The Arithmetic of Active Management," *Financial Analysts Journal* 47, 1 (1991), web.stanford.edu/~wfsharpe/art/active/active.htm.

3   You can browse salary levels for different professions in the United States using the US Bureau of Labor Statistics' Occupational Outlook Handbook tool: bls.gov/ooh/.

4   Esteban Ortiz-Ospina et al., *Time Use*, Our World in Data, 2020, ourworldindata. org/time-use.

5   S&P Dow Jones Indices, SPIVA, Results by Region: spindices.com/spiva/#/ reports.

6   Berlinda Liu and Gaurav Sinha, "SPIVA Canada Year-End 2020," S&P Dow Jones Indices, March 18, 2021, spglobal.com/spdji/en/spiva/article/spiva-canada.

7   Berlinda Liu and Gaurav Sinha, "U.S. Persistence Scorecard Year-End 2020," S&P Dow Jones Indices, May 11, 2021, spglobal.com/spdji/en/spiva/article/ us-persistence-scorecard.

8   Srikant Dash and Rosanne Pane, "Standard & Poor's Indices versus Active Funds Scorecard, Year End 2008," Standard & Poor's, April 20, 2009, spglobal.com/ spdji/en/documents/spiva/spiva-us-year-end-2008.pdf.

9   David H. Bailey et al., "Evaluation and Ranking of Market Forecasters," SSRN, revised July 22, 2017, doi.org/10.2139/ssrn.2944853.

10   Ken Fisher, *Markets Never Forget (but People Do): How Your Memory Is Costing You Money and Why This Time Isn't Different* (Hoboken, NJ: John Wiley & Sons, 2012); updated unemployment figures (post-2011) came from Trading Economics, using data from the US Bureau of Labor Statistics: tradingeconomics.com/united-states/unemployment-rate.

11   John Cassidy, "Mastering the Machine," *New Yorker*, July 18, 2011, newyorker.com/magazine/2011/07/25/mastering-the-machine.

12   Andrew Hallam, "The Naked Emperors Cost Investors Billions," AssetBuilder.com, August 1, 2019, assetbuilder.com/knowledge-center/articles/these-naked-emperors-cost-investors-billions.

13   "Scion Asset Management, LLC—Investor Performance," Fintel, fintel.io/ip/scion-asset-management-llc.

14   Reed Stevenson, "*The Big Short*'s Michael Burry Explains Why Index Funds Are Like Subprime CDOs," *Bloomberg*, September 4, 2019, bloomberg.com/news/articles/2019-09-04/michael-burry-explains-why-index-funds-are-like-subprime-cdos.

15   Dash and Pane, "Standard & Poor's Indices versus Active Funds Scorecard, Year End 2008."

16   James J. Rowley et al., *Setting the Record Straight: Truths about Indexing*, Vanguard Investments Research, March 2018, vanguardcanada.ca/documents/truth-about-indexing-en.pdf.

17   "Garzarelli to Liquidate Her 6-Month-Old Fund," *Los Angeles Times*, November 6, 1997, latimes.com/archives/la-xpm-1997-nov-06-fi-50727-story.html.

18   Dan Dorfman, "Go-Go Guru Is Bullish on 2008," *New York Sun*, December 7, 2007, nysun.com/business/go-go-guru-is-bullish-on-2008/67694/.

19   Andrew Hallam, "Why *The Big Short*'s Michael Burry Is Wrong about Index Funds," AssetBuilder.com, September 18, 2019, assetbuilder.com/knowledge-center/articles/why-the-big-shorts-michael-burry-is-wrong-about-index-funds.

20   Brian Chappatta, "Meredith Whitney Was Flat-Out Wrong about Municipal Bonds," *Bloomberg*, October 30, 2018, bloomberg.com/opinion/articles/2018-10-30/meredith-whitney-was-flat-out-wrong-about-municipal-bonds.

21   The twelve topics are known collectively as the Financial Planning Body of Knowledge (FP-BoK), FP Canada, fpcanada.ca/bok; one topic is Investment Styles: fpcanada.ca/en/bok/bok-statement?topicUrl= investments& articleUrl=investment-styles.

22 Juhani T. Linnainmaa et al., "The Misguided Beliefs of Financial Advisors," *Journal of Finance* 76, 2 (2021), doi.org/10.1111/jofi.12995.

Chapter 8: Set It and Forget It

1   Kathleen D. Vohs, "Money Priming Can Change People's Thoughts, Feelings, Motivations, and Behaviors: An Update on 10 Years of Experiments," *Journal of Experimental Psychology* 144, 4 (2015), doi.org/10.1037/xge0000091.

2   Myles Udland, "Fidelity Reviewed Which Investors Did Best and What They Found Was Hilarious," *Business Insider*, September 4, 2014, businessinsider.com/forgetful-investors-performed-best-2014-9.

3   Andrew Hallam, "Seven-Year Old Investor Beats Harvard's Endowment Fund," AssetBuilder.com, March 15, 2018, assetbuilder.com/knowledge- center/articles/seven-year-old-investor-beats-harvards-endowment- fund.

4   "Number of Exchange Traded Funds (ETFs) in the United States from 2003 to 2020," Statista, February 18, 2021, statista.com/statistics/350525/number-etfs-usa/. Statista reports 2,204 ETFs in the United States in 2020.

5   Barry Schwartz, *The Paradox of Choice: Why More Is Less—How the Culture of Abundance Robs Us of Satisfaction* (New York: Harper Perennial, 2004). See also Schwartz's TED Talk, "The Paradox of Choice," TED Global 2005, 19:24, ted.com/talks/barry_schwartz_the_paradox_of_choice? language=en#t-505374.

6   Adam Grant, *Give and Take: A Revolutionary Approach to Success* (New York: Viking, 2013).

7   Aye M. Soe, "Does Past Performance Matter? The Persistence Scorecard," S&P Dow Jones Indices, June 2014, spglobal.com/spdji/en/documents/spiva/persistence-scorecard-june-2014.pdf.

8   *Barron's* Top 100 Financial Advisors is updated annually. You can find the most recent list here: barrons.com/report/top-financial-advisors/100.

9   In the United States, check an advisor's Form ADV on the SEC's Investment Adviser Public Disclosure website: adviserinfo.sec.gov/.

10 In the United States, check an advisor's history with regulatory organizations on the North American Securities Administrators Association (NASAA) website: nasaa.org/.

11 In Canada, check an advisor's history on the Investment Industry Regulatory Organization of Canada (IIROC) website: iiroc.ca/.

12 In the United Kingdom, check an advisor's or firm's history on Financial Conduct Authority's (FCA's) services register: register.fca.org.uk/s/.

13   Eugene F. Fama and Kenneth R. French, "A Five-Factor Asset Pricing Model," Fama-Miller Working Paper, *SSRN*, doi.org/10.2139/ssrn.2287202.

14   Jeffrey Ptak, "Success Story: Target-Date Fund Investors," Morningstar, February 19, 2018, morningstar.com/articles/850872/success-story- targetdate-fund-investors.

15   "Vanguard Target Retirement Funds," Vanguard, investor.vanguard.com/mutual-funds/target-retirement/#/.

16   Find more information on BlackRock's website at blackrock.com/ca.

17   "New Vanguard ETFs Offer Diversified Portfolios in One Trade," Vanguard Australia, vanguardinvestments.com.au/au/portal/articles/insights/mediacentre/new-vanguard-etfs.jsp.

18   Find more information on the Vanguard UK website: vanguardinvestor.co.uk/.

19   Find more information on You&Yours Financial's website: youandyours financial.com/.

Chapter 9: How Well Do You Know Yourself?

1   "Vanguard Portfolio Allocation Models," Vanguard, investor.vanguard.com/investing/how-to-invest/model-portfolio-allocation.

2   "FIRE (Financial Independence, Retire Early)," TechTarget, whatis.techtarget.com/definition/FIRE-Financial-Independence-Retire-Early.

3   William Bernstein, *If You Can: How Millennials Can Get Rich Slowly* (Efficient Frontier Publications, 2014). You can access the booklet for free on Bernstein's website: efficientfrontier.com/ef/0adhoc/ifyoucan.pdf.

4   Warren Buffett, "1997 Chairman's Letter," February 27, 1998, berkshirehathaway.com/letters/1997.html.

5   Chelsea Brennan, "I Spent 7 Years Working in Finance and Managed a $1.3 Billion Portfolio—Here Are the 5 Best Pieces of Investing Advice I Can Give You," *Business Insider*, October 5, 2018, businessinsider.com/money-investing-advice-former-hedge-fund-manager-2018-10#index-fund-investing-is-the-easiest-way-to-win.

6   Jeff Berman, "Report of Retirees Fleeing Market Due to Coronavirus Was Greatly Exaggerated," ThinkAdvisor, June 22, 2020, thinkadvisor.com/2020/06/22/report-of-retirees-fleeing-market-due-to-coronavirus-was-greatly-exaggerated/.

7   You can test out Vanguard's Retirement Nest Egg Calculator here: retirement plans.vanguard.com/VGApp/pe/pubeducation/calculators/RetirementNestEggCalc.jsf.

8 Brad M. Barber and Terrance Odean, "Boys Will Be Boys: Gender, Overconfidence, and Common Stock Investment," *Quarterly Journal of Economics* 116, 1 (2001), doi.org/10.2139/ssrn.139415.

9 Ibid.

10 "Fidelity Investments Survey Reveals Only Nine Percent of Women Think They Make Better Investors Than Men, Despite Growing Evidence to the Contrary," press release, Fidelity Investments, May 18, 2017, fidelity.com/about-fidelity/ individual-investing/better-investor-men-or-women.

11 Tracie McMillion and Veronica Willis, *Women and Investing: Building on Strengths*, Wells Fargo Investment Institute, January 2019, https://www08.wellsfargomedia. com/assets/pdf/personal/investing/investment-institute/women-and-investing-ADA.pdf.

12 "Are Women Better Investors Than Men?" Warwick Business School, June 28, 2018, wbs.ac.uk/news/are-women-better-investors-than-men/.

13 Allison Chin-Leong, "Why Women Make Great Investors," Wells Fargo, July 25, 2017, stories.wf.com/women-make-great-investors/.

14 Yan Lu and Melvyn Teo, "Do Alpha Males Deliver Alpha? Facial Width-to-Height Ratio and Hedge Funds," *Journal of Finance and Quantitative Analysis*, revised December 15, 2020, doi.org/10.2139/ssrn.3100645.

Chapter 10: Happy Planet, Happy People

1 Samuel M. Hartzmark and Abigail B. Sussman, "Do Investors Value Sustainability? A Natural Experiment Examining Ranking and Fund Flows," *Journal of Finance* 74, 6 (2019), doi.org/10.1111/jofi.12841.

2 Michael Schröder, "Is There a Difference? The Performance Characteristics of SRI Equity Indices," *Journal of Business Finance & Accounting* 24, 1-2 (2007), doi.org/10.1111/j.1468-5957.2006.00647.x.

3 "Thematic Investing: Sustainable," Fidelity Investments, fidelity.com/mutual-funds/investing-ideas/socially-responsible-investing.

4 Explore sustainable iShares ETFs on BlackRock's website: blackrock.com/ca/ investors/en/products/product-list#!type=ishares&style=AlL&Fst=50586&view =perfNav.

5 See Andrew Hallam, "Are Canadians Wasting Billions on Currency-Hedged ETFs?" *Globe and Mail*, updated September 8, 2020, theglobeandmail.com/ featured-reports/article-are-canadians-wasting-billions-on-currency-hedged-etfs/.

6 Visit Vanguard Australia's website here: vanguard.com.au.

7   Kirk Warren Brown and Tim Kasser, "Are Psychological and Ecological Well-Being Compatible? The Role of Values, Mindfulness, and Lifestyle," *Social Indicators Research* 74 (2005), doi.org/10.1007/s11205-004-8207-8.

8   Josephine Moulds, "Costa Rica Is One of the World's Happiest Countries. Here's What It Does Differently," World Economic Forum, January 31, 2019, https://www.weforum.org/agenda/2019/01/sun-sea-and-stable-democracy-what-s-the-secret-to-costa-rica-s-success/.

9   Mary Jo DiLonardo, "Costa Rica Has Doubled Its Forest Cover in the Last 30 Years," Treehugger, updated May 24, 2019, mnn.com/earth-matters/wilderness-resources/blogs/costa-rica-has-doubled-its- forest-cover-last-30-years.

10   "Costa Rica Unveils Plan to Achieve Zero Emissions by 2050 in Climate Change Fight," *The Guardian*, February 25, 2019, theguardian.com/world/2019/feb/25/costa-rica-plan-decarbonize-2050-climate-change-fight.

11   Valerie Volcovici, "Americans Demand Climate Action (as long as It Doesn't Cost Much): Reuters Poll," Reuters, June 26, 2019, reuters.com/article/us-usa-election-climatechange-idUSKCN1TR15W.

12   Annie Leonard, "The Story of Stuff," YouTube, April 22, 2009, 21:16, youtube.com/watch?v=9GorqroigqM.

13   Victor Lebow quoted in David Suzuki, "Consumer Society No Longer Serves Our Needs," David Suzuki Foundation, January 11, 2018, davidsuzuki.org/story/consumer-society-no-longer-serves-needs/#:~:text=Retailing%20analyst%20victor%20Lebow%20famously,our%20ego%20satisfaction%20in%2.

14   Sabrina Helm et al., "Materialist Values, Financial and Pro-environmental Behaviors, and Well-Being," *Young Consumers* 20, 4 (2019), doi.org/10.1108/YC-10- 2018-0867.

15   Countries with Biocapacity Reserve vs. Countries with Biocapacity Deficit (interactive map), Global Footprint Network, data.footprintnetwork.org/?_ga=2.75676629.1953053049.1607448135-275758098.1607448135&_gac=1.2662.

16   Xiaoqian Gao and Hong-Sheng Wang, "Impact of Bisphenol A on the Cardio-vascular System—Epidemiological and Experimental Evidence and Molecular Mechanisms," *International Journal of Environmental Research and Public Health* 11, 8 (2014), doi.org/10.3390/ijerph110808399.

17   "Ethylene Oxide," National Cancer Institute at the National Institutes of Health, updated December 28, 2018, cancer.gov/about-cancer/causes-prevention/risk/substances/ethylene-oxide.

18   Joe Schwarcz, "Pollution from Incinerators," McGill Office for Science and Society, March 20, 2017, mcgill.ca/oss/article/science-science-everywhere/pollution-incinerators#:~:text=Incinerators%20may%20reduce%20the%20volume,toxic%20chemicals%20known%20to%20science.

19   Annie Leonard (interview with Patty Satalia), "Annie Leonard: The Story of Stuff—Conversations," YouTube, November 6, 2010, 56:51, youtube.com/watch?v=P5BcJb3BBz8.

20   Tara Shine, *How to Save Your Planet One Object at a Time* (London, UK: Simon & Schuster, 2020).

21   Rebecca Hersher and Allison Aubrey, "To Slow Global Warming, U.N. Warns Agriculture Must Change," NPR's *The Salt*, August 8, 2019, npr.org/sections/thesalt/2019/08/08/748416223/to-slow-global-warming-u-n-warns-agriculture-must-change.

22   "Teapigs Awarded Plastic-Free Trust Mark," *Tea and Coffee Trade Journal*, May 17, 2018, teaandcoffee.net/news/19760/teapigs-awarded-plastic-free-trust-mark/#:~:text=Teapigs%20tea%20brand%20is%20the,temples%20have%20always%20been%20biodegradable.

23   "Coffee Consumption Worldwide from 2012/13 to 2020/21," Statista, January 2021, statista.com/statistics/292595/global-coffee-consumption/.

24   *Assessment of Fairtrade Coffee Farmers' Income: Rwanda, Tanzania, Uganda, Kenya, India, Indonesia and Vietnam,* Fairtrade International and True Price, August 2017, https://files.fairtrade.net/standards/2017-08_At_a_Glance_Assessment_coffee_household_income_updated.pdf.

25   "Per Capita Consumption of Bottled Water Worldwide in 2018," Statista, July 2019, statista.com/statistics/183388/per-capita-consumption-of-bottled-water-worldwide-in-2009/#:~:text=In%202018%2C%20Mexico%20and%20Thailand,capita%20consumption%20in%20that%20year.

26   Annie Leonard, "The Story of Bottled Water: Fear, Manufactured Demand and a $10,000 Sandwich," *HuffPost*, updated December 6, 2017, huffpost.com/entry/the-story-of-bottled-wate_b_507942.

27   Paul L. Younger, *Water: All That Matters* (London, UK: Quercus, 2012); Younger quoted in "Bottled Water Is More Dangerous Than Tap Water," *Business Insider*, January 2, 2013, businessinsider.com/bottled-water-is-more-dangerous-than-tap-water-2013-1.

28   "Taste Test: Is Bottled Water Better Than Tap?" CTV *News Atlantic*, March 22, 2012, atlantic.ctvnews.ca/taste-test-is-bottled-water-better-than-tap-1.785329.

29   Eric Teillet et al., "Consumer Perception and Preference of Bottled and Tap Water," *Journal of Sensory Studies* 25, 3 (2010), doi.org/10.1111/j.1745-459X.2010.00280.x.

30 Annie Leonard, "The Story of Bottled Water," YouTube, March 17, 2010, 8:04, youtube.com/watch?v=Se12y9hsOMo.

31 Laura Parker, "A Whopping 91 Percent of Plastic Isn't Recycled," *National Geographic*, July 5, 2019, nationalgeographic.org/article/whopping-91-percent-plastic-isnt-recycled/#:~:text=Of%20the%208.3%20billion%20metric,the%20natural%20environment%20as%20litter.

32 Lynette Cheah et al., "Manufacturing-Focused Emissions Reductions on Footwear Production," *Journal of Cleaner Production* 44 (2013), doi.org/10.1016/j.jclepro.2012.11.037.

33 *The Life Cycle of a Jean: Understanding the Environmental Impact of a Pair of Levi's 501 Jeans*, Levi Strauss & Co., 2015, levistrauss.com/wp-content/uploads/2015/03/Full-LCA-Results-Deck-FINAL.pdf.

34 "UN Alliance for Sustainable Fashion Addresses Damage of 'Fast Fashion,'" press release, UN Environment Programme, March 14, 2019, unenvironment.org/news-and-stories/press-release/un-alliance-sustainable-fashion-addresses-damage-fast-fashion.

35 Ibid.

36 Nathalie Remy et al., "Style That's Sustainable: A New Fast-Fashion Formula," McKinsey & Company, October 20, 2016, mckinsey.com/business-functions/sustainability/our-insights/style-thats-sustainable-a-new-fast-fashion-formula.

37 Francesca Street, "What Happened on the Qantas Flight to Nowhere," CNN, October 12, 2020, cnn.com/travel/article/qantas-flight-to-nowhere-passenger-experience/index.html.

38 Rachel Hosie, "Singapore Airlines Has Cancelled Its Proposed 'Flights to Nowhere' after Criticism from Environmental Campaigners," *Business Insider*, October 1, 2020, insider.com/singapore-airlines-drops-flights-to-nowhere-after-environmental-concerns-2020-10.

39 Tatiana Schlossberg, "Flying Is Bad for the Planet. You Can Help Make It Better," *New York Times*, July 27, 2017, nytimes.com/2017/07/27/climate/airplane-pollution-global-warming.html.

40 Chris Jones quoted in "Is It More Environmentally Friendly to Drive a Used Car or a Tesla? The Answer Might Surprise You," Gumtree, July 10, 2018, blog.gumtree.com.au/environmentally-friendly-used-car-tesla/.

41 Jennifer Dunn quoted in David Common and Jill English, "Electric Vehicles Are Supposed to Be Green, but the Truth Is a Bit Murkier," CBC News, December 29, 2019, cbc.ca/news/technology/ev-electric-vehicle-carbon-footprint-1.5394126.

42   Fossil Fuels: What Share of Electricity Comes from Fossil Fuels? (interactive map), Our World in Data, 2020, ourworldindata.org/electricity-mix#fossil-fuels-what-share-of-electricity-comes-from-fossil-fuels.

43   "Electricity Facts," Government of Canada, updated October 6, 2020, nrcan.gc.ca/science-data/data-analysis/energy-data-analysis/energy-facts/electricity-facts/20068.

44   "Environmental Impacts of Hydro Power," Environment and Climate Change Canada, updated March 30, 2010, energybc.ca/cache/runofriver/www.ec.gc.ca/energie-energy/defaultc410.html#:~:text=In%20addition%20to%20methane%2C%20hydropower,disrupting%20the%20natural%20river%20flows.

45   See, for example, Sarah Gardner and Dave Albee, "Study Focuses on Strategies for Achieving Goals, Resolutions," press release 266, Dominican University of California, February 2, 2015, scholar.dominican.edu/news-releases/266/; more about Dr. Gail Matthews' study can be found here: dominican.edu/sites/default/files/2020-02/gailmatthews-harvard-goals-researchsummary.pdf.

Chapter 11: From Little Acorns...

1   Amy Chua, *Battle Hymn of the Tiger Mother* (New York: Penguin, 2011).

2   The Braun Research poll and University of Minnesota study are discussed in Jennifer Breheny Wallace, "Why Children Need Chores," *Wall Street Journal*, March 13, 2015, wsj.com/articles/why-children-need-chores-1426262655; more on the U of M study can be found in "Involving Children in Household Tasks: Is It Worth the Effort?" University of Minnesota College of Education and Human Development, revised May 8, 2013, ww1.prweb.com/prfiles/2014/02/22/11608927/children-with-chores-at-home-University-of-Minnesota.pdf.

3   G.E. Vaillant and C.O. Vaillant, "Natural History of Male Psychological Health, X: Work as a Predictor of Positive Mental Health," *American Journal of Psychiatry* 138, 11 (1981), doi.org/10.1176/ajp.138.11.1433.

4   Julie Lythcott-Haims, *How to Raise an Adult: Break Free of the Overparenting Trap and Prepare Your Kid for Success* (New York: Henry Holt and Company, 2015).

5   Philip Zimbardo and Nikita D. Coulombe, *Man, Interrupted: Why Young Men Are Struggling & What We Can Do about It* (Newburyport, MA: Conari Press, 2016).

6   Vicky Rideout, *The Common Sense Consensus: Media Use by Teens and Tweens*, Common Sense Media, 2015, commonsensemedia.org/sites/default/files/uploads/research/census_researchreport.pdf.

7   Daniel Goleman, *Social Intelligence: The New Science of Human Relationships* (New York: Bantam Books, 2006).

8   Damon E. Jones et al., "Early Social-Emotional Functioning and Public Health: The Relationship between Kindergarten Social Competence and Future Wellness," *American Journal of Public Health* 105, 11 (2015), doi.org/10.2105/AJPH.2015.302630.

9   Nick Bilton, "Steve Jobs Was a Low-Tech Parent," *New York Times*, September 10, 2014, nytimes.com/2014/09/11/fashion/steve-jobs-apple-was-a-low-tech-parent.html?_r=0.

10   Anna Attkisson, Teaching Kids about Money: An Age-by-Age Guide," *Parents*, updated March 31, 2021, parents.com/parenting/money/family-finances/teaching-kids-about-money-an-age-by-age-guide/.

11   Walter Mischel, *The Marshmallow Test: Mastering Self-Control* (New York: Little, Brown Spark, 2014).

12   Denise Appleby, "IRA Contributions: Deductions and Tax Credits," Investopedia, updated June 28, 2021, investopedia.com/articles/retirement/05/022105.asp.

13   "Junior ISA," Vanguard UK, vanguardinvestor.co.uk/investing-explained/stocks-shares-junior-isa; "Junior SIPP," Fidelity International, fidelity.co.uk/junior-sipp/.

14   Malcolm Gladwell (interview with Adam Grant), "Malcolm Gladwell on the Advantages of Disadvantages," *Knowledge@Wharton*, December 3, 2013, knowledge.wharton.upenn.edu/article/david-goliath-malcolm-gladwell-advantages-disadvantages/.

15   Susie Poppick, "Should You Pay for Your Child's College Education?" CNBC April 1, 2016, cnbc.com/2016/03/10/should-you-pay-for-your-kids-college-education.html.

16   Laura Hamilton et al., "Providing a 'Leg Up': Parental Involvement and Opportunity Hoarding in College," *Sociology of Education* 91, 2 (2018), doi.org/10.1177/0038040718759557.

17   Check out the costs of various schools at College Tuition Compare: collegetuitioncompare.com/edu/166027/harvard-university. You can find salary information with PayScale's College Salary Report database: payscale.com/college-salary-report.

18   Stacy Berg Dale and Alan B. Krueger, "Estimating the Payoff to Attending a More Selective College: An Application of Selection on Observables and Unobservables," National Bureau of Economic Research, working paper 7322, August 1999, doi.org/10.3386/w7322.

19   PayScale's College Salary Report database: payscale.com/college-salary-report.

Chapter 12: Rethink Retirement

1   Sam Roberts, "Shigeaki Hinohara, Longevity Expert, Dies at (or Lives to) 105," *New York Times*, July 25, 2017, nytimes.com/2017/07/25/science/shigheaki-hinohara-dead-doctor-promoted-longevity-in-japan.html.

2   *Pensions at a Glance 2017: OECD and G20 Indicators*, OECD, 2017, doi.org/10.1787/19991363.

3   "Japan's Silver Human Resources Centers: Undertaking an Increasingly Diverse Range of Work," International Longevity Center–Japan, accessed July 2021, longevity.ilcjapan.org/f_issues/0702.html.

4   Kenneth D. Kochanek et al., "Mortality in the United States, 2016," NCHS Data Brief 293, US Department of Health and Human Services, December 2017, cdc.gov/nchs/data/databriefs/db293.pdf.

5   "Life Expectancy for Japanese Men and Women Rises in 2019," Nippon, August 17, 2020, nippon.com/en/japan-data/h00788/.

6   Chenkai Wu et al., "Association of Retirement Age with Mortality: A Population-Based Longitudinal Study among Older Adults in the USA," *Journal of Epidemiology and Community Health* 70 (2016), doi.org/10.1136/jech-2015-207097.

7   "Working Later in Life Can Pay Off in More Than Just Income," Harvard Health, June 1, 2018, health.harvard.edu/staying-healthy/working-later-in-life-can-pay-off-in-more-than-just-income#:~:text=A%202016%20study%20of%20about,study%20period%2C%20regardless%20of%20health; Diana Kachan et al., Health Status of Older US Workers and Nonworkers, National Health Interview Survey, 1997–2011," *Preventing Chronic Disease* 12 (2015), doi.org/10.5888/pcd12.150040.

8   Carole Dufouil, "Older Age at Retirement Is Associated With Decreased Risk of Dementia," *European Journal of Epidemiology* 29, 5 (2014), doi.org/10.1007/s10654-014-9906-3.

9   Steve Vernon, "Rethinking a Common Assumption about Retirement Spending," CBS News, updated December 27, 2017, cbsnews.com/news/rethinking-a-common-assumption-about-retirement-spending/.

10   William Meyer and William Reichenstein, *Social Security Strategies: How to Optimize Retirement Benefits*, 3rd ed. (self-published, 2017).

11   "Life Expectancy for Men at the Age of 65 Years in the U.S. from 1960 to 2018," Statista, October 2020, statista.com/statistics/266657/us-life-expectancy-for-men-aat-the-age-of-65-years-since-1960/#:~:text=Now%20men%20in%20the%20United,20.7%20more%20years%20on%20average.&text=As%20of%202018%2C%20the%20average,United%20states%20was%2078.54%20years.

12 "Countries Ranked by Life Expectancy," Worldometer, accessed July 2021, worldometers.info/demographics/life-expectancy/#countries-ranked-by-life-expectancy.

13 Learn more about WWOOFing here: wwoof.net/.

14 Kelly Hayes-Raitt, *How to Become a Housesitter: Insider Tips from the HouseSit Diva* (Living Large Press, 2017).

15 Cost of Care Survey (interactive map), Genworth Financial, genworth.com/aging-and-you/finances/cost-of-care.html.

16 Richard A. Friedman, "Fast Time and the Aging Mind," *New York Times*, July 20, 2013, nytimes.com/2013/07/21/opinion/sunday/fast-time-and-the-aging-mind.html?_r=0.

Conclusion

1 Paul K. Piff et al., "Higher Social Class Predicts Increased Unethical Behavior," *PNAS* 109, 11 (2012), doi.org/10.1073/pnas.1118373109.

Appendix

1 S&P 500 Return Calculator, with Dividend Reinvestment, DQYDJ: dqydj.com/sp-500-return-calculator/.

INDEX

Note: Page numbers in italics refer to tables

Ron Dlutz

ABOUT THE AUTHOR

WHEN ANDREW HALLAM isn't getting eaten by mosquitoes in tropical jungles, cycling up a mountain during a downpour with his wife, or trying to drive to Argentina in a van, he's speaking and writing about happiness and personal finance. The former high school teacher wrote the international bestselling books *Millionaire Teacher* and *Millionaire Expat*. Profiled by media such as CNBC and the *Wall Street Journal*, he's the first person to have a #1 selling finance book on Amazon USA, Amazon Canada, and Amazon UAE. He has written columns for the *Globe and Mail, Canadian Business*, AssetBuilder.com, *MoneySense*, and Swissquote. Find him online at andrewhallam.com.

LET'S TAKE THIS RELATIONSHIP TO THE NEXT LEVEL

Custom editions and bulk sales

We can create a custom edition paperback, ebook, or both for your business, complete with your corporate logo on the cover and a letter from your company's most esteemed voice—whether that's the CEO or that popular person who serves food in the cafeteria.

Speaking

I give talks around the world in person, on Zoom, or via any online communication service that's in vogue.

Contact

If you would like to book me for a speaking engagement, or you want boxes of customized (or non-customized) books, please contact me at millionaireteacherspeaks@gmail.com. There's also a "Book Andrew" tab on my website, andrewhallam.com.

Maintain balance and cherish every day.

Andrew ☺